FOCUS ON GRAMMAR

An **INTRODUCTORY** Course for Reference and Practice

Irene E. Schoenberg

Jay Maurer

Longman

FOCUS ON GRAMMAR: An Introductory Course for Reference and Practice

Pearson Education, 10 Bank Street, White Plains, NY 10606

Vice president, director of publishing: Allen Ascher
Executive editor: Louisa Hellegers
Development director: Penny Laporte
Director of design and production: Rhea Banker
Senior development editor: Françoise Leffler
Development editor: Marietta Urban
Senior production manager: Alana Zdinak
Executive managing editor: Linda Moser
Senior production editor: Christine Lauricella
Director of manufacturing: Patrice Fraccio
Senior manufacturing buyer: David Dickey
Photo research: Iris Bodre-Baez and Andrea Bryant
Cover design: Rhea Banker
Text design: Charles Yuen
Text composition: Preface, Inc.
Illustrators: Ronald Chironna: pp. 2, 36–37, 81, 115, 127; Paul
    McCusker: pp. 3, 31, 42, 67, 85, 107, 119, 124, 131, 147, 167,
    179, 190, 199, 217, 219, 225, 233, 245, 251; Andy Myer:
    pp. 1–5, 10–12, 18, 24–25, 28, 30, 44, 48, 50, 58–59, 62–63,
    65–67, 70, 72, 77, 80, 88, 90–91, 94, 97, 99–100, 106, 110–111,
    114, 117, 120, 124, 126, 132, 135, 139–140, 144, 149–150,
    152–153, 158, 160, 166, 170, 172, 178, 185, 189–190, 192,
    195, 198, 201–202, 204, 207, 212, 218, 224, 227, 229–231, 236,
    238, 241, 244, 250, 253; Dusan Petricic: pp. 7, 9, 17, 25, 31,
    35, 45, 49, 51, 55, 59, 71, 95, 105, 121, 131, 137, 153, 173,
    187, 205, 213, 216, 222–223, 225, 251; Tom Sperling: pp. 19,
    22, 26, 64, 73, 89, 101, 107, 121, 122, 141, 159, 165, 179, 219,
    237, 239, 254.
Photo credits: see p. xii

Library of Congress Cataloging-in-Publication Data

Schoenberg, Irene
    Focus on grammar. An introductory course for reference and practice / Irene E. Schoenberg,
Jay Maurer.
        p.   cm.
    Includes index.
Summary: Provides listening, speaking, reading, and writing exercises to develop proficiency
in parts of speech, usage, tense, and other basics of English grammar.
    ISBN 0-201-61979-2
    1. English language—Grammar—Problems, exercises, etc. 2. English language—Textbooks
for foreign speakers. [1. English language—Grammar—Problems, exercises, etc.
2. English language—Textbooks for foreign speakers.]   I. Maurer, Jay.   II. Title.

PE1112 .S344 2001
428'.24—dc21   20001038872
                                                                                    CIP

Printed in the United States of America
7 8 9 10—CRK—07 06 05

CONTENTS

APPENDICES

INTRODUCTION

THE **FOCUS ON GRAMMAR** SERIES

Focus on Grammar: An Introductory Course for Reference and Practice is the latest addition to the **Focus on Grammar** series. Written by practicing ESL professionals, the series focuses on English grammar through lively listening, speaking, reading, and writing activities. Each book can stand alone as a complete text in itself, or it can be used as part of the series.

Both Controlled and Communicative Practice

Research in applied linguistics suggests that students expect and need to learn the formal rules of a language. However, students need to practice new structures in a variety of contexts in order to internalize and master them. To this end, **Focus on Grammar** provides an abundance of both controlled and communicative exercises so that students can bridge the gap between knowing grammatical structures and using them. The many communicative activities in each unit enable students to personalize what they have learned in order to talk to each other with ease about hundreds of everyday issues.

A Unique Four-Step Approach

The series follows a unique four-step approach. In the first step, **grammar in context,** new structures are shown in the natural context of conversations and narratives. This is followed by a **grammar presentation** of structures in clear and accessible grammar charts, notes, and examples. The third step is **focused practice** of both form and meaning in numerous and varied controlled exercises with objective answers. In the fourth step, **communication practice,** students use the new structures freely and creatively in motivating, open-ended activities.

A Complete Classroom Text and Reference Guide

A major goal in the development of **Focus on Grammar** has been to provide Student Books that serve not only as vehicles for classroom instruction but also as resources for reference and self-study. In each Student Book, the combination of grammar charts, grammar notes, and expansive appendices provides a complete and invaluable reference guide for the student. And exercises in the focus practice sections of each unit are also ideal for individual study.

Thorough Recycling

Underpinning the scope and sequence of the series as a whole is the belief that students need to use target structures many times in many contexts at increasing levels of difficulty. For this reason new grammar is constantly revisited so that students will feel thoroughly comfortable with it.

Comprehensive Testing Program

SelfTests at the end of each part of the Student Book allow for continual assessment of progress. In addition, diagnostic and final tests in the Teacher's Manual provide a ready-made, ongoing evaluation component for each student.

THE **INTRODUCTORY** STUDENT BOOK

Focus on Grammar: An Introductory Course for Reference and Practice is a course or reference book for beginners or weak false-beginning students of English. The book is divided into eleven parts comprising thirty-eight units. Each part concludes with a Review or SelfTest.

Grammar in Context

Every unit presents the grammar focus of the unit in a natural context. The texts, all of which are recorded, present language in various formats. These include conversations, e-mail messages, news articles, questionnaires, quiz shows, and phone calls. Each text is followed by two activities: **Words and Expressions** highlights lexical items from the Grammar in Context to help students increase their fluency by focusing on common words, phrases, idioms, and formulaic expressions; **With a Partner** gives students a chance to practice the grammar focus in a way that connects to the real world. For example, students can talk about world capitals, well-known people, or famous places.

Grammar Presentation

This section is made up of grammar charts, notes, and examples. The **Grammar Charts** focus on the form of the unit's target structure. Clear and easy-to-understand boxes present each grammatical form in all its combinations. These charts provide students with a clear visual reference for each new structure. The **Grammar Notes** explain the grammar shown in the preceding chart. These notes give definitions, describe the form, offer distinctions between the spoken and written language, and point out potential problems. Every note includes at least one example, and reference notes provide cross-references to related units and the Appendices.

Focused Practice

This section provides practice of the form and meaning of the structures presented in the Grammar Presentation. In the first exercise, **Discover the Grammar**, students indicate their awareness and recognition of the grammar. After this activity, students do a variety of contextualized exercises that progress from more controlled to more productive. Exercises are cross-referenced to the appropriate grammar notes so that students can review the notes if necessary. In addition, **Listening Practice** activities provide another dimension in which students can practice and incorporate the target grammar. The Focused Practice section ends with an **Editing** exercise in which students are asked to find and correct several mistakes. A complete **Answer Key** is provided in a separate booklet.

Communication Practice

The Communication Practice activities give students an opportunity to use the structures in open-ended, creative ways, allowing them to express their own thoughts and opinions in pair or group work. Through games, discussions, problem-solving activities, and information gap activities, students gain confidence in the target structure as well as many other aspects of the language.

Review or SelfTest

After the last unit of each part, there is a review section that can be used as a self-test. The exercises test the form and use of the grammar content of the part. These tests include questions in the format of the Structure and Written Expression sections of the TOEFL®. An **Answer Key** is provided at the back of the book.

Appendices

The appendices provide useful information including a current map of the world; lists of the days, months, and numbers; common irregular verbs; common non-count nouns; modals with their meaning and examples; tense form charts; and spelling and pronunciation rules of tenses.

Glossary of Grammar Terms

The Glossary of Grammar Terms provides definitions and examples of the grammatical terms used in *Focus on Grammar: An Introductory Course for Reference and Practice.*

SUPPLEMENTARY **COMPONENTS**

Audio Program

All the Grammar in Context passages and many of the Focused Practice exercises are recorded on cassettes and CDs. These include clozes, task-based listening, and pronunciation exercises. The symbol 🎧 appears next to these activities. The scripts appear in the Teacher's Manual and may be used as an alternative way of presenting these activities.

Teacher's Manual

The Teacher's Manual, divided into five parts, contains a variety of suggestions and information to enrich the material in the Student Book. The first part gives general suggestions for each section of a typical unit. The next part offers practical teaching suggestions and cultural information to accompany specific material in each unit. The Teacher's Manual also provides ready-to-use diagnostic and final tests for each of the eleven parts of the Student Book. In addition, a complete script of the audio program is provided, as is an answer key for the diagnostic and final tests.

TO THE STUDENT

We wrote this book with the hope that you learn a lot of English and have fun, too.

Here are a few suggestions:

- Don't worry about your mistakes. Mistakes are natural at this time. You can learn from your mistakes.

- Listen to the tapes again and again. Each time you listen, you learn something new.

- Read English. Don't worry if you don't understand every word.

- Practice English. Don't worry if you learn and forget. That's natural.

- Speak English to your classmates.

- Write new words and expressions in a notebook. Read and reread your notebook.

If you have any questions or comments about this book, please write to us at Pearson Education, 10 Bank Street, White Plains, New York 10606. We will be happy to answer your letters.

Good luck with English. We enjoyed writing the book. We hope you enjoy using it.

I.E.S. and J.M.

CREDITS

Photographs

Grateful acknowledgment is given to the following for providing photographs:

p. 10 *(left)* Image provided by Eyewire, Inc., *(right)* Mary Levin, University of Washington; **p. 12** *(left)* Image provided by Eyewire, Inc., *(center left)* David Bartruff/FPG International LLC, *(center right)* Mark Downey/PhotoDisc, Inc., *(right)* Hugh Sitton/Stone; **p. 18** © CORBIS; **p. 19** © CORBIS; **p. 25** *(left)* Cecil Stoughton, White House/John F. Kennedy Library, Boston, *(center)* © Hulton/Archive, *(right)* © Hulton/Archive; **p. 45** *(left)* Everett Collection, *(center)* TM and Copyright © 20th Century Fox Film Corp. All rights reserved. Courtesy: Everett Collection, *(right)* © Lucasfilm/Everett Collection; **p. 50** Image provided by Eyewire, Inc.; **p. 67** DENNIS THE MENACE®, used by permission of Hank Ketcham and © by North America Syndicate; **p. 81** *(left)* Everett Collection, *(center left)* © Mitchell Gerber/CORBIS, *(center right)* Reuters/Yves Herman/Hulton/Archive, *(right)* Associated Press AP; **p. 95** *(left)* Associated Press AP, *(center)* IHA/AP/Wide World Photos, *(right)* © Mitchell Gerber/CORBIS; **p. 104** *(left)* Satoru Ishikawa/ICM Artists, Ltd. – The Midori Foundation, *(right)* Photo: Susan Johann; **p. 115** *(top)* © Mitchell Gerber/CORBIS, *(bottom)* New York Times Co./Stephen Matteson, Jr./Archive Photos; **p. 141** Associated Press AP; **p. 151** *(top left)* Science VU/National Library of Medicine/Visuals Unlimited, *(top right)* © CORBIS, *(bottom left)* © Bettmann/CORBIS, *(bottom right)* Tony Vaccaro/Hulton/Archive; **p. 167** *(left)* © Paul Almasy/CORBIS, *(center)* Associated Press AP, *(right)* Tim Crosby/ Liaison Agency, Inc.; **p. 172** *(top)* © Copyright 1998 Tony Stone Images/ Jeremy Horner, *(bottom)* Jack Stein Grove/PhotoEdit; **p. 175** Richard Nowitz/Richard & Varda Nowitz Photography; **p. 176** Tom Bross/Stock Boston; **p. 202** Image provided by Eyewire, Inc.; **p. 213** AP/Wide World Photos; **p. 244** Associated Press AP; **p. 245** David Young-Wolfe/Stone; **p. 249** *(top left)* Kroll, Eric/Omni-Photo Communications, Inc., *(top center)* AP/Wide World Photos, *(top right)* Martial Colomb/PhotoDisc, Inc., *(bottom left)* © Duomo/CORBIS, *(bottom center)* © CORBIS, *(bottom right)* Corbis Digital Stock; **p. 278** *(left)* Bernard Gotfryd/Hulton/Archive, *(center left)* Associated Press AP, *(center right)* Jan Ali/George Hales/Hulton/Archive, *(right)* © Bettmann/CORBIS.

ACKNOWLEDGMENTS

The challenge of writing a beginning language book for adults is one of balancing the level with material that is interesting, clear, and accurate. We wish to thank the many people who helped us try to stay on track.

Consultants

Thanks to **Sandra Heyer**, University of Wisconsin, Whitewater, Wisconsin, for her superb grasp of what works at this level; **Alison Rice**, The International English Language Institute, Hunter College, CUNY, New York, for her insightful comments on the initial manuscript; and **Ellen Shaw**, University of Nevada, Las Vegas, Nevada, for her perceptive comments.

Reviewers

Thanks to **Irene Badaracco**, Fordham University, New York; **Pina Capone**, Bronx Community College, CUNY, Bronx, New York; **Martha Compton**, University of California at Irvine, Irvine, California; **Rosemary Hiruma**, California State University, Long Beach, California; **Michael I. Masey**, Saint Leo University, Saint Leo, Florida; **Gabriella Morvay**, Bronx Community College, CUNY, Bronx, New York; **Jackie Saindon**, University of Georgia, Athens, Georgia; and **Cynthia Smith**, Lynn University, Boca Raton, Florida; as well as **Tomomi Nada** for her well-taken comments on the manuscript from a student point of view. Their excellent suggestions helped guide us in the early stages of the book.

We are also grateful to **Christine Lauricella**, for her work in preparing the book for production; **Penny Laporte**, development director, for her fine eye for detail; and **Iris Bodre-Baez** for her efforts in moving the manuscript along in its later stages.

Finally, our very special thanks to the following people for their invaluable assistance:

- **Marietta Urban**, our developmental editor, for her tireless work and perceptive suggestions.
- **Marjorie Fuchs** for her many thoughtful recommendations for improving the manuscript in its later stages.
- **Françoise Leffler** for her amazing eye for how material should look on the page, for her surgical skills at keeping the manuscript the right length, and for her sense of humor.

Above all, we know that no project can be completed without a good director. We owe a debt of gratitude to **Louisa Hellegers** for her unwavering support and skillful management of this project.

I.E.S. and J.M.

ABOUT THE AUTHORS

Irene E. Schoenberg has taught ESL for over twenty-five years at Hunter College's *International English Language Institute* and for eighteen years at Columbia University's *American Language Program*. She has trained ESL and EFL teachers at Columbia University's Teacher's College and the New School for Social Research. She has lectured at conferences, English language schools and universities in Brazil, Dubai, El Salvador, Guatemala, Japan, Mexico, Nicaragua, Taiwan, Thailand, and the United States. She is the author of ***Talk about Trivia; Talk about Values; Focus on Grammar: A Basic Course for Reference and Practice;*** and the co-author with Jay Maurer of the ***True Colors*** series. Ms. Schoenberg holds an MA in TESOL from Columbia University. ***Focus on Grammar: An Introductory Course for Reference and Practice*** has grown out of the author's experience as a practicing teacher of English.

Jay Maurer has taught English in binational centers, colleges, and universities in Portugal, Spain, Mexico, the Somali Republic, and the United States. In addition, he taught intensive English at Columbia University's American Language Program. He was also a teacher of college composition, literature, speech, and drama for sixteen years at Santa Fe Community College and Northern New Mexico Community College. He is the co-author of the three-level ***Structure Practice in Context*** series; co-author with Irene Schoenberg of the five-level ***True Colors*** series; co-author of the ***True Voices*** video series; and author of ***Focus on Grammar: An Advanced Course for Reference and Practice***, First and Second Editions, and CD-ROM. Currently he writes and teaches in Seattle, Washington.

Getting Started

Classroom Instructions

Verbs

Look at page 1.

Listen to the CD.

Read the sentence.

Write the word.

Circle the word.

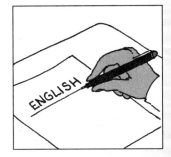

Underline the word.

Number the words 1, 2, 3, 4.

Match the words and the pictures.

1

Complete the sentence.

Point to the board.

Ask a question.

Answer the question.

Practice the conversation.

Nouns

a **word**

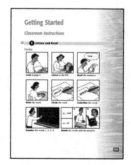

a **sentence**

a **page**

a **book**

a **CD**

a **tape**

a **VCR**

a **partner**

a **group**

a **class**

2 Work with a Partner

Student A, read a sentence.

Student B, point to the sentence.

Take turns.

UNIT

1 Imperatives

Relax!

Grammar **in Context**

🎧 *Listen and read the conversation.*

STEVE: Can I sit here?

JUDY: Sure. Please sit down.

STEVE: Hi, I'm Steve Beck.

JUDY: Nice to meet you. I'm Judy Johnson.

STEVE: Oops! Sorry.

JUDY: That's okay. Nervous?

STEVE: I guess so. It's my first day here. I'm a new teacher.

JUDY: Oh. Don't be nervous . . .

JUDY: Here. Listen to this.

STEVE: What is it?

JUDY: A tape.

STEVE: Uh . . . No, thanks.

JUDY: Try it. It's short. It's fun. [*Joking*] And it's free.

STEVE: Well, okay.

JUDY: Well, how are you now?

STEVE: Good.

JUDY: Don't worry. Repeat ten times, "I'm a good teacher." And have a good class.

STEVE: Okay, Judy. Thanks. Bye.

Words and Expressions

Do you know these words and expressions? Write new words and expressions in your notebook.

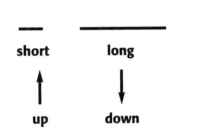

short   long

music

up   down

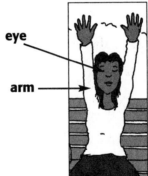

eye

arm

1. **A:** Hi, I'm Steve Beck / Judy Johnson.
   B: Nice to meet you.

2. **A:** How are you?
   B: Good. / Not so good. / Nervous.

3. **A:** Can I sit here?
   B: Sure. Please sit down.

4. **A:** Sorry.
   B: That's okay.

With a Partner

A. *Practice the conversation with a partner.*

B. *Listen. Follow the instructions.*

   Relax. Close your eyes.
   Listen to the music.
   Move your arms up and down. Slowly.
   Breathe. Relax. That's good. Relax.

C. *Ask your partner, "How are you now?"*

Grammar **Presentation**
Imperatives

Affirmative	Negative
Open your eyes. **Relax.**	**Don't open** your eyes. **Don't relax.**

Notes

Examples

1. Use the imperative for **instructions**, **requests**, and **suggestions**.

   In the imperative, the verb tells you what to do.

   • **Answer** the questions. *(instruction)*
   • Please **sit down**. *(request)*
   • **Relax.** *(suggestion)*

2. Use the **base form** of the verb for the imperative.

   • **Open** your eyes.

3. Use *do not* + the **base form** for the negative form of the imperative.

   Don't is the short form (contraction) of *do not*.

   • **Do not worry.**

   • **Don't worry.**

4. *Please* makes an imperative more **polite**. *Please* comes at the beginning or at the end of the sentence.

   • **Please** sit down.
     OR
   • Sit down, **please**.

Focused Practice

 Discover the Grammar

Read these sentences. Underline the imperative sentences.

I'm Steve Beck.   Please sit down.   Don't worry.

Listen to this.   It's fun.   Don't be nervous.

2 Instructions and Requests
Grammar Notes 1–4

Complete the sentences. Use the words in the box.

ask	relax	good class
the teacher	worry	nervous

1. Please sit down and _____relax_____.

2. Listen to _____.

3. Don't be _____.

4. _____ your partner a question.

5. Please don't _____.

6. Have a _____!

3 What Are They Saying?
Grammar Notes 1–4

Look at the pictures. What are the people saying? Choose a sentence in the box.
Write the answer.

Don't be nervous.	Please sit down.	Close the window, please.
Don't read this book.	Listen to this CD.	Please turn to page 6.

1. Please sit down.

2.

3.

4.

5.

6.

4 Follow Instructions

Grammar Notes 1–4

Read the instructions in Column A. Then read the sentence in Column B.
Follow the instructions.

Column A: Instructions

Column B: Sentences

1. Change "Do not" to the short form.

~~Do not~~ Don't open the door.

Write the new sentence.

_____

2. Add "please."

Open the door.

Write the new sentence.

_____

3. Change the word "window" to the word "door."

Open the window.

Write the new sentence.

_____

4. Complete the sentence.

Please close _____

5 What's the Homework?

Grammar Notes 1–3

A. *Listen and repeat the numbers.*

| 1 = one | 2 = two | 3 = three | 4 = four | 5 = five |
| 6 = six | 7 = seven | 8 = eight | 9 = nine | 10 = ten |

B. *Now listen to Steve. What's the homework?*

> ### Homework
>
> Read pages 1 to ___ .
> Study _____ on page ___ .
> _____ questions on page ___ .
> _____ question _____ .

6 Editing

Correct these sentences. There are six mistakes.

1. Please ~~not to~~ don't open your book.

2. You no sit here.

3. Study please page 3.

4. Completes the sentences.

5. Don't please worry.

6. No close the window.

Communication Practice

7 Make Requests

Work with a partner. Take turns. Make requests. Use the words in the box.

Verbs

close   open   move   answer   ask   read   write

Nouns

your name   your e-mail address   your arms   a question   your book
your address   your phone number   your eyes   a sentence   your dictionary

Examples: Close your eyes.
                 Please write your e-mail address.

8 The Telephone Game

*Work in large groups. Student A whispers one imperative sentence to Student B.
Student B whispers it to Student C. The last person says the sentence to the group.*

9 A Relaxation Tape

A. *Work with a partner. Listen to the music. Write the instructions for your relaxation tape.*

(Look at Appendix 3 on page 261 for more parts of the body.)

Example: Move your arms up and down.
                Touch your toes.

_____

_____

B. *Read your instructions to the class. The class follows the instructions. Ask the
class, "How are you now?"*

This is / These are; Subject Pronouns

This is Seattle.

Grammar in Context

🎧 *Listen and read.*

This is Seattle. It's a city in the state of Washington.

This is the University of Washington. Steve Beck works here. He's a teacher.

Steve lives here with his parrot, Charlie, and his cat, Buster. The apartment is small, but they're happy.

These are my parents.

Mary and Bill Beck live
in a small house.

This is my sister, Jessica.
She's a TV reporter.

Jessica and her family live
in a big house.

This is her husband,
Tim Olson.

These are their children,
Jeremy, Ben, and Annie.

Words

🎧 *Do you know these words? Write new words in your notebook.*

A Family

parents

father   mother

children

son   daughter

husband   wife

brother   sister

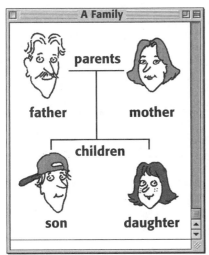

big

small

With a Partner

Work with a partner. Name the cities. Choose from the names in the box.
Check your answers on page 280.

Bangkok	Istanbul	Quebec	New York

This is New York. _____ _____ _____

Grammar **Presentation**
This is / These are

Singular		Plural	
This is my friend Pedro.		**These are** my friends Maria and Pedro.	
This is my seat.		**These are** our seats.	
Is this your seat?		**Are these** your seats?	

Subject Pronouns

Subject Pronouns	Example Sentences
I	**I**'m Steve Beck.
you	Hi, Maria. How are **you**?
he	**He**'s a teacher.
she	**She**'s a reporter.
it	This is my apartment. **It**'s in Seattle.
we	The apartment is small, but **we**'re happy here.
you	Hi, Mom and Dad. How are **you**?
they	**They**'re a nice family.

Notes	Examples
1. Use *this is* to introduce or talk about **one** person or thing **near** you.	• **This is** my friend Pedro. • **This is** my seat.
2. Use *these are* to introduce or talk about **two or more** people or things **near** you.	• **These are** my friends Maria and Pedro. • **These are** our seats.
3. To make **questions** with *this* and *these*, put *is* before *this* and *are* before *these*.	• **Is this** your cat? • **Are these** your books?
4. *Singular* means "one." *Plural* means "more than one." Most **plural nouns** end in *–s* or *–es*. Note: **Nouns** are names of people, animals, places, things, and ideas.	• This is my **friend**. *(one friend)* • These are my **friends**. *(more than one friend)* • This is my **class**. *(one class)* • These are my **classes**. *(more than one class)*
5. *I*, *you*, *he*, *she*, *it*, *we*, and *they* are **subject pronouns**. They replace a subject noun. Note: Use *it* or *he* or *she* to talk about an animal.	• *Jessica* is a TV reporter. **She** works in Seattle. • *Mary and Bill Beck* are my parents. **They** live in Seattle. • **It**'s a big cat! or **He**'s a big cat! or **She**'s a big cat!

Pronunciation Note
Some nouns that end in *–es* have an extra syllable: 1   1   2
class   class**es**

Reference Notes
1. Look at Unit 4 for more about the plural of nouns.
2. Look at Appendix 4 on page 262 for more about the spelling and pronunciation of plural nouns.

Focused Practice

1 Discover the Grammar

A. *Read* Grammar in Context *again. Underline two sentences with* **this is** *and two sentences with* **these are**.

Example: <u>This is Seattle.</u>

B. *Circle five of the subject pronouns.*

Example: (It)'s a city in the state of Washington.

2 My Photos

Complete the sentences. Use **this** *or* **these**.

1. _____These_____ are my photos.
2. _____ is my mother.
3. _____ are my sisters.
4. _____ is my father.

5. _____ is my apartment.
6. _____ are my friends.
7. Is _____ your cat?
8. Are _____ your seats?

3 Talk about People

Complete the sentences with **I**, **you**, **he**, **she**, **it**, **we**, *or* **they**.

Seattle is a city in the state of Washington. ___It___ is a beautiful city. Mary and Bill
                                                  1.

Beck live in Seattle. _____ are the parents of Steve Beck and Jessica Olson. Steve
                         2.

works at the University of Washington. _____ is a journalism teacher. Jessica works in
                                          3.

downtown Seattle. _____ is a TV reporter. Jessica and her husband have three children.
                     4.

_____ live in Redmond, a small city near Seattle. Jessica says, "Redmond is a good
   5.

place for our family. _____ 're happy here." Steve says, "_____ like Redmond,
                         6.   7.

but _____ love Seattle."
       8.

4 *This or These?*

A. *Listen. Check (✓)* **This** *or* **These**.

	This	These
1.	✓	❑
2.	❑	❑
3.	❑	❑
4.	❑	❑
5.	❑	❑

B. *Work with a partner. Say a sentence. Your partner points to the correct sentence.*

1. **a.** This is my friend.
2. **a.** These are my photos.
3. **a.** These are our tickets.
4. **a.** This is my sister.
5. **a.** Is this your key?

   b. These are my friends.
   b. This is my photo.
   b. This is our ticket.
   b. These are my sisters.
   b. Are these your keys?

5 Editing

Correct these conversations. There are four mistakes.

        This

1. **A:** ~~These~~ is my friend Pedro.

   B: Nice to meet you, Pedro.

2. **A:** This are my brothers.

   B: Hello.

3. **A:** This my partner, Ahmed.

   B: Hi, Ahmed.

4. **A:** Is these my books?

   B: No, they're not.

Communication Practice

6 Meet Your Classmates

Walk around the classroom. Meet three classmates. Make introductions.

Example:

Sun: Hi, I'm Sun Kim.
Victor: I'm Victor Gómez.
Sun: Nice to meet you, Victor. [*Sun walks over to Luis.*] Luis, this is Victor.
Luis: Nice to meet you, Victor.
Victor: Nice to meet you too.

7 My Family and Friends

Bring photos of your family or friends to class. Work in groups of four. Talk about the photos.

Examples:

A: Is this your mother?
B: Yes, this is my mother. She's in Lima.

C: This is my boyfriend. He's in Tokyo.
D: These are my friends, Emiko and Yuri.

8 A Game: Don't Repeat!

Work in groups. Don't use a dictionary.

Student A, touch something in the classroom and say, **This is a _____** *or* **These are _____.**

Student B, touch and name a different thing or different things. Continue.
The last person to name a different thing wins.

Review or SelfTest

I. *Complete the conversations. Circle the correct letter.*

1. STUDENT: What's the homework?   Ⓐ B C D
    TEACHER: _____
    (A) Answer questions 1–4   (C) I'm Steve Beck.
        on page 10.   (D) This is my mother.
    (B) Thank you.

2. STEVE: _____   A B C D
    MARK: Sorry.
    (A) Thanks.   (C) We're happy.
    (B) Nice to meet you.   (D) Don't sit here, please.

3. PEDRO: _____   A B C D
    MARIA: Nice to meet you, Steve.
    (A) This is the University   (C) They live in a big house.
        of Washington.   (D) This is my friend Steve.
    (B) I live in Seattle.

4. STEVE: _____   A B C D
    PEDRO: It's a good photo. They look great!
    (A) These are my parents.   (C) This is my seat.
    (B) Is this your cat?   (D) Are these your keys?

5. STEVE: How are you?   A B C D
    JUDY: _____
    (A) Bye.   (C) Not so good.
    (B) No, thanks.   (D) That's okay.

6. JESSICA: _____   A B C D
    STEVE: Thanks.
    (A) Open the door.   (C) Close the window, please.
    (B) Ask your partner a   (D) Have a good class.
        question.

II. *Complete the sentences. Use* **This is** *or* **These are**.

1. _____This is_____ my daughter.

2. _____ my sons.

3. _____ my classmate.

4. _____ my apartment.

5. _____ good photos.

6. _____ Steve Beck.

III. *Complete the sentences. Use* **He**, **She**, **It**, **We**, *or* **They**.

1. My daughter is a student. ___She___ is at the University of Washington.
2. My sons are in Seattle. _____ are reporters.
3. My apartment is small. _____ is near the university.
4. My brother is a student. _____ is on vacation now.
5. My mother is fine. _____ is in Florida.
6. My father and I are in Seattle. _____ are at the theater.

IV. *Look at each picture. What is the teacher saying? Choose a sentence from the box. Write it under the picture.*

Listen to the tape.	Write the homework in your notebook.
Practice with a partner.	Close your books.

1. _____

2. _____

3. _____

4. _____

V. *Correct the sentences. There are six mistakes.*

1. ~~Answers~~ the questions.   *Answer*
2. Dont write your name.
3. Don't to open the window.
4. These my new notebooks.
5. This are my parents.
6. No listen to the tape.

▶ *To check your answers, go to the Answer Key on page 282.*

UNIT

3 The Present of *Be*: Statements

We're from Australia.

Grammar **in Context**

🎧 *Listen and read the conversation.*

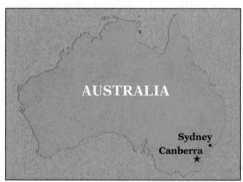

AUSTRALIA

Sydney
Canberra •
★

A kangaroo

MARK: Hi, Steve.

STEVE: Hi, Mark. Mark, this is my cousin Amy, and this is her friend Jenny. They're here on vacation.

MARK: Hi. Nice to meet you.

AMY: Nice to meet you too.

MARK: So you're not from around here?

AMY: No. We're from Australia.

MARK: Australia? Ah—the land of kangaroos and koalas.

AMY: And big business, and opera, and . . .

MARK: Right. Are you from the capital?

AMY: No. We're from Sydney. And our kangaroos and koalas are all . . .

MARK: In the zoo?

A koala

AMY: That's right. Are you from Seattle?

MARK: Yes, I am.

AMY: Jenny and I love Seattle. It's a beautiful city. It's not Sydney, of course, but it's clean. The people are friendly. And the coffee is delicious.

MARK: Is Sydney beautiful?

AMY: Yes, it's wonderful. And it's not because I live there.

The Sydney Opera House

Words and Expressions

🎧 *Do you know these words and expressions? Write new words and expressions in your notebook.*

clean

dirty

delicious

awful

1. A: Are you from around here?
B: No, I'm from Australia.

2. A: Are you here on business?
B: No, we're here on vacation.

With a Partner

A. *Practice the conversation with two partners.*

B. *One student reads the sentence on the left. The other student reads the correct sentence on the right. Take turns. Check your answers on page 280.*

Example: **A:** He's from Washington, D.C.

    B: It's the capital of the United States.

He's from Washington, D.C.   It's the capital of Taiwan.

She's from Lima.   It's the capital of the United States.

They're from Taipei.   It's the capital of Venezuela.

I'm from Canberra.   It's the capital of Australia.

She's from Caracas.   It's the capital of Brazil.

He's from Brasília.   It's the capital of Peru.

Grammar **Presentation**
The Present of *Be*: Statements

Affirmative Statements		
am	*is*	*are*
I **am** from Seattle.	He **is** from Seattle. She **is** from Sydney. It **is** clean. Seattle **is** clean.	We **are** from Sydney. You **are** cousins. They **are** friends. Jenny and I **are** from Sydney. Jenny and Amy **are** friends.
I am = I**'m**	he is = he**'s** she is = she**'s** it is = it**'s**	we are = we**'re** you are = you**'re** they are = they**'re**

Negative Statements		
am not	*is not*	*are not*
I **am not** from Sydney.	He **is not** from Sydney. She **is not** from Seattle. It **is not** dirty.	We **are not** from Seattle. You **are not** from here. They **are not** from here.

I am not = I**'m not**	he is not = he**'s not** OR
	            he **isn't**
	she is not = she**'s not** OR
	            she **isn't**
	it is not = it**'s not** OR
	            it **isn't**
		we are not = we**'re not** OR
		              we **aren't**
		you are not = you**'re not** OR
		              you **aren't**
		they are not = they**'re not** OR
		              they **aren't**

Notes

Examples

1. The **present of *be*** has three forms: *am*, *is*, *are*.	• I **am** from Seattle. • It **is** clean. • They **are** friendly.

2. Use the correct form of ***be* + *not*** to make a **negative statement**.	• I **am not** from Sydney. • It **is not** dirty. • We **are not** cold.

3. Use **contractions** (short forms) in speaking and informal writing.

NOTE: There are **two** negative contractions for *is not* and *are not*.

- **I'm** from Seattle.
- **I'm not** from Sydney.
- It**'s not** cold. OR It **isn't** cold.
- We**'re not** sad. OR We **aren't** sad.

4. Sentences have a subject and a verb.

The **subject** is a noun or a pronoun.

subject verb
noun
- **Amy**   **is**   my cousin.

pronoun
- **She**   **is**   from Australia.

Focused Practice

1 Discover the Grammar

Read the sentences. Write **A** *for affirmative and* **N** *for negative.*

__N__ **1.** She's not from around here.

_____ **2.** She's here with a friend.

_____ **3.** They're here on vacation.

_____ **4.** They aren't here on business.

_____ **5.** I'm not from the capital.

_____ **6.** We're from Sydney.

2 People and Places   Grammar Notes 1, 4

A. *Write* **She is**, **He is**, **It is**, **We are**, *or* **They are**.

1. Amy is a student. _____ _____ from Australia.

2. Amy and Jenny are students. _____ _____ here on vacation.

3. Sydney is a beautiful city. _____ _____ in Australia.

4. My friends and I are in school. _____ _____ in room 2.

5. Mark is a student. _____ _____ in Seattle.

B. *Say each sentence aloud. Use contractions.*

3 What's False?   Grammar Notes 1–2

A. *Check (✓) the false sentences. Change them to the negative. Write the full form.*

__✓__ **1.** I am a teacher.   _I am not a teacher._____

_____ **2.** I am a new student.   _____

_____ **3.** The Sydney Opera House is in Canberra. _____

_____ **4.** We are in room 2.   _____

(continued on next page)

_____ **5.** Mexico is the capital of Mexico City.   _____

_____ **6.** Mexico City is the capital of Mexico.   _____

_____ **7.** My parents are from around here.   _____

_____ **8.** It is hot here.   _____

B. *Read each negative sentence. Use contractions.*

4 A Postcard

Grammar Notes 1–4

🎧 *Listen and complete the postcard.*

Seattle

June 15

Dear Mum and Dad,
    Amy and I __are__ in Seattle. _____ _____ at the Western Hotel.
_____ at a youth hostel on Second Avenue. _____ _____ , and _____
_____ expensive. And all the people _____ _____.
    We love Seattle! _____ beautiful, and the hiking is wonderful. The food
_____ delicious, too—lots of Asian dishes. _____ cool at night, and _____
true—you need an umbrella! But _____ very happy to be here.
        Love,
        Jenny

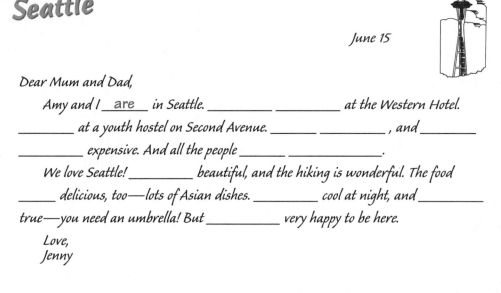

expensive

hiking

an Asian dish

an umbrella

5 No, She's Not.

Grammar Notes 1–3

Complete the sentences. Use the affirmative or negative form of **be.**

1. A: She's here on business.

   B: No. She_'s not_ here on business.
   She's here on vacation.

2. A: You're a student.

   B: No, I _____ a student.
   I'm a writer.

3. A: You're cold.

   B: Cold? We're not cold.
   We _____ fine.

4. A: They're from Austria.

   B: No, they're not. They _____
   from Australia.

5. A: It's cool today.

   B: Cool? It _____ cool. It's warm.

6. A: Egypt is the capital of Cairo.

   B: No, it _____. Cairo is the capital
   of Egypt.

6 Editing

Correct the conversations. There are seven mistakes.

1. A: Please close the window. I̶t̶ It's cold here.

   B: It's no cold. It's hot.

2. A: Please open the window. I be hot.

   B: Hot? It's not hot. Is cold.

3. A: My cousin from Tokyo. She's a student.

   B: My cousin from New York. She's a student too.

4. A: Seattle is the capital of Washington State.

   B: No, it's isn't. Olympia is the capital.

Communication Practice

7 True or False?

Listen and check (✓) **True**, **False**, *or* **No Information**.

> Matteo Milano
> Chef
>
> **Bellavista Restaurant**
> 20 First Avenue
> Seattle, Washington 98104

	True	False	No Information
1. The woman is from Australia.	✓	❑	❑
2. The woman's parents are from Australia.	❑	❑	❑
3. The man is from Italy.	❑	❑	❑
4. They are at a hotel.	❑	❑	❑
5. The woman thinks Italian food is delicious.	❑	❑	❑

8 I'm Not Here on Business.

Write true sentences. Read your sentences to your partner. Check (✓) sentences that are the same for you and your partner.

                                                                         Same

1. I / here on vacation.   *I'm not here on vacation.*   ✓

2. It / hot in class. _____ ❑

3. I / from Italy. _____ ❑

4. My teacher / from Australia. _____ ❑

5. I / happy to be here. _____ ❑

6. I / cold. _____ ❑

7. My parents / from Seattle. _____ ❑

8. It / noisy in class. _____ ❑

9. It / crowded. _____ ❑

That is / Those are; Possessive Adjectives; Plural Nouns

They're my grandchildren.

Grammar **in Context**

🎧 *Listen and read the conversation.*

ROSE: Okay. So who are those people?

MARY: My daughter, Jessica, and her husband, Tim. That's their house. Okay . . . Now here's the next slide.

ROSE: Is that their car? Look! Its tires are flat.

MARY: Well, it's Tim's car. It's his "baby." He's fixing it. That's Tim under the car.

ROSE: And who are the kids?

MARY: They're my grandchildren.

ROSE: What? You're a grandparent?

MARY: I sure am. That's Annie, my granddaughter. And that's Ben, my younger grandson.

ROSE: And who's that guy?

MARY: That's Jeremy, my older grandson.
His favorite things are computers and CDs.
He's a great kid!

Words and Expressions

🎧 *Do you know these words and expressions? Write new words and expressions in your notebook.*

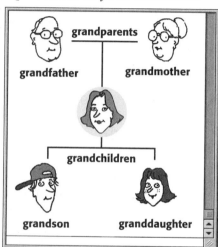

grandparents

grandfather   grandmother

grandchildren

grandson   granddaughter

1. **A:** Who are those kids?
   B: They're my grandchildren.

2. **A:** What? You're a grandparent?
   B: I sure am.

3. **A:** And who's that guy?
   B: That's Jeremy, my older grandson.

With a Partner

A. *Practice the conversation with a partner.*

B. *Look at the pictures. Who are the people? Talk about each group of people.*

Example: That's Joseph Kennedy with his children and his grandchildren.

Joseph Kennedy

Emperor Hirohito

Prince William

Grammar **Presentation**
That is / Those are

Singular	Plural
That is my grandson.	**Those are** my grandchildren.
That's his car.	**Those are** his cars.
Is that your key?	**Are those** your keys?

Possessive Adjectives

Subject Pronouns	Possessive Adjectives	Example Sentences
I	my	**I** am Mary. **My** name is Mary.
you	your	**You** are right. **Your** answer is correct.
he	his	**He** is Tim. **His** name is Tim.
she	her	**She** is Jessica. **Her** name is Jessica.
it	its	**It** is Tim's car. **Its** tires are flat.
we	our	**We** are Jessica's parents. **Our** daughter is Jessica.
you	your	**You** are both wrong. **Your** answers are wrong.
they	their	**They** are our children. **Their** names are Jessica and Steve.

Singular and Plural Nouns

Singular *(one)*	Plural *(more than one)*
one girl one boy	three girl**s** four boy**s**
one glass one dish	two glass**es** three dish**es**
one man one woman one child	two **men** two **women** three **children**

Notes

Examples

1. Use *that is* to talk about **one** person or thing **away** from you.

   We often contract *that is* to *that's* in informal speaking and writing.

- **That is** my grandson. *(there)*

- **That's** his car. *(there)*

2. Use *those are* to talk about **two or more** people or things **away** from you.

- **Those are** my grandchildren. *(there)*
- **Those are** their cats. *(there)*

3. To make **questions** with *that* and *those*, put *is* before *that* and *are* before *those*.

- **Is that** their car?
- **Are those** your keys?

4. Possessive adjectives are *my*, *your*, *his*, *her*, *its*, *our*, *their*. They tell who someone or something belongs to.

- This is **my** daughter.
- Those are **her** friends.

Pronunciation Note
Some words sound the same, but they are different in meaning and spelling:

- **Your** name is Maria.
- **You're** a student.
- **Its** name is Charlie.
- **It's** Steve's parrot.
- **Their** children are happy.
- **They're** happy.

5. Add *–s* to most **nouns** to make them **plural**.

Add *–es* to nouns that end in *s*, *z*, *ch*, *sh*, and *x*. Say an extra syllable.

- one cat, four cat**s**
- one house, two house**s**
- glass, glass**es**
- dish, dish**es**

6. Some nouns have **special plural** forms.

- one grandchild, two **grandchildren**
- one person, three **people**

Reference Notes
1. Look at Unit 2 for information about *this is* and *these are*.
2. Look at Appendix 4 on page 262 for more information about plural nouns.

Focused Practice

1 Discover the Grammar

A. *Read* Grammar in Context *again. Circle the uses of* **that** *and* **those**.

B. *Underline the possessive adjectives* (**my**, **your**, *etc.*).

C. *Check the seven plural nouns.*

Example: That's his car. Its tires are flat.

2 *That* or *Those*?   Grammar Notes 1–3

Complete the sentences with **that** *or* **those**.

1. __That__'s my new car.

2. Are _____ your grandchildren?

3. Look! _____'s a big umbrella!

4. _____ are my friends.

5. Is _____ your wallet on the table?

6. Are _____ your glasses?

3 Home Video   Grammar Note 4

Judy is showing a video about her visit home. Complete her sentences with **my**, **his**, **her**, **its**, *or* **our**.

That's me and ____my____ brother, Ken, with _____ parents in front of _____
                          1.   2.   3.

house. See those cars? The old one belongs to Ken—it's _____ first car. _____
                                                  4.   5.

battery is dead, so it doesn't run. But he loves it. The new car belongs to Dad. It's

_____ favorite thing. And the garden belongs to Mom. It's _____ favorite place.
 6.   7.

4 *Man* or *Men*?   Grammar Notes 4–5

A. *Listen to the conversations. Circle the word you hear.*

1. (woman)   women

2. man   men

3. grandchild   grandchildren

4. purse   purses

5. dish   dishes

6. key   keys

B. *Work with a partner. Say one of the words in each item. Your partner points to the word you say.*

5 Editing

Correct these conversations. There are seven mistakes.

1. **A:** Are those your ~~key~~ keys?

   B: No, they her keys.

2. **A:** That is my daughters.

   B: She's a beautiful women.

3. **A:** Are that your childs?

   B: Yes. That's our son, and that's our daughter.

4. **A:** Are it tires flat?

   B: Yes, they are.

Communication Practice

6 Are Those Your Children?

Listen to the conversation. Complete the sentences.

A: Are those ___your___ ___children___ ?
1.   2.

B: Yes. They're _____ _____, Jeremy and Ben.
3.   4.

   And that's _____ _____, Annie.
5.   6.

A: And is that _____ turtle?
7.

B: Yes. _____ name _____ Bozo.
8.   9.

A: Who are _____ other _____?
10.   11.

B: _____ friends.
12.

7 The Possessive Game

A. *Play this game with the class. Each student puts an item on the teacher's table. For example:*

a notebook	a jacket	a backpack	keys
a CD player	an earring	a watch	sunglasses

B. *The teacher picks up one thing and asks, "Who does it belong to?" A student points to the owner and says:*

   That's his / her _____.

Example:

Student 1: [*Pointing to Student 2*] That's his backpack.

Student 2: Right. It's my backpack.

   OR

   No, it's not my backpack. [*Pointing to Student 3*] It's her backpack.

The Present of *Be*: Yes/No Questions; Questions with *Who* and *What*

Is she married?

Grammar **in Context**

🎧 *Mark, Steve, and Kathy are at a wedding reception for Amanda and Josh. Listen and read these three conversations.*

STEVE: Mark?

MARK: Steve! Are you here for the wedding?

STEVE: Yes, I am. Amanda is my cousin. What about you?

MARK: Josh and I are good friends from school. It's a great wedding, isn't it?

STEVE: Yes, it is.

★

KATHY: Who's that man with Steve?

AMANDA: His name is Mark. He and Josh are friends.

KATHY: Hmm. Is he single?

AMANDA: Yes, he is.

KATHY: What does he do?

AMANDA: He's a writer. He writes travel books.

KATHY: Oh.

★

MARK: Who's that woman with Amanda?

STEVE: Her name is Kathy.

MARK: Is she married?

STEVE: No, she's not.

MARK: What does she do?

STEVE: She's a travel agent.

MARK: Oh.

Words and Expressions

🎧 *Do you know these words and expressions? Write new words and expressions in your notebook.*

married

single

a writer

a travel agent

1. A: I'm here for the wedding. What about you?
   B: I'm here for the wedding too.

2. A: What does she do?
   B: She's a travel agent.

With a Partner

A. *Practice the conversations with three partners.*

B. *Match the words and the pictures. Use your dictionary.*

> **an actor**   **an actress**   **an athlete**   **a scientist**   **a singer**

a singer
_____   _____   _____   _____

C. *Work with a partner. Take turns. Ask a question about a famous person. Use the words in the box.*

Example:

A: Is Antonio Banderas an actor?

B: Yes, he is. Is Cameron Diaz an athlete?

A: No, she's not. She's an actress.

Grammar **Presentation**
The Present of *Be*: *Yes / No* Questions

Yes / No Questions	Short Answers	
Singular	**Affirmative**	**Negative**
Am I right?	Yes, **you are.**	No, **you're not.** OR No, **you aren't.**
Are you a writer?	Yes, **I am.**	No, **I'm not.**
Is he a student?	Yes, **he is.**	No, **he's not.** OR No, **he isn't.**
Is she single?	Yes, **she is.**	No, **she's not.** OR No, **she isn't.**
Is your car new?	Yes, **it is.**	No, **it's not.** OR No, **it isn't.**

Plural	Affirmative	Negative
Are you happy?	Yes, **we are.**	No, **we're not.** OR No, **we aren't.**
Are we late?	Yes, **you are.**	No, **you're not.** OR No, **you aren't.**
Are they brothers?	Yes, **they are.**	No, **they're not.** OR No, **they aren't.**

The Present of *Be*: Questions with *Who* and *What*

Questions with *Who/What*	Short Answers	Long Answers
Who is that woman?	Kathy.	**That's** Kathy.
What's her name?	Kathy.	**It's** Kathy.

Notes

1. In a *yes / no* question with *be*, put *am*, *is*, or *are* before the subject.

2. Use contractions in **negative short answers**.

Don't use contractions in **affirmative short answers**.

Examples

- STATEMENT: I **am** right.
  (subject above "I")
- QUESTION: **Am** I right?
  (subject above "I")

A: Is she married?
B: No, she**'s not.** OR No, she **isn't.**

A: Are they brothers?
B: No, they**'re not.** OR No, they **aren't.**

A: Am I right?
B: Yes, **you are.** NOT ~~Yes, you're.~~

A: Is she single?
B: Yes, **she is.** NOT ~~Yes, she's.~~

3. Use *who* to ask for information about **people**. Use *what* to ask for information about **things** or **ideas**.

We often use the contractions *who's* and *what's* in speaking and informal writing.

- **Who** is that woman?
- **What** is her name?

- **Who's** that woman?
- **What's** her name?

Focused Practice

 Discover the Grammar

Read the conversations. Circle the questions with **be**. *Underline the short answers.*

1. **MARK:** She looks interesting. (Is she married?)
   STEVE: <u>No, she's not.</u>

2. **MARK:** Are you here for the wedding?
   STEVE: Yes, I am. Amanda is my cousin.

3. **KATHY:** I think he's single. Am I right?
   AMANDA: Yes, you are. And he's a nice guy.

4. **STEVE:** Are you a friend of Josh?
   MARK: Yes, I am. Actually, we're friends from school.

2 Questions   **Grammar Notes 1–2**

Match the questions and answers.

__c__ **1.** Is Amanda your sister?   **a.** No, he isn't.

_____ **2.** Are Mark and Helen teachers?   **b.** Yes, we are.

_____ **3.** Am I right?   **c.** No, she isn't. She's my cousin.

_____ **4.** Are you and Josh friends?   **d.** No, they aren't. They're writers.

_____ **5.** Is Mark married?   **e.** Yes, you are.

3 *Who* or *What*?   **Grammar Note 3**

Complete the conversations with **who** *or* **what**.

1. A: ____Who____ 's that woman with Mark?
   B: That's my mother.

2. A: _____'s her name?
   B: Mary.

3. A: _____'s that man with Judy?
   B: That's Mark.

4. A: _____'s the teacher in this class?
   B: Mr. Beck. Steve Beck.

5. A: _____'s the capital of Australia?
   B: Canberra.

6. A: _____'s the capital of Brazil?
   B: Brasília.

4 **Conversations**

Change the order of the words. Make conversations.

1. **A:** Steve / Portland / Is / from / ?

   B: not / No, / he's / .

2. **A:** today / the wedding / Is / ?

   B: Yes, / is / it / .

3. **A:** cousins / Are / they / ?

   B: aren't / No, / they / . / brothers / They're / .

4. **A:** man / that / Who / is / ?

   B: my / 's / teacher / He / .

5. **A:** Seattle / hot / Is / ?

   B: isn't / No, / it / .

6. **A:** you / here / for / Are / the wedding / ?

   B: I / am / Yes, / .

7. **A:** name / What's / his / last / ?

   B: Mason / It's / .

A: <u>Is Steve from Portland?</u>

B: <u>No, he's not.</u>

A: _____

B: _____

A: _____

B: _____

A: _____

B: _____

A: _____

B: _____

A: _____

B: _____

A: _____

B: _____

5 **Who's That Woman?**

🎧 *Listen. Complete the conversations.*

1. **A:** <u>Who's</u> that <u>woman</u> with Amanda?

   B: That's Kathy.

   A: _____ _____ married?

   B: _____, _____ _____.

2. **A:** _____ _____ your brother?

   B: _____, he _____.

   A: Is he _____ _____?

   B: _____, he's _____. _____ _____ _____.

6 **Editing**

Correct these conversations. There are ten mistakes.

1. **A:** ~~Is~~ ^{Are} you a singer?

   B: Yes, I'm.

2. **A:** What her last name is?

   B: It's Smith.

3. **A:** They students?

   B: No, they are.

4. **A:** Is he your father?

   B: No, he's.

5. **A:** Are your purse new?

   B: No, it old.

6. **A:** Who that man?

   B: He Steve Beck.

Communication Practice

⑦ Nice Wedding, Right?

🎧 *Listen to the conversation. Answer each question with a short answer.*

1. Is Susan a doctor? _____

2. Is she married? _____

3. Are Bobby and Mike brothers? _____

4. Is Laura single? _____

⑧ Game: Ten Questions

A. *Your classmates choose the name of a famous person. They write it on a piece of paper and put it on your back. You don't see the name.*

B. *Ask your classmates ten* yes / no *questions about the person. Your classmates answer with short answers.*

Example:

A: Am I a man?   **A:** Am I a writer?

B: No, you aren't.   **B:** No, you aren't.

C. *Guess who you are.*

Example:

A: Am I Céline Dion?

B: Yes, you are. OR No, you aren't.

The Present of *Be*: Questions with *Where*; Prepositions of Place

It's on First between Jackson and Main.

Grammar **in Context**

🎧 *Listen and read these e-mail messages.*

Yuko's birthday

Subj: Yuko's birthday
Date: Tuesday, November 2
From: JudyJohnson@UW.edu
To: MM@UW.edu

Hi Mark,

I want to go to Yuko's party, but I don't have her address. Where's her new apartment?

Judy

a birthday cake

Yuko's birthday

Subj: Yuko's birthday
Date: Wednesday, November 3
From: MM@UW.edu
To: JudyJohnson@UW.edu

Hi Judy,

Her apartment is on First Avenue between Jackson and Main. (I don't remember the address.) It's across from a library and next to a gym. She's on the second floor, Apartment 2A. Take the number 4 bus. It stops at the corner of First and Jackson. (Her phone number is 860-2343.)

See you Saturday.

Mark

By the way, any gift ideas?

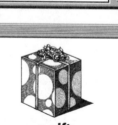

a gift

Words and Expressions

🎧 *Do you know these words and expressions? Write new words and expressions in your notebook.*

a supermarket

a gym

a library

an apartment building

1. A: Where's the gym?
   B: It's at the corner of First and Jackson.

2. A: What floor is she on?
   B: She's on the second floor.

Ordinal Numbers

1st = first	2nd = second	3rd = third	4th = fourth	5th = fifth
6th = sixth	7th = seventh	8th = eighth	9th = ninth	10th = tenth

With a Partner

Read the e-mail messages again. Look at the map. What's Yuko's address?

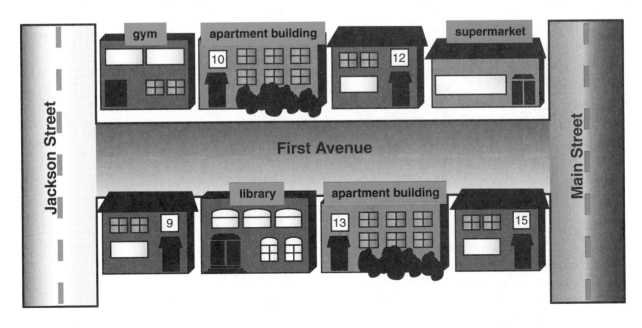

Grammar **Presentation**
The Present of *Be*: Questions with *Where*

Questions with *Where*	Short Answers	Long Answers
***Where* is** the art museum? ***Where* are** Yuko and Keiko from?	On First Avenue. Japan.	**It's** on First Avenue. **They're** from Japan.

Prepositions of Place

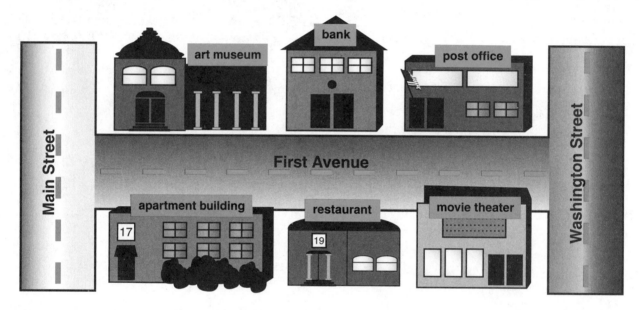

The restaurant is **on** First Avenue. It's **across from** the bank. The bank is **between** the art museum and the post office. The restaurant is **next to** the movie theater. The restaurant is **at** number 19 First Avenue.

Notes

Examples	

1. Use *where* to ask questions about **location**.

Where's is the short form for *where is*.

> **A: Where** is the restaurant?
> **B:** It's on First Avenue.
> **A: Where's** the bank?
> **B:** It's next to the museum.

2. *In, on, at, next to, between,* and *across from* are **prepositions of place**. They tell the **location** of places and things.

> • My school is **in** Seattle.
> • It's **on** Main Street.
> • It's **next to** a bank.

3. Use:

at + street address

on + street name

on the + floor

in + city, state, country, or continent

NOTE: We don't always say "street" or "avenue" in informal speaking or writing.

- My school is **at** 15 Main Street.
- It is **on** Main Street.
- My English class is **on the** 2nd floor.
- It is **in** Seattle.

A: Where's your school?

B: It's on **Main**. OR It's on **Main Street**.

4. Use **ordinal numbers** for streets and floors.

- It's at **First** Avenue and **Tenth** Street.
- She's on the **second** floor.

Reference Note

Use the **imperative** to give **directions**: *Take the number 4 bus to the museum.* Look at Unit 1 for more about the imperative.

Focused Practice

Discover the Grammar

Read Mark's e-mail message to Judy on page 36. Underline the six prepositions of place.

Example:

Her apartment is <u>on</u> First Avenue . . .

2 A Business Card   **Grammar Notes 3–4**

Look at Yuko's business card. Complete the sentences.

Yuko Shinohara
10 First Avenue, Apt. 2A
Seattle, Washington 98104

1. Yuko lives (city, state) _____.

2. She lives _____ Avenue.

3. Her building is at _____.

4. Her apartment is _____ floor.

3 **Locations**

Look at the map. Match the questions and answers that follow.

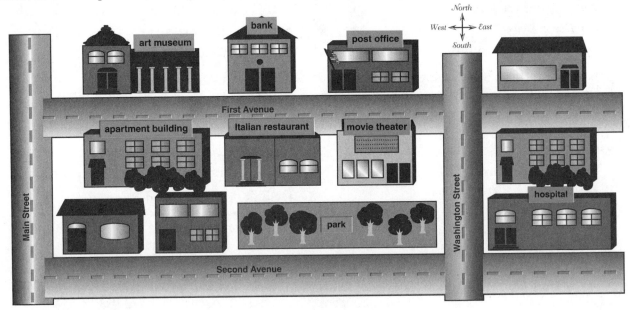

_____ b _____ **1.** Where's the art museum?

_____ **2.** Where's the hospital?

_____ **3.** Where's the restaurant?

_____ **4.** Where's the park?

a. It's across from the hospital.

b. It's next to the bank.

c. It's between the movie theater and an apartment building.

d. It's on the northeast corner of Second and Washington.

4 **Where's the Post Office?**

A. *Complete the conversation. Use the sentences in the box.*

a. Is it on Main Street?

b. Turn left at the corner.

c. Where's First Avenue?

d. Is this Main Street?

MAN: Excuse me. _____

WOMAN: Yes, it is.

MAN: I'm looking for the post office. _____

WOMAN: No, it's not. It's on First Avenue.

MAN: Oh. _____

WOMAN: Walk to the corner of this street. _____
The post office is next to the bank.

B. *Listen and check your work.*

C. *Look at the map in Exercise 3. Where are the man and woman now?*
Put an X on the street.

5 **Editing**

Correct the conversations. There are eight mistakes.

1. **A:** ~~Where's~~ *Where* are you from?

   B: I'm from Bogotá.

   A: Where Bogotá?

   B: It's on Colombia.

2. **A:** Is your apartment in this floor?

   B: No, it's on the eight floor.

3. **A:** Where's the bank?

   B: It's First Avenue.

   A: Is it next the museum?

   B: Yes, it is.

4. **A:** Is the library in Main Street and Washington Street?

   B: No, it's between Main and Jackson.

Communication Practice

6 **Where Is the Supermarket?**

*Look at the map in Exercise 3. Listen to the conversation. Write **supermarket** and **flower shop** on the correct buildings.*

7 **Information Gap: What's the Address?**

Work in pairs.

Student B, look at the Information Gap on page 274. Follow the instructions there.

Student A, look at business cards 1 and 2 on this page. Ask Student B questions and complete the cards. Then answer Student B's questions about cards 3 and 4.

1.

China Palace
_____ Main Street
_____, _____ 48104
U.S.A.

2.

Turkish Delights
213 East _____ Street
New York, _____ 10021
U.S.A.

3.

THE FITNESS CENTER

80 West Street
Ottawa, Ontario
Canada

4.

Jim's Gym
18 North Avenue
Vancouver, British Columbia
Canada

Example:

A: Where's China Palace?

B: In Ann Arbor, Michigan.

A: What street is it on?

B: . . .

Review or SelfTest

I. *Complete the conversations. Circle the correct letter.*

1. **MARK:** Are you from around here?   A Ⓑ C D
   AMY: No, I'm _____.
   (A) from here   (C) not here
   (B) here on vacation   (D) happy to meet you

2. **KATHY:** Are you a businessman?   A B C D
   MARK: No, _____.
   (A) I'm not from around here   (C) I'm on vacation
   (B) I'm a businessman   (D) I'm a writer

3. **MARK:** Is he a travel agent?   A B C D
   STEVE: Yes, _____.
   (A) he is   (C) she's a doctor
   (B) he's   (D) she's not

4. **ROSE:** Is she your daughter?   A B C D
   MARY: No, _____.
   (A) she's your friend   (C) he's my son
   (B) he isn't   (D) she's my granddaughter

5. **STEVE:** What does he do?   A B C D
   MARK: _____
   (A) He's married.   (C) He's here on business.
   (B) He's a singer.   (D) He's from Australia.

II. *Look at the pictures. Complete each question with **Is this**, **Is that**, **Are these**, or **Are those**.*

1. _____ your daughter?   2. _____ your snowboard?

3. _____ your children?   4. Kevin, _____ your books?

III. *Complete the paragraph. Use* **his**, **her**, *or* **their**.

You know the Becks and the Olsons. Bill Beck is married to Mary Beck.

Mary is _____his_____ second wife. Steve Beck and Jessica (Beck) Olson are
            1.

_____ children. Steve Beck is _____ son. Jessica Olson is _____
   2.   **3.**   **4.**

daughter. Jessica is married. Tim Olson is _____ husband. Jeremy, Annie,
                                              5.

and Ben Olson are _____ children.
                    6.

IV. *Look at the map. Complete the sentences. Use* **is** *or* **are** *and* **in**, **on**, **next to**,
between, *or* **across from**.

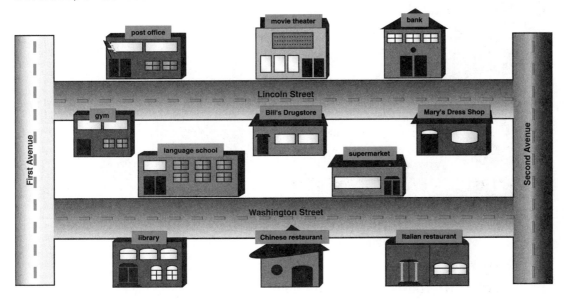

1. Lincoln Street _____is between_____ First Avenue and Second Avenue.

2. The library _____ Washington Street.

3. The gym _____ Lincoln Street _____ the post office.

4. The movie theater _____ Lincoln Street _____ the
   post office and the bank.

5. Bill's Drugstore _____ Mary's Dress Shop.

6. Mary's Dress Shop and Bill's Drugstore _____ the bank and the
   movie theater.

7. The language school _____ Washington Street _____
   the library.

8. The Italian restaurant and the Chinese restaurant _____ Washington
   Street.

9. The Chinese restaurant _____ the Italian restaurant.

▶ *To check your answers, go to the Answer Key on page 282.*

UNIT

The Past of *Be*: Statements, Yes/No Questions

Were you alone?

Grammar **in Context**

🎧 *Listen and read the conversation.*

Today (April 15)

Yesterday (April 14)

[Phone rings]

KATHY: Hello?

AMANDA: Hi, Kathy. This is Amanda.

KATHY: Hi, Amanda. How's it going?

AMANDA: Fine. Hey, Josh and I stopped by your house last night, but you weren't there. Or were you asleep?

KATHY: Actually, I wasn't home last night. I was at a movie.

AMANDA: Were you alone?

KATHY: Uh, no. I was with . . . someone. The movie was great. Really exciting. And funny too.

AMANDA: Really! What movie was it?

KATHY: *Frankenstein's Uncle.*

Kathy was at a movie **last night**.

Words and Expressions

🎧 *Do you know these words and expressions? Write new words and*
expressions in your notebook.

alone

asleep

funny

exciting

1. A: Hi, Kathy. This is Amanda.
   B: Hi, Amanda. How's it going?
   A: Fine.

2. A: We stopped by your house last night,
      but you weren't there.
   B: Actually, I wasn't home last night.
      I was at a movie.

With a Partner

A. *Practice the conversation with a partner.*

B. *Now look at the pictures. Talk about the movies. Use* **was** *and* **were**.

Example:

Matt Damon and Robin Williams were in the movie *Good Will Hunting*. Matt Damon
was Will Hunting. Robin Williams was Sean McGuire.

Starring Matt Damon as
Will Hunting and Robin
Williams as Sean McGuire.

Starring Leonardo DiCaprio
as Jack Dawson and Kate
Winslett as Rose DeWitt
Bukater.

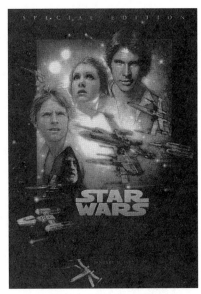

Starring Mark Hamill as
Luke Skywalker, Carrie
Fisher as Princess Leia, and
Harrison Ford as Han Solo.

Grammar **Presentation**
The Past of *Be*: Statements, *Yes / No* Questions

Affirmative Statements	
was	*were*
I **was** at a movie last night. He **was** at home. She **was** at the gym. It **was** hot.	We **were** at a party yesterday. You **were** wonderful in the play. You and Ryan **were** both wonderful. They **were** at the soccer game.

Negative Statements	
was not	*were not*
I **was not** at home last night. He **wasn't** at a movie. She **wasn't** at the library. It **wasn't** cold yesterday.	We **were not** at home last night. You **weren't** in class yesterday. They **weren't** at the library yesterday.

Yes / No Questions	Short Answers	
was / were	Affirmative	Negative
Was I right?	Yes, you **were**.	No, you **weren't**.
Was he at home?	Yes, he **was**.	No, he **wasn't**.
Was she at the game?	Yes, she **was**.	No, she **wasn't**.
Was it cold yesterday?	Yes, it **was**.	No, it **wasn't**.
Were we right?	Yes, you **were**.	No, you **weren't**.
Were you at home?	Yes, I **was**. Yes, we **were**.	No, I **wasn't**. No, we **weren't**.
Were they at a movie?	Yes, they **were**.	No, they **weren't**.

Notes / Examples

1. The past of *be* has two forms: *was* and *were*.
   - I **was** at a movie last night.
   - The girls **were** at the library yesterday.

2. Use *was* or *were* + *not* to make negative statements.
   - I **was not** alone.
   - You **were not** at home.

3. Use the contractions *wasn't* and *weren't* in speaking and informal writing.

- I **wasn't** alone.
- You **weren't** at home.

4. To ask a *yes / no question*, put *was* or *were* before the subject.

- **Was** the movie interesting?
  subject
- **Were** you alone at the movie?
  subject

5. Use a pronoun and *was*, *wasn't*, *were*, or *weren't* in short answers.

A: Was Mary at the library yesterday?
B: Yes, **she was**.

A: Were your friends at home last night?
B: No, **they weren't**.

Focused Practice

1 Discover the Grammar

A. *Read* Grammar in Context *again. Underline the past forms of* **be**. *Circle the subjects.*

Example:

. . . (you) weren't there.

B. *Match the questions and answers.*

____d____ **1.** Were you at home yesterday?

_____ **2.** Was Ryan in class yesterday?

_____ **3.** Was the concert good?

_____ **4.** Was the movie interesting?

_____ **5.** Was Susan at the library yesterday?

a. No, it wasn't. The music was pretty bad.

b. Yes, she was. We were both there.

c. Yes, it was. Matt Damon is a great actor.

d. No, I wasn't. I was at a concert.

e. No, he wasn't. He was sick.

2 Who Was in That Movie?　　　　Grammar Notes 1–3

Look at the movie posters on page 45. Complete the sentences with **was**, **wasn't**, **were**, *or* **weren't**.

1. Matt Damon and Robin Williams _____were_____ in *Good Will Hunting*. They _____ in *Titanic*.

2. Kate Winslett _____ in *Titanic*. She _____ in *Star Wars*.

3. Carrie Fisher and Harrison Ford _____ in *Star Wars*, but they _____ in *Good Will Hunting*.

3 **Last Night**

Look at the pictures. Where were these people last night? Complete the sentences.
*Use **was** or **were**.*

at a concert

at a movie

at a play

at a party

at a soccer game

at home

1. Last night, Tim and Jessica _____were at a movie_____ .

2. Mary, Annie, and Ben _____ .

3. Jeremy _____ .

4. Mark _____ .

5. Bill and Steve _____ .

6. Judy _____ .

4 **Editing**

Correct the note from Kathy. There are seven mistakes.

Mark,

              wasn't
    Sorry I ~~was~~ home last night. I were at a basketball game.
Amanda and Josh was with me. It were really exciting.

      Where were you on Tuesday afternoon? Susan, Brent, and
I are at the soccer game, but you were there. That's too bad.
It is really exciting.

     I'll talk to you soon. Call me.

                Kathy

Communication Practice

5 What's the Message?

Listen to the message on the answering machine. Check (✓) **True, False,** *or* **No Information.**

	True	False	No Information
1. Mark is at home now.	❏	❏	❏
2. Josh was at the movies last night.	❏	❏	❏
3. Amanda was at home last night.	❏	❏	❏
4. Josh was alone at the movies.	❏	❏	❏
5. The movie was very long.	❏	❏	✓
6. The movie was *Tarzan*.	❏	❏	❏

Hello, this is Mark . . .

6 Yesterday

Work with a partner. Answer the questions. Give more information.

1. Were you late to class yesterday?
2. Were you at a concert yesterday?
3. Were you at home last night?

4. Were you at the library yesterday?
5. Were you at a movie last night?
6. Were you at school yesterday?

Example:

A: Were you late to class yesterday?
B: I was. The bus was late.

7 Talk about an Event

Tell a partner about a movie, a play, a concert, or a game.
How was it? Use the following words.

Example:

A: You weren't home last night
(last Sunday / yesterday / etc.).
B: No, I was at a movie. *The Sixth Sense*.

A: Was it good?
B: Yes! It was exciting—and scary.

funny

exciting

boring

scary

interesting

The Past of *Be*: *Wh-* Questions

How was your vacation?

Grammar **in Context**

🎧 *Listen and read the conversation.*

JASON: Hi, Mark. Welcome back. How was your vacation?

MARK: Great.

JASON: You look good. Where were you?

MARK: In Spain.

JASON: Nice. How long were you there?

MARK: Ten days. Ten wonderful days.

JASON: How was the weather?

MARK: Hot and sunny. But it was cool at the beach.

JASON: Were you on a tour?

MARK: No, but I was with a guide.

JASON: A guide? Who was your guide?

MARK: Remember Kathy? At Amanda's wedding? The travel agent?

JASON: Sure. She was your guide?

MARK: Yes. She was in Barcelona last week.

JASON: You lucky man!

A beach near Barcelona

Words and Expressions

🎧 *Do you know these words and expressions? Write new words and expressions in your notebook.*

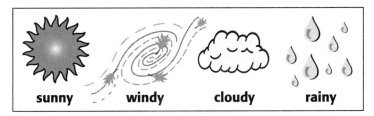

sunny   **windy**   **cloudy**   **rainy**

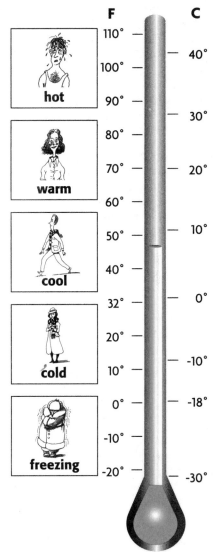

1. A: Welcome back.
   B: Thanks.

2. A: How long were you on vacation?
   B: Two weeks.

3. A: How was the weather?
   B: Fine. It was warm and sunny.

4. A: Remember Kathy? (Do you remember Kathy?)
   B: Sure.

With a Partner

A. *Practice the conversation with a partner.*

B. *Ask your partner these questions about December 31, 1999. Your partner chooses an answer.*

1. A: Where were you?   **B:** I was _____.
                                          (at the beach / at home / at a party / at a concert)

2. A: Who were you with?   **B:** I was _____.
                                          (with friends / with my family / alone)

3. A: How was the weather?   **B:** It was _____.
                                          (hot / warm / cool / cold)

4. A: How was your evening?   **B:** It was _____.
                                          (wonderful / okay / so-so / awful)

5. A: How long were you there? **B:** I was there _____.
                                          (until midnight / until 2:00 A.M. / until the morning)

Grammar **Presentation**
The Past of *Be*: *Wh*- Questions

Wh- Questions	Short Answers	Long Answers
Where **were** you?	(In) Spain.	I was in Spain.
Who **were** you with?	Friends.	I was there with friends.
How **was** the weather?	Hot.	It was hot.
How long **were** you there?	Ten days.	I was there for ten days.

Wh- Questions about the Subject	Short Answers	Long Answers
Who **was** in Spain?	Mark (was).	Mark was in Spain.

Notes

Examples

Notes	Examples
1. *Wh*- questions start with words like *where*, *when*, *who*, *what*, *how*, *how long*. These words ask for information. In informal conversation, **answers** are usually **short**.	**A:** *How* was your vacation? **B:** Great! **A:** *When* were you in Spain? **B:** Last week.
2. Use *where* to ask about a **location**. Use *when* to ask about a **time**.	**A:** *Where* were you? **B:** In Spain. **A:** *When* were you there? **B:** In June.
3. Use *who* to ask about a **person**.	**A:** *Who* was in Spain? **B:** Mark. **A:** *Who* were you with? **B:** A friend.
4. Use *how* to ask for a **description**.	**A:** *How* was your vacation? **B:** Wonderful!
5. Use *how long* to ask for a **length of time**.	**A:** *How long* was the game? **B:** Two hours.

6. NOTE: Use *it* to talk about the <u>weather</u>. *It* is the subject of this sentence.

> **A:** How was the weather?
>
> **B: It** was hot.

Focused Practice

1 Discover the Grammar

A. *Read* Grammar in Context *again. Find three more* wh- *questions. Write the questions below.*

1. ___How was your vacation?___ *who were you with?*
2. ___How was the weather___
3. ___How ~~was~~ long were you there___ *were you on a tour?*
4. ___what was your vacation___ *when were you in Spain?*

yes or No

2 Conversations   Grammar Notes 1–6

Put the words in the right order. Make conversations.

1. **A:** How / your weekend / was / ?   **A:** ___How was your weekend?___
   B: was / It / great / .   **B:** ___It was great.___

2. **A:** How / the weather / was / ?   **A:** ___How was the weather?___
   B: It / awful / was / .   **B:** ___It was awful.___

3. **A:** you / were / Where / ?   **A:** ___where were you?___
   B: a jazz concert / At / .   **B:** ___At a jazz concert___

4. **A:** the musician/ Who / was / ?   **A:** ___who was the musician?___
   B: was / Wynton Marsalis / It .   **B:** ___It was___

5. **A:** the concert / long / was / How / ?   **A:** ___How long was the concert?___
   B: two hours / It / was / .   **B:** ___It was two hours.___

3 What's the Question?   Grammar Notes 1–6

Write questions about the <u>underlined</u> *words.*

How many miles?

1. **A:** ___How was the weather___?
   B: It was <u>sunny</u>.

2. **A:** ___Who was___ at a movie?
   B: <u>Mark</u> was.

3. **A:** ___Where was___ Pierre on Monday?
   B: He was <u>in Paris</u>.

4. **A:** ___where was steve?___?
   B: Steve was <u>at work</u>.

5. **A:** ___How was the the house?___?
   B: The movie was <u>wonderful</u>.

6. **A:** ___How long was___ the movie?
   B: The movie was <u>three hours long</u>.

long — time
How / far — size → short – small, measurement (Length)
much (many) → distance
nice
How long
How far

4 Editing

Correct the conversations. There are eight mistakes.

1. **A:** How ~~were~~ was your weekend?

   B: Saturday evening was great.

   A: Where was you?

   B: At a soccer game.

   A: How the game was?

   B: Exciting and long.

   A: How long were it?

   B: Three hours.

2. **A:** How were your vacation?

   B: Okay.

   A: Where you were?

   B: Was at the beach.

   A: How the weather was?

   B: Cool and rainy.

   A: That's too bad.

Communication Practice

5 How Was Jason's Weekend?

Listen to the conversation about Jason's weekend. Complete the sentences.

1. Jason's weekend was _____great_____.
   a. good   **b.** great   **c.** bad

2. He was at _____.
   a. the beach   **b.** a movie   **c.** home

3. The weather was _____.

   a. sunny and cool   **b.** sunny and hot   **c.** sunny and cold

6 Information Gap: How Was the Weather on Sunday?

A. *Listen and repeat the names of the days of the week.*

Sunday	Monday	Tuesday	Wednesday	Thursday	Friday	Saturday

B. *Work in pairs.*

Student B, look at the Information Gap on page 275. Follow the instructions there.

Student A, complete this chart. Ask Student B questions about the weather in Tokyo. Then answer Student B's questions about the weather in Rio.

Example:

A: How was the weather in Tokyo last Sunday?

B: It was sunny and warm.

	Tokyo	Rio de Janeiro
Sunday		
Monday		
Tuesday		

7 **Game: Who Was Really There?**

A. *Work in groups of three. Choose a place where only one student was.*

All three students say, "I was in _____."

Example:

A: I was in Kyoto.

B: I was in Kyoto.

C: I was in Kyoto.

B. *The class asks the three students questions.*

Examples:

When were you there?

How was the weather?

Who were you with?

Were you on a tour?

How long were you there?

C. *Students A, B, and C answer the questions. The class guesses who was really there.*

Review or SelfTest

I. *Complete the conversations. Circle the correct letter.*

1. AMANDA: Where were you last night?
   KATHY: _____
   (A) Yes, I was.   (C) Were you alone?
   (B) At a movie.   (D) For two hours.

A Ⓑ C D

2. MARK: Was she at the gym?
   STEVE: _____
   (A) No, she was.   (C) Who was at the gym?
   (B) Yes, she was.   (D) No, they weren't.

A B C D

3. KATHY: _____
   AMANDA: Where were you?
   (A) Sorry I wasn't   (C) Are you at the gym?
       home last night.   (D) Mark and I are at
   (B) Were you at home?   a soccer game.

A B C D

4. JASON: How long were you there?
   MARK: _____
   (A) Fine, thanks.   (C) Yesterday.
   (B) By car.   (D) Four days.

A B C D

5. JASON: _____
   MARK: It was cool.
   (A) How was the weather?   (C) How long was it?
   (B) How are you?   (D) Where were you?

A B C D

6. JASON: _____
   MARK: No, I wasn't. I was alone on a tour.
   (A) Were you with friends? (C) Where were you?
   (B) How were you?   (D) What movie was it?

A B C D

7. AMANDA: _____
   KATHY: It was scary.
   (A) How long was the movie? (C) How was the movie?
   (B) How is the movie?   (D) Who was in the movie?

A B C D

II. *Complete the conversations. Use* **was, were, wasn't, weren't,**
I, you, he, she, it, *and* **they** *in your answers.*

1. A: Was I right?
   B: Yes, ____you____ ___were___.

2. A: Was it hot in Mexico City?
   B: No, _____ _____. It was cool.

3. A: Were they in Madrid?
B: No, _____ _____. They were in Barcelona.

4. A: Were you at home?
B: Yes, _____ _____ at home all day.

5. A: Was Tom Hanks in *Saving Private Ryan*?
B: Yes, _____ _____.

6. A: Was your aunt in Hawaii?
B: No, _____ _____ in Fiji.

III. *Complete the questions about a photo. Use the words in the box.*

| How | How long | When | What | Where | Who |

A: _____Who_____'s that woman?
1.
B: My sister.

A: _____ is she?
2.
B: In Bryce.

A: _____'s Bryce?
3.
B: It's a national park in Utah. We were there with her on a family vacation.

A: _____ were you there?
4.
B: Last year.

A: _____ were you there?
5.
B: Three days.

A: _____ was the weather?
6.
B: Hot.

IV. *Complete the letter from Judy to her family. Use the present or past of* **be.**

Hi Everyone,

Last week _____was_____ terrible. It _____ exam week. My friends and
1.   2.
I _____ at the library every day. But this week is easy. We _____
3.   4.
free to read and relax. No homework, no exams.

How _____ everyone at home? Mom, how _____ your flowers?
5.   6.
Beautiful, I _____ sure. And Ken, how _____ your arm? I hope it
7.   8.
_____ okay. Remember! Basketball _____ just a game. Dad, thanks
9.   10.
for the check. My classes _____ terrific this year, especially journalism.
11.
Send my love to Grandma and Grandpa.

Love,

Judy

▶ *To check your answers, go to the Answer Key on page 282.*

9 The Present Progressive: Statements

She's dreaming about her office.

Grammar **in Context**

🎧 *Listen and read the conversation.*

Tim: Those pictures are from the company picnic.

Al: That's a funny picture. Who's that man?

Tim: It's me.

Al: You're kidding.

Tim: No. Really! I'm not wearing my glasses.

Al: Oh. Well, what are you doing?

Tim: My assistant and I are playing Frisbee.

Al: You're wearing a funny hat.

Tim: Yeah. It's not my hat. The sun was very hot.

Al: Who are the other people?

Tim: That's our vice president. He's barbecuing chicken. And our president is talking to our new salespeople. They're all listening carefully. She's the boss.

AL: Where was this picnic?

TIM: In West Park. It's a great place for a company picnic.

AL: It looks like fun.

TIM: It was . . . Well, it was fun for everyone but Sabrina. Sabrina's our receptionist. Look at this picture. She's *not* enjoying the picnic. She hates picnics, and she hates hot weather. She's dreaming about her cool office.

Words and Expressions

🎧 *Do you know these words and expressions? Write new words and expressions in your notebook.*

They're having a picnic.

He's barbecuing chicken.

She's running after a Frisbee.

The receptionist is wearing glasses.

1. A: You're kidding!
   B: No. Really.

2. A: It looks like fun.
   B: It was.

With a Partner

A. *Practice the conversation with a partner.*

B. *Close your eyes. Relax. Daydream. Tell the class your daydream.*

Examples:

I'm dreaming about Hawaii.

I'm dreaming about dinner.

Grammar **Presentation**
The Present Progressive: Statements

Affirmative Statements		
am	*is*	*are*
I **am listening**.	He **is eating**. She **is talking**. It **is raining**.	We **are listening**. You **are talking**. They **are talking**.
I**'m** listening.	He**'s** talking. She**'s** listening. It**'s** snowing.	We**'re** listening. You**'re** talking. They**'re** listening.

Negative Statements		
am not	*is not*	*are not*
I **am not talking**.	He **is not listening**. She **is not reading**. It **is not snowing**.	We **are not working**. You **are not listening**. They **are not working**.
I**'m not** talking.	He**'s not** listening. OR He **isn't** listening. She**'s not** talking. It**'s not** snowing.	We**'re not** talking. OR We **aren't** talking. You**'re not** talking. They**'re not** talking.

Notes

Examples

Notes	Examples
1. Use the **present progressive** to talk about an event that is **happening now**. 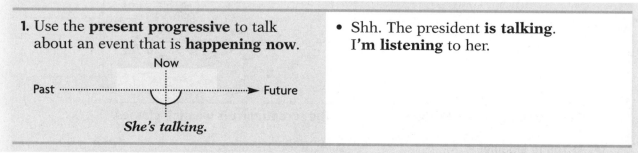	• Shh. The president **is talking**. **I'm listening** to her.

2. Use a form of *be* + the **verb** + *–ing* to form the present progressive.

NOTE: If the **base verb ends in** *–e*, drop the *–e* and add *–ing*.

If the **base verb is one syllable** and it ends in a consonant + a vowel + a consonant, **double the last consonant**. Then add *–ing*.

	base verb
• I **am listening**.	listen
• She **is talking**.	talk
• He is writ**ing**.	write
• She is run**ning**.	run
• They're sit**ting** on the grass.	sit

3. Use **contractions** in speaking and informal writing.

- He**'s** playing Frisbee.
- I**'m** reading.
- They**'re** smiling.

4. Use a form of *be + not +* the **verb** *+ –ing* for **negative statements**.

There are **two contractions** for *is not* and *are not*.

- I**'m not wearing** a hat.

- He**'s not** talking. OR He **isn't** talking.
- They**'re not** reading. OR They **aren't** reading.

Focused Practice

① Discover the Grammar

Read Grammar in Context *again. Find and write four affirmative sentences and two negative sentences in the present progressive.*

Affirmative sentences:

He's barbecuing chicken.

_____

_____

_____

Negative sentences:

_____

_____

② Affirmative or Negative?   Grammar Notes 2–4

Is the sentence affirmative or negative? Write **A** *or* **N**.

_N_ **1.** I'm not wearing my glasses.

_____ **2.** We're playing Frisbee.

_____ **3.** He's not cooking.

_____ **4.** She's talking to our new salespeople.

_____ **5.** You're wearing a funny hat.

_____ **6.** Sabrina isn't playing Frisbee.

_____ **7.** It's raining.

3 **A Family Scene**

A. *Complete the chart. Write the base form or the –ing form of the verbs.*

Base Form	-*ing* Form	Base Form	-*ing* Form
1. eat	eating	**6.** _____	playing
2. _cook_	cooking	**7.** bake	_____
3. _____	reading	**8.** drink	_____
4. wear	_____	**9.** _____	sleeping
5. write	_____	**10.** sit	_____

B. *Look at the picture. Write about the people and the cat. Use the present progressive form of the verbs above.*

1. Jessica _____ chicken.

2. Tim ___is sitting___ at a desk and ___is writing___ a letter.

3. Jeremy ___is eating___ pasta. He ___is drinking___ soda.

4. Ben and Annie ___are playing___ cards.

5. The cat _____ a hat and ___reading___ a book.

4 **Clothes for Work**   Grammar Notes 1–4

Tim Olson works for Arthur Andrews Company.
Read this article from his company newsletter.

Five years ago

Today

Arthur Andrews Company
EMPLOYEE NEWS & VIEWS

Fall 2001   Vol. 8 Issue 3

Goodbye Suits, Hello Sweaters

Look at us five years ago. Now take a look at us today. What's the difference? That's right. We're not wearing suits. We're all wearing "casual" clothes. Some men are wearing turtleneck sweaters. Some are wearing shirts. Some women are wearing pants with sweaters. Others are wearing skirts.

Tim Olson says,

"Casual clothes are great. I'm saving money. And I'm much more comfortable." Pam Cooper says, "I love the new look. I love the new policy."

But not everyone likes the change. Todd Stuart says, "I'm not happy. I like to wear a suit."

Are casual clothes here to stay? At this time, we just don't know.

*True or false? Write **T** or **F** on the line.*

___F___ **1.** Five years ago: No one at Arthur Andrews Company is wearing a suit.

___F___ **2.** Today: The men are wearing suits, but the women aren't.

___F___ **3.** Everyone is happy with the new policy.

___T___ **4.** Tim Olson is happy. He's saving money.

5 **Tickets to a Concert**   Grammar Notes 1–4

🎧 *Listen and complete the conversation.*

JEREMY: Hi, guys. Are you busy?

ANNIE: Well, _____.

BEN: And _____ TV.

JEREMY: Too bad. I have tickets to a rap concert.

ANNIE: Tickets to a rap concert? _____ anymore.

BEN: And _____.

JEREMY: Well, come on. Let's go. The concert is in twenty minutes. Just one thing . . .

ANNIE: What?

JEREMY: Don't tell Mom and Dad about our report cards. Wait a week.

BEN AND ANNIE: _____.

6 Editing

Correct the sentences. There are ten mistakes.

1. Annie ∧ wearing a new T-shirt today.   *(is)*

2. We no are eating pasta now.

3. They're cook chicken right now.

4. He reading the newspaper now.

5. It no is raining today.

6. I no drinking water. I drinking soda.

7. She isn't talk. She's listen.

8. You not listening to me.

Communication Practice

7 Where Is Everyone?

🎧 *Listen to the conversation. Listen again and complete the chart.*

	Where are they?	**What are they doing?**
Dad	In the living room.	Reading the paper.
Mom		
Grandma		
Grandpa		

8 Personal Responses

A. *Check (✓) the true statements.*

❏ I'm wearing a sweater.

❏ Our teacher is wearing a suit.

❏ Our classmates are listening to music.

❏ The person on my left is wearing glasses.

❏ The sun is shining today.

❏ It's raining today.

❏ I'm not wearing a sweater.

❏ Our teacher isn't wearing a suit.

❏ Our classmates aren't listening to music.

❏ The person on my left isn't wearing glasses.

❏ The sun isn't shining today.

❏ It's not raining today.

B. *Read your sentences. Compare them with a partner.*

9 What Are They Wearing?

A. *Work with a partner. Look at the second picture in Exercise 4. Label the clothes.*

a shirt	a sweater	a skirt	a vest
a blouse	a turtleneck	pants	

B. *Describe one of the people in the picture. Your partner points to the person.*

Example:

This person is wearing a turtleneck sweater.

10 At a Barbecue

Study the two pictures. Find five differences.

Picture A

Picture B

Example:

In Picture A Tim Olson is cooking hot dogs. In Picture B he's cooking chicken.

10 The Present Progressive: Yes/No Questions

Is Annie sleeping?

Grammar **in Context**

🎧 *Listen and read the conversations.*

TIM: Hi, hon. Everyone okay at home?

JESSICA: I hope so. Jeremy's at a ball game with Steve.

TIM: Oh. Is Mrs. Brody watching the kids?

JESSICA: No. She has the flu. Kelly Brown's babysitting.

TIM: Who's that?

JESSICA: Mrs. Brody's granddaughter. She's thirteen.

TIM: Hmm. A bit young, isn't she? Well, let's enjoy the meal. Call her after dinner.

[Later]

KELLY: Hello?

JESSICA: Hi, Kelly. This is Mrs. Olson. How's it going? Are the children listening to you?

KELLY: Oh, yes. Everything's great.

JESSICA: Good. Is Ben doing his homework?

KELLY: No, not now. He's baking. We're making cookies.

JESSICA: Oh? Well, that's nice. Just remind him about his homework. What about Annie? Is she sleeping?

KELLY: No. Her friend Gail is here. The girls are playing. They're having fun.

JESSICA: Hmm. Well, I'm sure they're okay. But please go and check.

KELLY: Sure, Mrs. Olson. Don't worry. Everything's cool. Enjoy your anniversary.

JESSICA: Thanks, Kelly. See you around eleven.

Words and Expressions

🎧 *Do you know these words and expressions? Write new words and expressions in your notebook.*

They're playing.

She's sleeping.

He's doing his homework.

1. A: How's it going?
  B: Great.

2. A: See you around eleven.
  B: Okay. See you.

3. A: Don't worry. Enjoy your anniversary.
  B: Thanks.

4. She has the flu.

With a Partner

A. *Practice the conversations with two partners.*

B. *Talk about the cartoon. What does it mean?*

DENNIS THE MENACE

"The sitter is sleeping. Now you need to pay me. Right?"

Grammar **Presentation**

The Present Progressive: *Yes / No* Questions

Yes / No Questions	Short Answers	
Am I **dreaming**?	Yes, you **are**.	No, you**'re not**. OR No, you **aren't**.
Is he **sleeping**?	Yes, he **is**.	No, he**'s not**. OR No, he **isn't**.
Are they **playing**?	Yes, they **are**.	No, they**'re not**. OR No, they **aren't**.

Notes

Examples

1. In a *yes / no* **question**, put *am*, *is*, or *are* before the subject.

- STATEMENT: You **are** working.

  (subject above You)
- QUESTION: **Are** you working?

  (subject above you)

2. Use **short answers** in speaking and informal writing.

A: Are you doing your homework?

B: Yes, I am. OR **Yes.**

C: No, I'm not. OR **No.**

3. Don't use contractions in affirmative short answers.

A: Is he reading?

B: Yes, **he is.** NOT ~~Yes, he's.~~

4. REMEMBER: There are **two contractions** for *is not* and *are not*.

- She**'s not** reading. OR
  She **isn't** reading.
- We**'re not** working. OR
  We **aren't** working.

Focused Practice

 Discover the Grammar

Read Grammar in Context *again. Underline the four* yes / no *questions in the present progressive.*

Example:

Is Mrs. Brody watching the kids?

2 Questions and Answers   Grammar Notes 1–3

Match the questions and the answers.

__i__ **1.** Are you kidding?   **a.** No, go to the other line.

_____ **2.** Is it raining?   **b.** Yes, you are.

_____ **3.** Are we standing in the right line? **c.** No, they're wearing jeans.

_____ **4.** Are you still reading?   **d.** No, he's doing his homework.

_____ **5.** Are they wearing suits?   **e.** Yes, I am. It's a long book.

_____ **6.** Am I doing the right exercise? **f.** No, she's crying.

_____ **7.** Is she smiling?   **g.** No, but it's cloudy.

_____ **8.** Is he playing?   **h.** No, Amy is watching them.

_____ **9.** Is Mrs. Burns watching the kids? **i.** Yes, of course. I'm not a hundred years old.

3 A Phone Call for Kelly   Grammar Notes 1–3

A. *Write statements and* yes / no *questions in the present progressive. Use the words in parentheses.*

KELLY: Hello.

SUSAN: Kelly?

KELLY: Uh-huh. Susan?

SUSAN: Yes, it's me. So, tell me. Is he there?

KELLY: You mean . . .

SUSAN: Jeremy, of course.

KELLY: Uh . . . sure. Right here with me.

SUSAN: Oh, you're so lucky. _____?
                                    1. (you / watch TV together)

KELLY: Yeah. _____.
                    2. (we / watch / a video)

SUSAN: _____?
              3. (you/ watch a romance)

KELLY: Uh-huh. _____ *Love Story*.
                    4. (We / watch)

SUSAN: Awesome. _____?
                        5. (Jeremy / wear / that cool cap)

KELLY: Sure. And he wants to take me to a concert.

SUSAN: Wow!

KELLY: Hey Susan. _____. _____ here
                        6. (I / kid)   7. (Jeremy / not / sit)

with me. _____ together. He isn't even here.
            8. (We / watch a video / not)

_____ a silly basketball game. And he doesn't
   9. (Jeremy and his uncle / watch)

know I exist.

B. *Listen and check your work.*

4 Photos

🎧 *Listen and complete the conversation.*

JESSICA: How are the photos?

TIM: This one is _____.

JESSICA: You're right. It is. _____?

TIM: No. _____.

He's doing magic tricks.

JESSICA: Oh. Well, look at this photo.

That's me in New York.

TIM: _____?

JESSICA: Tim! I'm not wearing a hat. That's my

_____!

TIM: Oh. Sorry.

5 Editing

Correct these conversations. There are fifteen mistakes.

1. **A:** ~~He~~ He's playing cards.

   B: No, he not. He's doing magic tricks.

2. **A:** Are you wear my T-shirt?

   B: Yes, I am. Is that okay?

3. **A:** Is raining?

   B: Yes, it's.

4. **A:** Are they read in the living room?

   B: No. They read in the bedroom.

5. **A:** Oh, I'm sorry. Am I use your dictionary?

   B: Yes. It's my dictionary, but it's okay.

6. **A:** Steve working hard?

   B: Yes, is he.

7. **A:** Am wearing a good outfit?

   B: It's perfect.

8. **A:** Is she do her homework?

   B: I don't know.

9. **A:** Are we sit in the right seats?

   B: Yes, we're.

10. **A:** I'm read a wonderful book.

    B: Oh? What's the title?

Communication Practice

6 A Telephone Conversation

🎧 *Listen to the telephone conversation between Steve and his sister, Jessica. Then listen again and check* **Yes**, **No**, *or* **No Information**.

	Yes	No	No Information
1. Is Steve working hard?	❏	❏	❏
2. Is Tim listening to the conversation?	❏	❏	❏
3. Is Steve writing for a newspaper and teaching?	❏	❏	❏
4. Are Jessica and Steve talking about their parents?	❏	❏	❏

7 How's Your Memory?

A. *Look at the* Dennis the Menace *cartoon on page 67. Label these items in the picture.*

a sandwich	glasses	a coat
a glass of milk	a sofa	shoes

B. *Write five yes / no questions about the cartoon. Use the present progressive.*

1. Is Dennis wearing a coat? _____
2. _____
3. _____
4. _____
5. _____

C. *Ask classmates your questions. Answer their questions.*

8 Game: Charades

A. *Write a sentence in the present progressive. Use one of these verbs.*

bake	cook	daydream	drink	eat	write
listen to	play	read	sleep	watch	clean

B. *Give your sentence to a classmate. That classmate acts out your sentence.*

C. *The class asks yes / no questions to guess the action.*

Example:

CLASS: Are you playing cards?

YOU: Yes, I am.

The Present Progressive: Wh- Questions

What are you making?

Grammar **in Context**

🎧 *Listen and read the conversations.*

ANNIE: Hey, Mom. Dad's driving down the street. Where's he going?

JESSICA: To the store.

ANNIE: Why is he going to the store now?

JESSICA: Because we're out of milk.

ANNIE: Oh. What's for dinner?

JESSICA: Your favorite!

ANNIE: My favorite? Really? What?

JESSICA: Broccoli.

ANNIE: Mom! Come on! Are you kidding?

JESSICA: Yes, I'm kidding.

[*Later*]

JEREMY: Hi, Mom. Who are you talking to?

JESSICA: Dad. He's at the supermarket.

JEREMY: What are you making?

JESSICA: Spaghetti.

JEREMY: With meat sauce?

JESSICA: Yes. Of course with meat sauce.

JEREMY: Mmm. Good deal. I'm starved. What's for dessert?

JESSICA: Apple pie with ice cream.

JEREMY: What flavor? Chocolate chip?

JESSICA: Sorry. It's vanilla. Now, Jeremy, don't forget about your guitar lesson.

JEREMY: That's tomorrow, Mom. I have a date tonight.

Words and Expressions

🎧 *Do you know these words and expressions? Write new words and expressions in your notebook.*

out of milk

broccoli

spaghetti

apple pie

chocolate chip ice cream

a slice of pizza

1. A: What's for dinner?
   B: Spaghetti.
   A: Good deal. I'm starved.

2. A: Come on! Are you kidding?
   B: Yes, I'm kidding.

With a Partner

A. *Practice the conversations with two partners.*

B. *Look at the pictures. Ask and answer questions. Say what they are eating.*

Example:

A: What's he eating?
B: He's eating spaghetti. What's she eating?

Grammar **Presentation**
The Present Progressive: *Wh-* Questions

Wh- Questions About the Object	Short Answers
What **are** you **making**?	Spaghetti.
Where **are** you **going**?	To the store.
Why **is** Dad **going** to the store now?	We're out of milk.
Who **are** you **talking** to?	Dad.
How **are** you **doing**?	Fine.

Wh- Questions About the Subject	Short Answers
Who **is singing**?	Dad. OR Dad is.

Notes

Examples

Notes	Examples
1. Begin *wh-* **questions** in the present progressive with a question word like *what*, *where*, *why*, *who*, or *how*. Use *am*, *is*, or *are* + the *–ing* form of the verb.	Wh- word + *be* + subject + *-ing* form • *What* **are** you **making**? • *Where* **is** he **going**?
2. Use *who* to ask about a **person**.	A: *Who* is singing in the shower? B: Mom (is). A: *Who* are you talking to? B: Dad. He's at the supermarket.
3. Use *why* to ask for **reasons**.	A: *Why* is Dad going to the store now? B: Because we're out of milk.
4. In informal conversation, **answers** are often **short**.	A: Who's singing? B: **Dad (is).** A: Where's Dad going? B: **To the store.**

Pronunciation Note

In *yes / no* questions, your voice goes up at the end of the question:

Are you watching TV now?

In *wh-* questions, your voice goes up and down at the end:

What are you watching?

Focused Practice

1 Discover the Grammar

A. *Read* Grammar in Context *again. Underline the* wh- *questions in the present progressive.*

Example:

A: Where's he going?

B. *Match the* wh- *questions and the short answers.*

<u>f</u> **1.** What are you making?   **a.** Uncle Steve is. He's really tired.
_____ **2.** Who's playing the guitar?   **b.** Mom is working late.
_____ **3.** How's it going?   **c.** Jeremy is. He's practicing for his concert.
_____ **4.** Where's Jessica going?   **d.** To work. It's 8:30.
_____ **5.** Why is Dad making dinner?   **e.** Great. What about you?
_____ **6.** Who's sleeping in my bed?   **f.** Pizza. Your favorite.

2 Conversations   Grammar Notes 1–3

A. *Change the order of the words to make questions.*

B. *Match the questions and the short answers.*

Questions   **Answers**

1. wearing / you / black / are / Why / ?

   Why are you wearing black?   _____ **a.** My favorite kind of pie—apple.

2. shower / a / Who / taking / is / ?

_____   <u>1</u> **b.** It's my favorite color.

3. feeling / morning / this / you / are / How / ?

_____   _____ **c.** To his office.

4. is / What / making / Grandma / ?

_____   _____ **d.** Pretty sick.

5. Uncle / Steve / Where / going / is / ?

_____   _____ **e.** Jeremy is. He has a date.

③ Write Questions

Write questions in the present progressive for the following answers. Use the words in parentheses and **Where**, **How**, **What**, **Why**, *or* **Who**.

1. **A:** ___Why is Dad making___ dinner?   **B:** Because Mom's at work.
   (Dad / make)

2. **A:** _____?   **B:** To their favorite restaurant for dinner.
   (Grandma and Grandpa / go)

3. **A:** _____ you?   **B:** My cousin. He's from Hawaii.
   (visit)

4. **A:** _____?   **B:** Spaghetti with meat sauce. Your favorite.
   (you / make)

5. **A:** _____ in school?   **B:** Great. She loves it.
   (your daughter / do)

④ Editing

Correct the conversations. There are seven mistakes.

         is Uncle Steve

1. **A:** Why ~~Uncle Steve is~~ sleeping?
   B: He not feeling well.

2. **A:** Who singing in the shower?
   B: Jeremy is.

3. **A:** What you are studying, Jeremy?
   B: Biology. I have a test tomorrow.

4. **A:** Why you wearing a suit today?
   B: My other clothes are dirty.

5. **A:** Who you talking to?
   B: Dad. He's at the supermarket.

6. **A:** What she wearing?
   B: A blue suit.

⑤ Intonation

🎧 **A.** *Listen and read the questions. Write an up arrow (↑) if the voice goes up at the end. Write a down arrow (↓) if the voice goes down at the end.*

Example:

What are you doing? ↓
Is it broken? ↑

1. Is Jeremy taking a shower?
2. Why is Jeremy taking a shower?
3. Is Mom making dinner?
4. What's she making?

5. Are Grandpa and Grandma coming?
6. What's Uncle Steve doing?
7. Why is he sleeping now?
8. Is he sleeping in the living room?

🎧 **B.** *Listen again and repeat. Then read the questions to a partner. Take turns.*

Communication Practice

6 Again?

Listen. Then answer the questions. Use long answers.

1. Who is Annie talking to? _____

2. What is Jeremy doing? _____

3. Why? _____

4. What is Uncle Steve doing? _____

5. Why? _____

7 Information Gap: A Strange News Story

Work in pairs.

Student B, look at the Information Gap on page 276 and follow the instructions there.

Student A, complete the story below. Ask Student B wh- questions in the present progressive.

Example:

A: Where is Jessica Olson speaking from?

B: The park.

  Good afternoon. This is KZYX News, and I'm Jessica Olson. I'm speaking to you from

_____the park_____. Tightrope walker Alonzo Bonzo is walking across the

    1.

park on a tightrope! The tightrope is a hundred feet above the park. Alonzo is wearing

_____. There is a net under the tightrope. Firefighters and

    2.

doctors are waiting by the net. _____ is in the park watching him.

        3.

Why is Alonzo doing this? For money? No, says his wife. He's doing it because tightrope

walking is his favorite sport. Alonzo is walking _____. He's halfway

            4.

across! Now he's three-quarters of the way across! Now he's on the other side!

Congratulations to Alonzo Bonzo! Everybody is happy. Everybody is laughing.

  This is Jessica Olson, KZYX News.

Review or SelfTest

I. *Complete the conversations. Circle the correct letter.*

1. MAIKO: Hi, Jeremy. What are you doing?   (A) B   C   D
    JEREMY: I'm _____ the radio.
    (A) listening to   (C) listening
    (B) listen   (D) listen to

2. ANNIE: _____ Mom and Dad going?   A   B   C   D
    BEN: To the store. We need ice cream.
    (A) What are   (C) Why are
    (B) Where are   (D) How are

3. JEREMY: Who's taking a shower?   A   B   C   D
    BEN: _____
    (A) Is Dad   (C) It was Dad.
    (B) Dad's   (D) Dad is.

4. PEDRO: Why _____ laughing?   A   B   C   D
    MARIA: Because that joke is funny.
    (A) you   (C) you are
    (B) are you   (D) you're

5. STEVE: Is it raining there?   A   B   C   D
    TIM: _____
    (A) No, it's raining.   (C) Yes, it is.
    (B) No, it is.   (D) Yes, it was.

II. *The Johnson family is spending a quiet evening together. Complete the sentences. Use the present progressive forms of the verbs in the box. Use each verb once.*

watch	make	play	read	sing	sit	sleep	~~visit~~

Judy Johnson _____is visiting_____ her parents in Michigan this week.
                       1.

It's a typical evening. Mr. Johnson _____ dinner. Mrs. Johnson
                                       2.

and Judy _____ songs, and Mrs. Johnson _____
               3.   4.

the piano. Ken and his grandmother _____ on the sofa; he
                                     5.

_____ the newspaper, and she _____ television.
     6.   7.

Prince and Princess, the cats, _____ on different chairs.
                                     8.

III. *Write conversations. Use the words in parentheses in the correct order.*

1. **A:** (doing / Annie / what's / ?)   **A:** ___What's Annie doing?___

   B: (game / she's / a / playing / .)   **B:** _____

2. **A:** (playing / Ben / is / too / ?)   **A:** _____

   B: (playing / with / cat / the / he's / no, / .)   **B:** _____

3. **A:** (laughing / you / why / are / ?)   **A:** _____

   B: (the / is / cat / wearing / a / hat / .)   **B:** _____

4. **A:** (Jessica / going / is / where / ?)   **A:** _____

   B: (supermarket / the / going / to / she's / .)   **B:** _____

IV. *Aunt Hattie is calling Steve to wish him a happy birthday. Write questions with* **what**, **who**, *or* **why** *in the present progressive. Use the words in parentheses.*

STEVE: Hello?

HATTIE: Hi, Steve. This is Aunt Hattie. Happy birthday!

STEVE: Hi, Aunt Hattie! Thanks a lot. The family is here. We're having a little party.

HATTIE: That's great. _____What's everybody doing?_____
                              1. (everybody / do)

STEVE: Well, let's see. Annie and Ben are sitting on the floor. They're playing a game.

HATTIE: _____
                              2. (they / play)

STEVE: Cards. And Dad is making dinner.

HATTIE: _____
                              3. (he / make dinner)

STEVE: Because he's a great cook. Don't you remember?

HATTIE: Oh, yes. That's right. _____
                              4. (he / make)

STEVE: Turkey. And it smells delicious.

HATTIE: Good. You know, I hear music. _____
                              5. (sing)

STEVE: Mom and Jessica. They sound good, right?

HATTIE: They sure do. Well, say hello to everybody for me.

▶ *To check your answers, go to the Answer Key on page 283.*

UNIT

12 The Simple Present: Statements

Nick likes computers.

Grammar **in Context**

🎧 *Listen and read the conversation.*

JUDY: I need more coffee. Can I get you some?

MARK: Yes, please.

JUDY: Here you go.

MARK: Thanks.

JUDY: Oh! New photos?

MARK: Yep . . . Look at this one. This is my brother, Nick. He lives in Alaska.

JUDY: You look alike.

MARK: I know. We both have blond hair and blue eyes.

JUDY: And you're both tall.

MARK: But we're different in a lot of ways.

JUDY: How?

MARK: Well, I like people and parties. Nick likes computers. I don't like computers, and Nick doesn't like parties.

JUDY: Oh, really?

MARK: Yeah. And I speak Mandarin. Nick speaks Spanish. I read newspapers and magazines. Nick reads novels. I watch TV almost every night, but Nick goes online.

JUDY: Yeah? He sounds interesting.

Words and Expressions

🎧 *Do you know these words and expressions? Write new words and expressions in your notebook.*

look alike

go online

a novel

a newspaper

a magazine

1. **A:** Can I get you some coffee?
   B: Yes, please.
   A: Here you go.
   B: Thanks.

2. **A:** This is my sister.
   B: You look alike.

3. He sounds interesting.

With a Partner

A. *Practice the conversation with a partner.*

B. *Talk about these people with your partner.*

Example:

Jackie Chan comes from Hong Kong. He speaks Cantonese.

Jackie Chan
Hong Kong
Cantonese

Salma Hayek
Mexico
Spanish

Céline Dion
Canada
French and English

**Prince William and
Prince Harry**
Great Britain
English

Grammar **Presentation**
The Simple Present: Statements

Affirmative Statements		
Subject	**Verb**	
I You* We They	**come**	from Hong Kong.
He She It	**comes**	

Negative Statements			
Subject	***Do not /*** ***Does not***	**Base Form** **of Verb**	
I You* We They	**do not** **don't**	**come**	from Hong Kong.
He She It	**does not** **doesn't**		

You is both singular and plural.

Notes

Examples

Notes	Examples
1. Use the **simple present** tense to talk about **facts** or about things that **happen again and again**.	• I **live** in Alaska. *(fact)* • He **watches** TV almost every night. *(thing happening again and again)*
2. In **affirmative statements**, use the **base form** (dictionary form) of the verb with *I*, *you*, *we*, and *they*. Add *–s* or *–es* to the base form only with the third-person singular (*he*, *she*, *it*). Add *–s* to most verbs. Add *–es* to verbs that end in *ch*, *o*, *s*, *sh*, *x*, or *z*.	• We **live** in Redmond. • They **have** a house in Seattle. • He **reads** travel books. • She **watches** TV at night.

3. Use **do not** or **does not** + the **base form** of the verb to make a **negative statement**.

Use the contractions **don't** and **doesn't** in speaking and informal writing.

- They **do not live** in the city.
- He **does not speak** Chinese.
- They **don't live** in the city.
- He **doesn't speak** Chinese.

4. **Be**, **have**, **like**, **need**, and **want** are **non-action (stative) verbs**. We usually use these verbs in the **simple present**, not the present progressive.

NOTE: Look at Units 13 and 14 for more practice with these verbs.

- Mary **likes** spaghetti.
- She **doesn't like** pizza.
- I **need** water now.
- I **don't need** food.

5. **Be** and **have** are **irregular verbs**.

NOTE: Look at Unit 15 for more practice with be and have.

- I **am** a teacher. Steve **is** a teacher too.
- I **have** a lot of students. Steve **has** a lot of students too.

Reference Note
Look at Appendix 10 on page 268 for more on the spelling and pronunciation of the third-person singular.

Focused Practice

1 Discover the Grammar

A. *Check (✓) the sentences in the simple present.*

_____ **1.** She's speaking English now. She isn't speaking Spanish.

_____ **2.** Nick and I look alike. We're brothers.

_____ **3.** Jessica speaks Spanish. She doesn't speak Italian.

_____ **4.** I have brown eyes. I don't have blue eyes.

_____ **5.** They're not working. They're playing.

_____ **6.** Jeremy has a brother and a sister.

B. *Check (✓) the sentences in the third-person singular.*

_____ **1.** Annie and I don't like fish.

_____ **2.** Maryam speaks Arabic.

_____ **3.** It doesn't snow in Brazil.

_____ **4.** She doesn't speak Italian.

_____ **5.** Nick likes computers.

_____ **6.** They come from Hong Kong.

2 **Countries and Languages**

Write two sentences about these people.

1. **Name:** Heng

   Place: Beijing, China ___Heng lives in Beijing, China.___

   Language: Mandarin ___She speaks Mandarin.___

2. **Name:** Omar

   Place: Amman, Jordan _____

   Language: Arabic _____

3. **Names:** João and Rosa

   Place: Salvador, Brazil _____

   Language: Portuguese _____

4. **Name:** Elena

   Place: Santiago, Chile _____

   Language: Spanish _____

5. **Names:** Maureen and James

   Place: Dublin, Ireland _____

   Language: English _____

3 **At the Restaurant**

Complete the conversation with the correct form of **want**. *Use the affirmative or negative of the simple present tense.*

WAITER: Can I help you?

TIM: Yes, thanks. The children ___want___ ice cream. My son _____ chocolate.
                                     1.   2.

BEN: No, Dad. I _____ chocolate. I _____ vanilla.
                         3. (not)   4.

Annie _____ chocolate.
           5.

TIM: Okay. My son _____ vanilla. My daughter _____ chocolate.
                             6.   7.

WAITER: And you, sir?

TIM: I _____ ice cream. I just _____ soda.
                8. (not)   9.

WAITER: Is that all?

TIM: Yes, thanks.

WAITER: Okay. I'll be right back.

4 *Have, Like, Need,* and *Want*   **Grammar Notes 1, 3, 4**

Complete the sentences with affirmative or negative verbs.

1. The restaurant _____doesn't have_____
   (have)
   steak. They _____have_____ fish.

2. The people _____ fish.
   (like)
   They _____ steak.

3. The man _____ water.
   (need)
   He _____ pizza.

4. The girl _____ broccoli.
   (want)
   She _____ ice cream.

5 **Editing**

Correct the letter. There are eight mistakes.

Dear Mary,

    Spain is great! The Spanish people are very friendly, but they ~~speaks~~ speak so fast. Jim speak Spanish very well. He don't understand everything, but he understand a lot. I speak a little Spanish. I don't understand much yet.

    It's raining a lot. That's unusual. People say it don't usually rain much in the summer here. We are staying at my cousin's house. He and his wife lives in a beautiful apartment in Madrid. Juan work in an office downtown. His wife Alicia not works. She stays at home with the children.

    See you soon.

    Rose

Communication Practice

6 Everyone Speaks Three Languages

🎧 *Listen to the conversation between Tim Olson and a man he meets on a train. Then listen again and complete the sentences.*

1. They're going to _____.
   a. Chicago   **b.** Seattle   **c.** Bucharest

2. The man doesn't live in _____.
   a. Romania   **b.** Bucharest   **c.** Chicago

3. The man comes from _____.
   a. Rwanda   **b.** Russia   **c.** Romania

4. A lot of people in the man's country know some _____.
   a. English   **b.** Spanish   **c.** Arabic

5. The man speaks _____ languages.
   a. one   **b.** two   **c.** three

6. Tim doesn't speak _____.
   a. English   **b.** Spanish   **c.** Romanian

ROMANIA

Bucharest
★

Black Sea

7 What Do You Do?

🎧 *Listen to the next part of the conversation. Complete the sentences with simple present verbs.*

TIM: So do you live in Seattle?

MAN: For the moment—not permanently. My wife is teaching at the university this year.

TIM: Oh. What does she teach?

MAN: She _____ European literature. She also writes novels.
            1.

TIM: That _____ interesting.
            2.

MAN: Yes, it is. But it's also difficult. She _____ American English too well.
                                                        3.

   What about you? What do you do?

TIM: I'm a graphic artist. I _____ for an advertising agency.
                                        4.

MAN: And do you _____ in Seattle?
                            5.

TIM: We _____ in the city, but we _____ near it.
                    6.   7.

8 True Statements

A. *Write true statements about yourself.*

I live in _____.

I work _____.

I don't work _____.

I speak _____.

I don't speak _____.

I like _____.

I don't like _____.

I need _____.

I don't need _____.

I want _____.

I don't want _____.

B. *Now work with a partner. Tell your partner four things about yourself. Your partner tells another classmate about you.*

Example:

A [*to B*]:   I work in a department store. I speak two languages.
            I like chocolate ice cream. I don't like pizza.

B [*to C*]:   A works in a department store. She speaks two languages.
            She likes chocolate ice cream. She doesn't like pizza.

C [*to B*]:   That sounds interesting. What about you?

9 True or False?

A. *Work with a partner. Take turns. Use the words to make affirmative sentences in the simple present tense. Three of the statements are true, and four are false. Correct the false statements.*

Example:

Most people / in Beijing / speak Spanish

A: Most people in Beijing speak Spanish.

B: False. Most people in Beijing speak Mandarin.

1. Antonio Banderas / come from / Spain

2. Most people / in Thailand / eat with chopsticks

3. People / in Japan / drive / on the left

4. People / in Britain / drive / on the right

5. People / live / at the North Pole

6. Penguins / live / in deserts

7. It / snow / in Chile / in July

B. *Check your answers on page 280.*

13 The Simple Present: Yes/No Questions

Do you want a clock?

Grammar **in Context**

🎧 *Listen and read the conversation.*

STEVE: Hey Mark. Come on in.

MARK: Hi Steve. What's happening?

STEVE: Oh, not much.

MARK: Are you busy now?

STEVE: No, not really. I'm just cleaning my closet . . . Hey, do you want a clock?

MARK: A clock? Why?

STEVE: I have an extra one.

MARK: Well, sure.

MARK: Uh . . . Does it have a minute hand?

STEVE: No, it doesn't.

MARK: Does it have an alarm?

STEVE: No.

MARK: Does it work?

STEVE: I don't know. But Mark, it's a gift.

MARK: Oh . . . Well, then . . . thanks.

Words and Expressions

 Do you know these words and expressions? Write new words and expressions in your notebook.

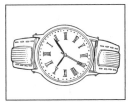

the minute hand

a watch　　　　　　**a clock**　　　　　　**an alarm**

1. A: Hey Mark. Come on in.
　　B: Hi Steve. What's happening?
　　A: Not much.

2. A: Are you busy?
　　B: No, not really. I'm just cleaning.

With a Partner

A. *Practice the conversation with a partner.*

B. *Discuss.*

　1. Do you think the clock is really a gift? Why or why not?

　2. Talk about gifts with your partner. Do you like or dislike _____?
　　a. CDs　　　　　　　　**c.** handmade gifts
　　b. clothes　　　　　　　**d.** money

Grammar **Presentation**
The Simple Present: *Yes / No* Questions

Yes / No Questions	Short Answers	
Do	Affirmative	Negative
Do I **know** him?	Yes, you **do**.	No, you **don't**.
Do you **want** this gift?	Yes, I **do**. Yes, we **do**.	No, I **don't**. No, we **don't**.
Do we **need** this clock?	Yes, you **do**.	No, you **don't**.
Do they **have** the time?	Yes, they **do**.	No, they **don't**.

Yes / No Questions	Short Answers	
Does	Affirmative	Negative
Does she **have** a watch?	Yes, she **does**.	No, she **doesn't**.
Does he **like** the clock?	Yes, he **does**.	No, he **doesn't**.
Does it **work**?	Yes, it **does**.	No, it **doesn't**.

Notes	Examples
1. Use *do* or *does* + a **subject** + the **base form** of the verb to ask *yes / no* **questions** in the simple present.	*do / does* subject base form • **Do** you **want** a clock? • **Does** Mark **have** a clock?
2. We usually use **short answers** in conversation. Sometimes we use **long answers**.	**A: Do** you **have** a digital watch? **B: No.** OR **No, I don't.** **B: No.** I **don't have a digital watch.**

Focused Practice

1 Discover the Grammar

Check (✓) the yes / no *questions in the simple present tense.*

_____ **1.** Are you wearing a watch?   _____ **4.** Are you watching the clock?

_____ **2.** Does your watch work?   _____ **5.** Don't be late.

_____ **3.** Do you have the time?   _____ **6.** Is it raining?

2 Questions   Grammar Note 1

Write yes / no *questions in the simple present tense. Use the words in parentheses and* **do** *or* **does**.

1. (you / like the color purple) _____?

2. (you / watch TV every day) _____?

3. (your best friend / have an unusual hobby) _____?

4. (your friends / like extreme sports) _____?

3 An Unusual Man   Grammar Notes 1–2

A. *Jessica is interviewing Alonzo Bonzo on TV. Complete the interview. Put the words in parentheses in the correct order.*

JESSICA: Alonzo, thank you for coming here today. You are amazing. Tell us more about yourself. We know you're a tightrope walker.

_____?

1. (you / Do / regular job / a / have)

ALONZO: Oh, yes, Jessica. I'm a librarian.

JESSICA: A librarian?

ALONZO: Yes. It pays the rent. But tightrope walking is my true love.

JESSICA: _____?
2. (practice / you / Do / at a gym)

ALONZO: No, I don't. I practice at home. I have a tightrope in my yard.

JESSICA: Really? In your backyard?

ALONZO: No. In my front yard.

JESSICA: Hmm. _____?
3. (complain / Do / the neighbors)

ALONZO: Oh, no. There's no law against tightrope walking.

JESSICA: How about your wife? _____?
4. (like / she / your / hobby / Does)

ALONZO: She worries, but she doesn't complain.

JESSICA: Tell me, Alonzo, _____?
5. (any other hobbies / have / you / do)

ALONZO: I knit. Scarves, socks, sweaters. You name it. I knit it. Here, Jessica. This is for you.

JESSICA: Why, Alonzo. It's beautiful! Thanks so much.
[*To the TV camera*] Ladies and gentlemen, this is one unusual man.

B. *Now listen and check your work.*

4 More Questions for Alonzo   Grammar Note 1

Read the end of the interview. Write the yes / no *questions in the simple present or present progressive.*

1. JESSICA: _____?

ALONZO: No, I don't sell my scarves.

2. JESSICA: Many of your scarves are purple.

_____?

ALONZO: Yes, I do. I like purple very much.

3. JESSICA: _____?

ALONZO: No, she doesn't. My wife doesn't knit.

4. JESSICA: _____?

ALONZO: Yes, she is. She's watching us right now.
[*To the TV camera*] Hi, Alice.

5. JESSICA: _____?

ALONZO: Yes, I do. I have two brothers and two sisters.
[*To the TV camera*] Hi, Scott. Hi, Russ. Hi, Jan. Hi, Lulu.

5 A Perfect Gift

🎧 *Listen and complete the conversation.*

JUDY: Are you going to the game?

MARK: No. It's my grandmother's birthday, and I need to get a gift.
_____?

JUDY: Let's see. _____?

MARK: I don't know.

JUDY: Well, _____?

MARK: I don't really know.

JUDY: _____?

MARK: I think so. I'm not sure.

JUDY: I know the perfect gift.

MARK: You do? What?

JUDY: _____.

MARK: That's not a gift.

JUDY: Yes, it is. _____.

6 Editing

Correct the conversation. There are seven mistakes.

CUSTOMER: I'm looking for a good novel.

SALESPERSON: ~~Does~~ you want a mystery?
                  Do

CUSTOMER: Yes. I love mysteries.

SALESPERSON: Here. This mystery is wonderful.

CUSTOMER: Thanks. I'm also looking for a book for my sister. She's fifteen.

SALESPERSON: Does she likes romance?

CUSTOMER: No, she don't.

SALESPERSON: She like mysteries?

CUSTOMER: No. She not like mysteries.

SALESPERSON: Well, does she like music?

CUSTOMER: Yes, she is. She love Ricky Martin. Do you have a book about him?

SALESPERSON: Sure. Over there.

CUSTOMER: Thanks.

Communication Practice

7 Ask Your Partner

Ask your partner the questions in Exercise 2. Answer your partner's questions.
Use short answers and add a sentence with more information.

Example:

A: Do you like the color purple?

B: Yes, I do. I have purple shoes, purple jeans, and a purple hat.

8 Find Someone Who . . .

A. *Write five* yes / no *questions. Use the ideas in the box. Ask four classmates your questions. Follow the example below.*

Example:

JUAN: Anna, do you like chocolate?

ANNA: Yes, I do.

JUAN: Pablo, do you like chocolate?

PABLO: No, I don't.

Find someone who. . .

likes the rain	knows a good joke	likes chocolate
has four brothers	likes extreme sports	speaks three languages
knits	plays soccer	likes to clean

Yes / No Questions		Student 1	Student 2	Student 3	Student 4
	Do you like chocolate?	Yes	No		
1.					
2.					
3.					
4.					
5.					

B. *Tell the class about your classmates.*

Example:

JUAN: *[To the class]* Anna likes chocolate. Pablo doesn't like chocolate.

The Simple Present: *Wh-* Questions

How do you like married life?

Grammar **in Context**

🎧 *Listen and read the conversation.*

KATHY: So . . . how do you like married life?

AMANDA: It's wonderful! But . . . really different.

KATHY: What do you mean?

AMANDA: Well, Josh and I are opposites. For one thing, he goes to bed early, and I stay up late.

KATHY: What time does he go to bed?

AMANDA: Eight-thirty or a quarter to nine. He starts work at 6:00 A.M.

KATHY: Where does he work?

AMANDA: At the airport.

KATHY: Oh, no wonder. What does he do?

AMANDA: He's a ticket agent.

KATHY: How late do *you* stay up?

AMANDA: At least until midnight.

KATHY: Yeah. That *is* different. What else?

At the airport

AMANDA: Well, he loves cooking, and I hate it. He doesn't like most sports, and I love them.

KATHY: Really? That's too bad. What do you have in common?

AMANDA: Talking. We talk for hours and hours. About everything.

KATHY: That's good.

Words and Expressions

🎧 *Do you know these words and expressions? Write new words and expressions in your notebook.*

go to bed early ⟵⟶ **stay up late**
opposites

cooking   **sports**

1. **A:** Josh and I are opposites.
   B: What do you mean?
   A: He's a morning person, and I'm a night person.

2. **A:** What else?
   B: He loves cooking, and I hate it.

3. **A:** What do you have in common?
   B: We talk about everything.

With a Partner

A. *Practice the conversation with a partner.*

B. *Ask and answer questions about the pictures.*

Example:

A: Who are they?
B: Venus and Serena Williams.
A: What do they do?
B: They're tennis players.
A: Where do they live?
B: In Florida. OR They live in Florida.

Venus and Serena Williams
tennis players
Florida

Emperor Akihito and Empress Michiko
Tokyo

Cameron Diaz
actress
Los Angeles

Grammar **Presentation**
The Simple Present: *Wh-* Questions

Wh- Questions	**Answers**
How **do** I **get** there? *Why* **do** you **go** to bed so early? *When* **do** we **leave**? *Where* **do** they **live**?	Take the number 3 bus. I start work at 6:00 A.M. After work. In Seattle.
What **does** he **do**? *How* late **does** she **stay up**? *What* time **does** it **start**?	He's a ticket agent. At least until midnight. At 7:00.

Wh- Questions about the Subject	**Answers**
Who **wakes** you up? Amanda? *What* **happens** on Saturday?	No. My alarm clock does. We sleep in.

Notes

Examples

1. *Wh-* **questions** ask for **information**. They often start with *when*, *why*, *how*, *where*, *what time*, *who*, or *what*.

   Use a *wh-* **word** + *do* or *does* + a subject + the base form of the verb.

   ▶ **BE CAREFUL!** Use *do* with *I*, *you*, *we*, and *they*. Use *does* with *he*, *she*, and *it*.

Wh- word	do / does	subject	base form
• *Where*	**do**	you	**work**?
• *What*	**does**	he	**make**?

2. To ask a **question about the subject**, use *who* or *what* + the third-person singular form of the verb. Do not use *do* or *does*.

   • *Who* **wakes** up first?
 NOT ~~Who does wake up first?~~

   • *What* **happens** on Sunday?

3. NOTE: To ask about the **meaning of a word**, say "*What does . . . mean?*"

   To answer, say, ". . . means . . ."

   A: *What* **does** "little" **mean**?
 NOT ~~What means "little"?~~
 NOT ~~What does mean "little"?~~

   B: "Little" **means** "small."

Pronunciation Note
REMEMBER: In pronunciation we use falling intonation for *wh-* questions:

Where do you live?

Focused Practice

1 Discover the Grammar

Read the conversation. Underline the wh- *questions in the simple present.*

MARK: So . . . <u>what do you think of married life?</u>

JOSH: Great. I love it. But it's really different.

MARK: What do you mean?

JOSH: Well, Amanda and I are opposites. She's a night person, and I'm a morning person.

MARK: What time do you go to bed?

JOSH: About 8:30 or 9:00.

MARK: Who wakes you up? Amanda?

JOSH: Amanda? No way! My alarm clock does.

MARK: So . . . are you happy?

JOSH: Totally. We talk all the time.

MARK: What do you talk about?

JOSH: Everything. Travel. Books. Movies.

MARK: That's great, man. Opposites attract!

2 Interview   Grammar Note 1

Josh's niece is asking him some questions for her school newspaper. Write her wh- *questions in the simple present.*

1. (Where / you / work / ?) _____ Where do you work? _____

2. (What time / you / start work / ?) _____

3. (What / you / do in your job / ?) _____

4. (What / Aunt Amanda / do / ?) _____

5. (Where / Aunt Amanda / work / ?) _____

6. (What sport / you / like / ?) _____

7. (Why / you / like it / ?) _____

8. (When / you / play it / ?) _____

3 What's the Question?

Write wh- *questions about the underlined words. Use* **who**, **what**, **where**, **why**, *or* **what time**.

1. **A:** Where do they live?
   B: They live on 40th Street in Redmond.

2. **A:** Jeremy, _____
   B: I go to bed at 10:30 or 10:45.

3. **A:** Tim, _____
   B: My wife cooks in our house.

4. **A:** Ben, _____
   B: I play soccer because it's really fun.

5. **A:** Mom, _____
   B: "Fascinating" means "very interesting".

4 Editing

Correct the conversation. There are four mistakes.

A: Hey! I have a new job.

B: Really? Where do you work?

A: At a bookstore.

B: What you do?

A: I'm a salesperson.

B: Does you like the work?

A: Yes. It's challenging.

B: Challenging? I don't know that word. What means "challenging"?

A: It means "hard but interesting."

Communication Practice

5 Ask Your Partner

Work with a partner. Student A, ask Student B questions from Exercise 2 on page 97. Student B, answer the questions.

Example:

A: Where do you work?

B: I work at a supermarket. Where do you work?

A: I work . . .

6 What Do You Do, Jason?

🎧 *Listen to the conversation in a cafeteria. Listen again and answer the questions with short answers.*

1. Who is new in the company?
_____ Jason (is). _____

2. What does Jason do? _____

3. What does Margaret do? _____

4. Does Jason like his job? _____

5. What does Jason dislike? _____

6. Where do Jason and Margaret live? _____

7. Does Margaret drive to work? _____

8. What time does Margaret catch the bus? _____

7 Information Gap: What Does "Tiny" Mean?

Work in pairs.

Student B, look at the Information Gap on page 277 and follow the instructions there.

Student A, ask Student B about the meaning of a word from your list. Write the answer. Then answer Student B's question. Choose an answer from the box below. Take turns.

Example:
A: What does "tiny" mean?
B: "Tiny" means "very small." What does "large" mean?

Student A's Words

1. tiny _____ very small _____   **5.** super _____

2. boring _____   **6.** unhappy _____

3. noon _____   **7.** terrible _____

4. midnight _____   **8.** nice _____

Student A's Answers

the children of your aunt or uncle   good-looking
your parents, brothers, sisters, etc.   intelligent
big   not married
between first and third   totally different

Check your answers on page 280.

The Simple Present: Be and *Have*

He has dark hair and big brown eyes.

Grammar **in Context**

🎧 *Listen and read the conversation. Judy and Mark are on a bus.*

JUDY: Look!

MARK: Where?

JUDY: There. On the second floor in the window . . . Never mind. The boy isn't there now.

MARK: What boy?

JUDY: I see a young boy in that window every day. He plays the violin.

MARK: Hmm. How old is he?

JUDY: About eight or nine.

MARK: What does he look like?

JUDY: He's a good-looking boy. He has dark hair and big brown eyes. He has a scar on his right cheek.

MARK: Does he have long arms and legs and curly hair?

JUDY: Yes, he does.

MARK: Is his hair a little long?

JUDY: I think so. Why?

MARK: He's famous. He was on the news just last night.

The young violinist

JUDY: Really?

MARK: Yes. And look at the paper. He's here too.

JUDY: Well, look at that! That's the boy.

antiques   أنتيكات

Words and Expressions

Do you know these words and expressions? Write new words and expressions in your notebook.

a window

a violin

a scar

curly hair

1. A: He was on the news just last night.
   B: Look at the paper. He's here too.
   A: Well, look at that! That's the boy.

2. A: What does he look like?
   B: He has curly hair and a scar on his cheek.

With a Partner

A. *Practice the conversation with a partner.*

B. *Read the story with a partner.*

Who Am I?

It is 1764. I am eight years old. I am from Austria. I am in England now with my family. My father is a violinist. I have an older sister. She is a violinist too. I play the violin and the harpsichord. I also write music. People say I have a beautiful voice. They say I am a child prodigy. The kings and queens of Europe love my music. My middle name is Amadeus. Who am I?

a harpsichord

C. *Check your answer on page 280.*

D. *Discuss.*

Do you like classical music? What kinds of music do you like?

Grammar **Presentation**
The Simple Present: *Be* and *Have*

Be		**Have**	
Affirmative Statements		**Affirmative Statements**	
I **am** short. He **is** tall. We **are** late.		I **have** brown eyes. She **has** blue eyes.	
Negative Statements		**Negative Statements**	
I**'m not** tall. He**'s not** short. OR He **isn't** short. We**'re not** early. OR We **aren't** early.		I **don't have** green eyes. She **doesn't have** green eyes.	
Yes / No **Questions**		*Yes / No* **Questions**	
Am I late? **Is** he ten years old? **Are** we early?		**Do** I **have** any gray hair? **Does** he **have** black hair?	
Wh- **Questions**		*Wh-* **Questions**	
What **am** I? *Where***'s** your violin? *Who* **is** tall?		*What* **do** I **have** in my hand? *Where* **does** he **have** a scar? *Who* **has** green eyes?	

Notes

Examples

1. Remember that *be* and *have* are common **irregular verbs**. *Be* has three forms in the simple present: *am*, *is*, and *are*. *Have* has two forms in the simple present: *have* and *has*. Use *have* for all persons except the third-person singular (*he, she, it*). Use *has* with *he, she, it*.	• I **am** short. • He **is** tall. • They **are** tall. • I **have** black hair. • You **have** blue eyes. • We **have** blond hair. • They **have** brown eyes. • He **has** brown hair. • She **has** blond hair. • It **has** green eyes.
2. In **negative statements** with *be*, use *am not*, *is not*, *are not*, or their contractions. In **negative statements** with *have*, use *do not have*, *does not have*, or their contractions.	• I**'m not** home. • She**'s not** tall. • We**'re not** tall. • I **don't have** blue eyes. • He **doesn't have** green eyes.

3. In a *yes / no* **question** with *be*, put *am*, *is*, or *are* before the subject.

In a *yes / no* **question** with *have*, use *do* or *does* + a subject + *have*.

> subject
> • **Are you** a student?
>
> • **Do you have** blue eyes?
> • **Does he have** brown eyes?

---

4. For *wh-* **questions** with *be*, use the question word + *yes / no* question word order.

Most *wh-* **questions** with *have* use the *wh-* question word + *do* or *does* + a subject + the base form of the verb.

Questions about the subject use statement word order. They do not use *do* or *does*.

> • *Where* **am** I?
> • *What* **is** her name?
> • *How* **are** his parents?
>
> • *What* **does** he **have** for lunch?
> • *When* **do** they **have** dinner?
>
> • *Who* **has** green eyes?
> • *What* **has** eight legs?

---

5. Use *be* to talk about **age**.

> **A:** How old **are** you?
> **B:** I **am** twenty-one years old.
> NOT ~~I have twenty-one years.~~

Focused Practice

 Discover the Grammar

*Read each sentence. Write **A** for affirmative statements, **N** for negative statements, and **Q** for questions. Does the sentence use a form of **be** or **have**? Write **be** or **have**.*

<u>N, be</u>	**1.** He isn't very tall.
<u>A, have</u>	**2.** He has long fingers.
_____	**3.** I am not ten years old.
_____	**4.** Do you have long hair?
_____	**5.** How old is he?
_____	**6.** Her brother doesn't have a piano.
_____	**7.** Who is twenty?
_____	**8.** Who has a violin?
_____	**9.** When do they have breakfast?
_____	**10.** Are they famous?

2 Midori

*Complete the questions about the violinist Midori. Use the words in parentheses and the correct form of **be** or **have**.*

As a child

Today

A: (Who / that woman / ?) _____ Who is that woman? _____

B: Her name is Midori. She's a violinist. She was a child prodigy.

A: (Where / she / from / ?) _____

B: She's from Osaka, Japan.

A: (she / in Japan / now / ?) _____

B: No. She lives in New York.

A: (she / any sisters or brothers / ?) _____

B: She has a brother, Ryu Goto.

A: (he / a violinist / ?) _____

B: Yes, he is. He's very talented and famous too.

A: (Midori / other interests / ?) _____

B: Yes, she does. She enjoys reading and working for the Midori Foundation.

A: (What / the Midori Foundation / ?) _____

B: It's a group that brings music to children at schools.

3 Editing

Correct the conversation. There are six mistakes.

JUDY: Who was on the phone?

MARK: My cousin Francisco.

JUDY: How old ~~has~~ is he?

MARK: Twenty-five.

JUDY: Where he from?

MARK: São Paulo.

JUDY: What does he do?

MARK: He a musician. He plays the piano.

JUDY: He cute?

MARK: Yes, like me.

JUDY: Does he has a girlfriend?

MARK: Yes, he do.

Communication Practice

4 Who Are They Talking About?

🎧 *Listen to the conversation. Look at the pictures. Who are they talking about? Circle the man.*

5 Who Am I Talking About?

Work with a partner. Describe one of the people in Exercise 4 to your partner. Your partner points to the person. Take turns.

6 Describe a Famous Person

A. *The class makes a list of famous people. Write their names on the board.*

B. *Work in groups. A student in each group talks about one of the people. The others in the group guess the person. Use the vocabulary in the box below.*

Example:

A: He's from Canada. He's about thirty-five. He's a hockey player. He's tall, and he's of average weight. He has light brown hair.

B: Is he Wayne Gretsky?

A: Yes, he is.

Personal Information

Country: *Look at map of the world on pages 258–259.*

Age: *See numbers in Appendix 2, page 260.*

Occupation: actor, athlete, hockey player, musician, singer, swimmer, writer

Height: tall, medium height, short

Weight: thin, average weight, heavy

Eye color: brown, black, blue, green, hazel, gray

Hair color: black, dark brown, light brown, red, blond, gray

Marital status: single, married, divorced

Adverbs of Frequency

Do you ever sleep late?

Grammar **in Context**

🎧 *Listen and read the conversation.*

JOSH: What's the matter, Steve? You look really tired.

STEVE: I *am* tired. I never have enough energy anymore.

JOSH: That's too bad. Any idea why?

STEVE: Well, maybe I'm not getting enough sleep.

JOSH: How much are you getting?

STEVE: Oh, about six hours a night.

JOSH: What time do you go to bed?

STEVE: Hmm . . . I usually stay up till 1:00. And I get up at 7:00.

JOSH: Do you ever sleep late?

STEVE: Sometimes—on the weekend.

JOSH: What about food? Do you eat three meals a day? Breakfast, lunch, and dinner?

STEVE: Well . . . not really. I'm usually in a hurry in the morning. So I skip breakfast.

JOSH: Not good, my friend. What about lunch and dinner?

STEVE: I always have a good dinner. But lunch . . . well, I usually go to a fast-food place near the university.

JOSH: Hmm. Not enough sleep. No breakfast. Fast food for lunch. You're living dangerously.

STEVE: Maybe. But I have one good habit. I exercise.

JOSH: Great. How often?

STEVE: Two or three times a year.

Words and Expressions

🎧 *Do you know these words and expressions? Write new words and expressions in your notebook.*

fast food

energy / no energy

enough / not enough

1. **A:** What's the matter?
   B: I never have enough energy anymore.

2. **A:** That's too bad. Any idea why?
   B: Well, maybe I'm not getting enough sleep.

With a Partner

A. *Practice the conversation with a partner.*

B. *Work with a partner. Look at the pictures. Say what you* **never**, **sometimes**, *or* **often** *eat.*

Example:

I never eat carrots.

I often eat fish.

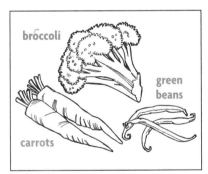

vegetables

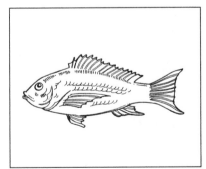

fish

rice

doughnuts

red meat

ice cream

Grammar **Presentation**
Adverbs of Frequency

Yes / No Questions
Do you **ever** stay up late?

Short Answers		
Yes, I	always usually often sometimes	do.
No, I	rarely never	

↑ 100% of the time

↓ 0% of the time

Adverbs of Frequency with *Be*

	Be	Adverb	
I	am	always usually often rarely	late.
He She It	is		
We You They	are		

Adverbs of Frequency with Other Verbs

	Adverb	Verb	
I	sometimes	skip	breakfast.
He	never	has	

Notes

Examples

---

1. Adverbs of frequency say **how often** something happens.

- I *often* **skip** breakfast.
- She *sometimes* **skips** lunch.

---

2. Adverbs of frequency come **after the verb *be***.

- I'm *usually* tired in the morning.
- The food at that restaurant **is *never*** very good.

---

3. Adverbs of frequency usually come **before other verbs**.

- He *usually* **goes** to a fast-food place near the theater.
- It *always* **rains** on the weekends.

4. Use *ever* in *yes / no* questions. *Ever* means "at any time."

NOTE: Do not use *ever* in affirmative statements.

A: Do you *ever* **sleep** late?
B: *Often*. OR I *often* do.

A: Are you *ever* late?
B: *Never.*

• I sleep late.
  NOT ~~I ever sleep late.~~

5. *How often* is a *wh-* question word. Use *how often* **to ask about frequency**.

A: **How often** do you exercise?
B: I *usually* exercise *three times a week*.

Focused Practice

1 Discover the Grammar

Read Grammar in Context *again. Circle all the adverbs of frequency.*

Example:

I (never) have enough energy anymore.

2 Conversations   Grammar Notes 2–3

Put the words in the correct order. Complete the conversation. Write questions and answers.

1. A: (late / ever / Do / up / stay / you / ?)

A: ___Do you ever stay up late?___

B: (do / Yes, / often / I / .)

B: _____

2. A: (tired / morning / you / Are / the / in / ever / ?)

A: _____

B: (always / I'm / tired / .)

B: _____

3. A: (often / exercise / How / you / do / ?)

A: _____

B: (week / a / five / usually / I / exercise / times / .)

B: _____

4. A: (usually / evenings / you / do / What / the / in / do / ?)

A: _____

B: (piano / the / practice / I / often / .)

B: _____

5. A: (here / hot / it / Is / ever / ?)

A: _____

B: (summer / sometimes / the / in / It's / hot / .)

B: _____

3 Jessica's Habits

Grammar Notes 2–3

Look at the pictures. Write sentences about Jessica Olson. Use **always**, **usually**, **sometimes**, *or* **never**.

	Sunday	Monday	Tuesday	Wednesday	Thursday	Friday	Saturday
	✓	✓	✓	✓	✓	✓	✓
		✓	✓		✓	✓	
		✓		✓		✓	

1. _____ (take a shower)

2. _____ (drive to work)

3. _____ (arrive on time to work)

4. _____ (cook dinner)

4 Editing

Correct Jessica's interview of sports star Domingo Rosario. There are seven mistakes.

                                                        often

JESSICA: Domingo, you're a great soccer player. How ∧ do you exercise?

DOMINGO: I exercise six or seven days a week.

JESSICA: Do ever you get tired of exercising?

DOMINGO: Sure I do. But always I do it.

JESSICA: Okay. How often do you travel?

DOMINGO: Often I travel. At least three times a month.

JESSICA: Does ever your wife get unhappy because you travel so much?

DOMINGO: No, she gets never unhappy. She travels usually with me.

JESSICA: That's great, Domingo. Now, good luck in your next game.

Communication Practice

5 A Phone Call from Grandma

🎧 *Listen to the conversation. Then listen to it again. Complete the statements.*

1. Grandma is calling Ken because tomorrow is <u>his birthday</u>.

2. Grandma is usually _____.

3. Ken is always _____.

4. Ken usually starts work at_____.

5. He never has time _____.

6. Ken sometimes stays up late _____.

7. Ken usually gets _____ of sleep.

8. Grandma says Ken needs _____ of sleep every night.

6 True Statements

A. *Write true statements about yourself. Use the words in parentheses and an adverb of frequency.*

1. (be on time to class) _____

2. (take a shower in the morning) _____

3. (eat breakfast) _____

4. (eat fast food) _____

5. (be happy) _____

6. (go to the movies) _____

7. (go dancing) _____

8. (take a bus) _____

9. (smoke) _____

10. (get enough sleep) _____

B. *Change the statements to* yes / no *questions. Ask your partner the questions. Tell the class three things about your partner.*

Review or SelfTest

I. *Complete the conversations. Circle the correct letter.*

1. **STUDENT:** Do you have the time?   A B Ⓒ D
   TEACHER: _____
   (A) Yes, you have. It's 9:30.   (C) Yes, I do. It's 9:30.
   (B) Yes, I am. It's 9:30.   (D) Yes, you do. It's 9:30.

2. **DAD:** Does he want chocolate ice cream?   A B C D
   ANNIE: _____
   (A) No, he does. He   (C) No, we don't. We
       wants vanilla.   want vanilla.
   (B) Yes, he does. He   (D) No, he doesn't. He
       wants vanilla.   wants vanilla.

3. **STEVE:** _____   A B C D
   MARK: Yes. Red is her favorite color.
   (A) Does she like red?   (C) Why does she like red?
   (B) What's her favorite color?   (D) Do we like red?

4. **PEDRO:** _____   A B C D
   MARIA: Very small.
   (A) How do you spell "tiny"?   (C) What does "tiny"
   (B) How do you pronounce   mean?
       "tiny"?   (D) Who's tiny?

5. **KATHY:** _____   A B C D
   AMANDA: At the airport.
   (A) When does he work?   (C) Why does he work?
   (B) Where does he work?   (D) Is he at the airport?

6. **KATHY:** _____   A B C D
   AMANDA: At 9:00.
   (A) Why does he go to   (C) Does he go to bed?
       bed at 9:00?   (D) What time does he
   (B) Who goes to bed at 9:00?   go to bed?

II. *Write sentences. Use the words in parentheses in the correct order.*

1. (John / late / always / is / .) _____ John is always late. _____

2. (at 9:00 / never / comes / he / .) _____

3. (arrives / at 9:15 / usually / he / .) _____

4. (eat / do / where / you / usually / ?) _____

5. (have / you / always / at noon / do / lunch / ?) _____

_____

III. *Complete the paragraph. Use the correct form of* **have** *or* **be**.

Dana ___is___ an artist. She _____ twenty-five years old. She
_{1.}   _{2.}

_____ from Ohio, but she lives in Florida now. She lives with four other
_{3.}

artists. They _____ a big house. It _____ a garden in the front. They
_{4.}   _{5.}

also _____ a turtle and a bird. The bird's name _____ Sammy. He
_{6.}   _{7.}

_____ loud and funny. He sits outside and says, "Please don't eat the flowers."
_{8.}

IV. *Complete the conversations. Use the words in parentheses.*

A. AMANDA: _____ *What does she do?* _____
                      _{1. (what / she / do / ?)}

    KATHY: She's a manager.

    AMANDA: _____
                      _{2. (where / she / work / ?)}

    KATHY: At a bank.

    AMANDA: _____
                      _{3. (what time / she / start / ?)}

    KATHY: She starts at nine.

    AMANDA: _____
                      _{4. (how long / she / stay / ?)}

    KATHY: She stays until six.

    AMANDA: That sounds like a good job.

B. MATT: _____
                      _{1. (who / live / in that house / ?)}

    PETER: Tim and Jessica Olson.

    MATT: _____
                      _{2. (what / they / do ?)}

    PETER: He's a graphic artist, and she's a TV news reporter.

    MATT: _____
                      _{3. (they / have / children / ?)}

    PETER: Yes, they do. They have two sons and a daughter.

    MATT: _____
                      _{4. (the boy on the bike / their son / ?)}

    PETER: Yes, that's Ben. He's a nice kid.

▶ *To check your answers, go to the Answer Key on page 283.*

UNIT

Possessive Nouns;
This / That / These / Those

I like those shoes.

Grammar **in Context**

🎧 *Listen and read the conversation.*

JUDY: Mark, you look sharp! What's the occasion?

MARK: Dinner—with Kathy and her parents. It's her parents' anniversary. Is the jacket okay?

JUDY: It's fine.

MARK: It's my brother's.

JUDY: I like those shoes.

MARK: They're my roommate's. How about this tie? Does it match these suspenders?

JUDY: It's a perfect match.

MARK: The tie is Steve's. The suspenders are his too.

JUDY: Is *anything* yours?

MARK: Sure. This new goatee. It's all mine.

JUDY: Oh. I see. Well, that goatee makes you look like a doctor.

MARK: Good. Now I need to remember— Kathy's mom is Liz, and her dad is Russ, not Ross. When I'm nervous, I forget names.

JUDY: Mark, you look wonderful. Don't be nervous. And just don't call Kathy's dad Rose.

Words and Expressions

🎧 *Do you know these words and expressions? Write new words and expressions in your notebook.*

a tie

a sports jacket

slacks

shoes

A: What's the occasion?

B: It's Kathy's parents' anniversary.

OR

It's Mark's birthday.

OR

It's Judy's graduation.

With a Partner

A. *Practice the conversation with a partner.*

B. *Read these paragraphs. Who are these people?*

1. This American man of Irish descent was a magazine publisher. His father was a United States President. His mother was a famous beauty. His uncle is a United States Senator. This man's first name was John. His father's first name was John too.

Who was he? _____

2. This African-American woman is a poet, writer, actress, playwright, producer, and director. She speaks French, Spanish, and West African Fanti. Her husband was a South African freedom fighter. This woman's book about her childhood, *I Know Why the Caged Bird Sings*, was a 1970 bestseller. This woman's first name is Maya.

Who is she? _____

C. *Check your answers on page 280.*

Grammar **Presentation**
Possessive Nouns; *This / That / These / Those*

Possessive Nouns	
Singular	**Plural**
My **sister's** car is red. The **actress's** name is Rosa.	My **parents'** car is blue. Her **daughters'** names are Tina and Marie.

This / That / These / Those	
Pronouns	**Adjectives**
This is my cell phone. **That** is your jacket. **These** are my keys. **Those** are your keys.	**This** cell phone is great. **That** tie is Steve's. **These** keys don't work. **Those** keys are Steve's.

Notes

Examples

Notes	Examples
1. Possessive nouns show **belonging**.	• I'm wearing my **roommate's** shoes. *(The shoes belong to my roommate.)*
2. To show possession: Add an **apostrophe (')** + *–s* to a singular noun or an irregular plural noun. Add only an **apostrophe (')** to a plural noun ending in *–s*.	• That's my **father's** jacket. • That's **Kathy's** mom. • That's **Steve Beck's** tie. • Where's the **women's** restroom? • It's her **parents'** anniversary. • It's the **Becks'** house.
3. *This*, *that*, *these*, and *those* can be **pronouns** or **adjectives**. REMEMBER: *This* and *that* are **singular**; *these* and *those* are **plural**. Use *this* and *these* for things that are **near**. Use *that* and *those* for things that are **away** from you.	• *This* is my cell phone. *(pronoun)* • *This* **cell phone** is new. *(adjective)* • *These* are my sunglasses. *(pronoun)* • *Those* **sunglasses** on *that* **table** over there are Robert's. *(adjective)*

Pronunciation Note
The **'s** in a possessive noun sounds like **/s/**, **/z/**, or **/ɪz/**:
/s/ : *This is my aunt's telephone number.*
/z/ : *When's your uncle's birthday?*
/ɪz/ : *Those are Ross's glasses.* (Note that **/ɪz/** makes an extra syllable.)

Reference Note
Look at Units 2 and 4 for more practice with *this*, *that*, *these*, and *those* as pronouns.

Focused Practice

1 Discover the Grammar

Read Grammar in Context *again. Circle the possessive nouns. Underline* **this**, **that**, **these**, *and* **those**.

Example:

It's her (parents') anniversary.
I like those shoes.

2 At the Restaurant
Grammar Note 3

Mark and Kathy are having dinner with Kathy's parents. Complete the conversations.
Use **this**, **that**, **these**, *or* **those**.

1. **KATHY:** Mom, Dad, _____ is Mark. Mark, _____ are my parents.

    MARK: Nice to meet you.

      LIZ: Good to meet you.

    RUSS: Hello, Mark.

2. **RUSS:** Liz, is _____ your phone?

      LIZ: No, Russ. I think it's Kathy's.

    KATHY: It is, Dad. Sorry.

3. **MARK:** _____'s an unusual ring.

      LIZ: Thanks. _____ ring was my
great-grandmother's.

4.   **LIZ:** How do you like the food?

    MARK: _____ steak is delicious!

    KATHY: And _____ vegetables melt in your mouth.

3 What's in a Woman's Name?   Grammar Note 2

Complete the reading. Use the words in parentheses in the possessive.

Women in the United States are free to choose their family name when they marry.

Many women change their name to their _____husband's family name_____. For example,
1. (husband / family name)

before_____ married Bill Beck, she was Mary Meyers. After her
2. (Steve Beck / mother)

marriage, she became Mary Beck.

But some women don't change their names. _____, Liz Harlow,
3. (Kathy White / mother)

married Russ White. She is still Liz Harlow after thirty years of marriage. Today some

women are keeping their name and adding their _____. For example,
4. (husband / name)

_____, Jill, is married to Joe Smith. Her married name is Jill
5. (Kathy / sister)

White-Smith. So a woman's name doesn't always tell you who she's married to.

4 Pronunciation

🎧 *Listen to the sentences. Write the possessive noun. Listen again. Check (✓) the final sound of the possessive noun.*

Possessive Noun	/s/	/z/	/ɪz/
1. mother's		✓	
2.			
3.			
4.			
5.			
6.			

5 Editing

Correct this student's essay. There are six mistakes.

> ~~~~~~~parents'~~~~~~~
> My family loves to eat out. On my ~~parents~~ anniversary we go
> to a Chinese restaurant. That's because my parent's love Chinese
> food. On my brother birthday we go to an Italian restaurant.
> My brother loves Italian food. On my sister birthday we go to
> a Mexican restaurant. That's because her favorite food come's
> from Mexico. And on my birthday we go to a different restaurant
> every year because I like to try different places. These year I
> want to try a Brazilian restaurant.

Communication Practice

6 Compliments

Work in groups. Compliment your classmates.

Example:

> **ALI:** Maria, those earrings are beautiful!
>
> **MARIA:** Thanks. They were a present from my grandmother. That's a very nice sweater, Ali. Is it new?
>
> **ALI:** Thank you. Yes, it is.

7 What's Different?

A. *Look at the pictures. What's different in Picture B?*

Meg Juan Renee Amy Ari

Picture A

Meg Juan Renee Amy Ari

Picture B

Example:

In Picture B, Meg is wearing Amy's earrings and necklace.

Juan is wearing . . .

B. *One student leaves the classroom. The other students exchange glasses, backpacks, watches, shoes, etc. The student returns and talks about the changes.*

Count and Non-count Nouns; *Some* and *Any*

I usually have a bagel and coffee.

Grammar **in Context**

🎧 *Listen and read the news interviews.*

JESSICA: Hello, everyone. This morning we're interviewing people about their eating habits. Here's our first person. Sir, do you eat breakfast?

MAN: Yes, I do.

JESSICA: What do you have?

MAN: I have a bagel and a cup of coffee.

JESSICA: That's all?

MAN: Yes. I'm always in a hurry. 'Bye!

JESSICA: Okay. Thanks. 'Bye.

JESSICA: Now, here's our next person. Ma'am, what do you have for breakfast?

WOMAN 1: I never eat breakfast.

JESSICA: Nothing at all?

WOMAN 1: No. I'm on a diet.

JESSICA: Okay. Thank you . . .

JESSICA: And what about you, ma'am? What do you have for breakfast?

WOMAN 2: Oh, I usually have a bowl of cereal and some yogurt with fruit—a banana, a peach or an orange, or some strawberries. And I have a glass of juice.

JESSICA: Hmm. That sounds healthy.

WOMAN 2: Yes, I always eat a good breakfast.

JESSICA: All right, thanks. Let's see what our next person says . . .

Words and Expressions

🎧 *Do you know these words and expressions? Write new words and expressions in your notebook.*

a bagel

a cup of coffee

fruit

an orange
a banana
strawberries
a peach

cereal

yogurt

a sandwich

a salad

a slice of toast

eggs

1. A: I'm in a hurry. 'Bye!
   B: 'Bye. See you later.

2. A: I never eat breakfast.
   B: Nothing at all?
   A: No. I'm on a diet.

With a Partner

A. *Practice the interviews with three partners.*

B. *Tell your partner what you usually have for breakfast.*

Example:

I usually have toast and eggs and coffee for breakfast.

Grammar **Presentation**
Count and Non-count Nouns; *Some* and *Any*

Count Nouns		Non-count Nouns
Article + Singular Noun	**Plural Noun**	
a banana **an** orange **a** sandwich	banana**s** orange**s** sandwich**es**	bread yogurt water

Quantifiers: *Some* and *Any*	
Count Nouns	**Non-count Nouns**

A: Do you have **any** oranges?
B: Yes, I have **some**.   OR
     No, I don't have **any**.
	A: Do you have **any** bread?
	B: Yes, I have **some**. OR
	     No, I don't have **any**.

Notes

1. Count nouns refer to separate things. It is **easy to count** them.

To form the plural of most count nouns, add *–s* or *–es*.

2. Non-count nouns refer to things that are **difficult to count**.

We use **quantifiers** to help us count non-count nouns. Some quantifiers are:

a cup of (coffee)

a slice of (bread)

a bowl of (cereal)

a bottle of (mineral water)

a glass of (water)

Some and *any* are also quantifiers.

3. Use **singular verbs** with **non-count nouns**.

Examples

- *one* orange, *two* eggs, *three* bagels
- orange   orange**s**
- sandwich   sandwich**es**

- I love **coffee**.
- Bring me *a cup of* **coffee**.

- Ben likes **bread**.
- Please bring him *a slice of* **bread**.

- I want **cereal**.
- Please bring me *a bowl of* **cereal**.

- I want *some* **cereal**. I don't want *any* **bread**.

- Rice **is** good for you.
  NOT ~~Rice are good for you.~~

4. Use *a* or *an* before **singular count nouns**. Use *a* before words that start with consonant sounds. Use *an* before words that start with vowel sounds.

Use *some* (or nothing) with **plural count nouns** and **non-count nouns**.

- Steve wants **a banana**.
  (starts with a consonant sound)

- I want **an orange**.
  (starts with a vowel sound)

  plural count noun
- We have **(some) oranges** in the refrigerator.

  non-count noun
- I drink **(some) juice** every morning.

---

5. Use *some* in **affirmative statements**. Use *any* in **negative statements** and in **questions**.

NOTE: You can use *some* in a **question** when you are offering something.

- I have **some** fruit.
- I don't have **any** fruit.
- Do you have **any** fruit?

- Do you want **some** fruit? *(offer)*

---

6. Use **plural count nouns** or **non-count nouns** to talk about things you **like or dislike** in general. (Don't use *a* or *an*.)

- I like **oranges**. I don't like **yogurt**.

  NOT ~~I like an orange. I don't like some yogurt.~~

Reference Notes
1. Look at Appendix 4 on page 262 for more information about plural nouns.
2. Look at Appendix 5 on page 263 for a list of non-count nouns and quantifiers.

Focused Practice

 Discover the Grammar

Read Grammar in Context *again. Find the different kinds of food. Write them in the correct column. Use* **a** *or* **an** *and* **some** *or another quantifier.*

Count Nouns	Non-count Nouns with a Quantifier
a bagel	a cup of coffee

2 At the Restaurant

Complete the conversation. Choose the correct word in parentheses.

WAITER: All right, folks. What would you like?

MARY: I'd like _____ spaghetti and
1. (a bag of / some)

_____ coffee.
2. (a bag of / some)

WAITER: Of course. And for you, young man?

BEN: I want _____ peanut butter
3. (a / some)

sandwich. Is that okay, Grandma?

MARY: Yes, that's fine. But how about _____ salad to go with it?
4. (a slice of / some)

BEN: I don't like _____ salad, Grandma.
5. (a / Ø*)

MARY: All right. But you need something green. Or maybe some fruit.
Maybe _____ banana?
6. (a / some)

BEN: Okay, Grandma. I like _____ bananas.
7. (Ø / some)

WAITER: All right. For you, young lady?

ANNIE: I'd like _____ pizza. And _____ orange.
8. (a slice of / a bowl of)   9. (a / an)

WAITER: Of course. And to drink?

MARY: Can you bring them each _____ milk?
10. (a / a glass of)

WAITER: Certainly. Be right back with your drinks.

_____
*Ø = no article or quantifier

3 A Party

*Complete the conversation. Use **some** or **any** and the nouns in parentheses.*

AMANDA: Josh, we need _____ for the party tonight. Can you go to
1. (things)

the store now?

JOSH: Sure. I know we don't have _____. And we don't have
2. (soda)

_____. What else?
3. (chips)

AMANDA: We need _____. And we need _____. But let me
4. (fruit)   5. (olives)

check . . . Oh, yes! Get _____. Don't get _____.
6. (black olives)   7. (green olives)

JOSH: Okay. Anything else? Do you want _____?
8. (ice cream)

AMANDA: Good idea. Get _____.
9. (chocolate ice cream)

4 Editing

Correct the conversations. There are five mistakes.

1. **A:** Do you like a̶ ̶b̶a̶g̶e̶l̶?̶ (bagels)

    B: No, I don't. But I like a sandwich.

2. **A:** Can I bring you some coffee?

    B: No, thanks. I don't like a coffee.

3. **A:** Are we having eggs for breakfast?

    B: Yes, we are. We're also having a yogurt.

4. **A:** Can I bring you a hamburger?

    B: Yes, please. I like a hamburger.

Communication Practice

5 I Can't Believe This Place!

*Listen to Mark and Judy talk with a waiter. Then read the statements. Listen again. Check **T (True)**, **F (False)**, or **NI (No Information)**. Correct the false statements.*

	T	F	NI	
1. The restaurant is serving lunch now.	☐	☑	☐	The restaurant isn't serving lunch now.
2. Judy wants chips and salsa.	☐	☐	☐	_____
3. The restaurant has iced tea.	☐	☐	☐	_____
4. Mark likes tea.	☐	☐	☐	_____
5. The restaurant is out of salsa.	☐	☐	☐	_____
6. The restaurant has mineral water.	☐	☐	☐	_____
7. The soda is expensive.	☐	☐	☐	_____
8. Mark and Judy like the restaurant.	☐	☐	☐	_____

6 What Do You Like to Eat?

Write about the kinds of food you like and don't like. Compare your likes and dislikes with a partner. Which are the same? Which are different?

Example:

A: I like chips and salsa. I don't like peas. I hate green olives!

B: I don't like chips and salsa. But I hate green olives too!
    What I like to eat is pizza and chocolate ice cream.

A / An and The; One / Ones

I really like the blue one.

Grammar **in Context**

🎧 *Listen and read the conversation.*

CLERK: May I help you?

KEN: Yes, I'm looking for a new blazer. I have an interview tomorrow.

CLERK: Oh, you're in luck! We're having a sale on blazers.

KEN: You are? Great!

CLERK: What size?

KEN: Forty-two.

CLERK: Okay. Be right back.

CLERK: All right. Do you like any of these?

KEN: Yes! I really like the blue one.

CLERK: Do you want to try it on?

KEN: Sure.

CLERK: How does it feel?

KEN: Very comfortable. How does it look, Laura?

LAURA: Well, it's pretty bright. And it's casual. How about that black one? It's more formal.

KEN: All the black ones are dull—really boring.

LAURA: Okay. It's up to you.

Words and Expressions

Do you know these words and expressions? Write new ones in your notebook.

a blazer

a sale

try on

two sizes

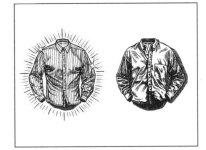

bright / dull

formal / casual

1. A: You're in luck.
   B: Great!

2. A: Do you want to try it on?
   B: Sure.

3. A: How does it feel?
   B: Very comfortable.

4. A: How does it look?
   B: It looks fine.

5. It's up to you.

With a Partner

A. *Practice the conversation with two partners.*

B. *Look at the pictures. Which item do you like? Tell your partner.*

Example:

I like the expensive suit. I don't like the cheap one.

expensive / cheap

big / small

bright / dull

formal / casual

Grammar **Presentation**
A / An and *The*; *One* / *Ones*

Indefinite Articles (*A / An*)	
Singular Nouns	**Plural Nouns**
I'm looking for *a* **blazer**. I have *an* **interview** tomorrow.	**Blazers** are expensive. I don't like **interviews**.

The Definite Article (*The*)	
Singular Nouns	**Plural Nouns**
I like *the* blue **blazer**.	I don't like *the* black **blazers**.

One and *Ones*	
Singular Pronouns	**Plural Pronouns**
I like **the** blue *one*.	I don't like **the** black *ones*.

Notes

Examples

---

1. Use *a* or *an* to talk about an **indefinite** (nonspecific) **singular count noun**.

REMEMBER: Use *a* before a word that begins with a consonant sound. Use *an* before a word that begins with a vowel sound.

Don't use an article to talk about **indefinite plural count nouns**.

- I'm looking for *a* **blazer**.
- I have *an* **interview** tomorrow.

- **Blazers** are expensive.
  (*indefinite—in general*)

---

2. When we mention something for the **first time**, it is usually **indefinite**.

When we mention something for the **second time**, it is usually **definite** (specific). Use *the* with a **definite noun**.

- I have *an* **interview** tomorrow.

- *The* **interview** is at 10:00 A.M.

---

3. When something is **unique** (when it is the only one), it is **definite**. Use *the* with the noun.

- I really like *the* **blue blazer**.
  (*There is only one blue blazer in the store.*)

- *The* **sun** is bright today.
  (*There is only one sun.*)

4. Use *the* with **definite nouns**, both **singular** and **plural**.

- *The* blue **blazer** is bright.
- *The* black **blazers** are dull.

5. *One* is a singular pronoun. *Ones* is plural. We can sometimes use *one* or *ones* to **replace a noun**.

- They have three **blazers** on sale. I like the blue *one*. I don't like the black *ones*.

Pronunciation Note
The word *the* has two pronunciations.
Pronounce it "thee" (like "be") before a word that begins with a vowel sound: *the interview*
Pronounce it "the" (like "a") before a word that begins with a consonant sound: *the blazer*

Reference Note
Look at Appendix 6 on page 264 for more information about articles.

Focused Practice

1 Discover the Grammar

Read the conversations. Circle the correct answer.

1. A: The sun is bright today! (one sun / more than one sun)

   B: Yes. We need sunglasses. (specific sunglasses / sunglasses in general)

2. A: Where's the cat? (more than one cat / one cat)

   B: She's sleeping in the bedroom. (one bedroom / more than one bedroom)

3. A: Do you have a car? (a specific car / a car in general)

   B: No, I don't. Cars are expensive. (cars in general / specific cars)

4. A: Do you like the blazers? (some of the blazers / all of the blazers)

   B: I like the red one. (one red blazer / more than one red blazer)

2 Pronunciation

 Listen to the conversations. Write **a** *or* **an** *in each blank.*

1. A: What do you want for your birthday, Mary?

   B: I want _____ good novel. And I want _____ umbrella—_____ red one.

2. A: Annie, is someone at the door?

   B: Yes, there's _____ man outside. He's _____ old man.

3. A: Grandma, I have _____ interview tomorrow.

   B: Oh, good, Ken. I hope it's _____ good interview.

3 Ken and Laura

Complete the next part of Ken and Laura's conversation. Choose from the words in parentheses.

CLERK: Do you need anything else?

KEN: Yes, I need _____Ø_____ dress shoes.
1. (a / the / Ø*)

CLERK: Okay. _____ dress shoes are over here.
2. (A / The)

CLERK: What size?

KEN: Ten medium.

LAURA: I like _____ black ones. What do you think?
3. (a / the / Ø)

KEN: No. They're dark and formal. And I don't like _____ style.
4. (a / the / Ø)

CLERK: What about these?

KEN: Cool! I like them.

CLERK: Do you want to try them on?

KEN: Yes, please.

CLERK: How do they feel?

KEN: Perfect. Laura, what do you think?

LAURA: Well, _____ shoes look nice. But they're casual.
5. (a / the / Ø)

This is for _____ interview.
6. (a / an / Ø)

KEN: They're fine.

_____
*Ø = no article or quantifier

4 Editing

Correct the letter. There are ten mistakes.

Dear Kathy,
    Josh and I have ~~an~~ᵃ great house! House is very big, but it's also a old one. It needs work. It has the nice living room, but the colors are terrible. Each wall is the different color. There's a orange wall, an yellow wall, a blue wall, and the red wall. We need to repaint.
    We want you to see a house. Give me the call.

Love,
    Amanda

Communication Practice

5 Let's Go Out Tonight

Listen to the conversation. Circle the correct answers.

1. There is (one / more than one) concert.

2. Josh and Amanda have (one / more than one) dog.

3. They have (one / more than one) photograph.

4. They have (one / more than one) house.

5. They have (one / more than one) umbrella.

6. They have (one / more than one) car.

6 Styles

Work with a partner. Look at the pictures. Tell your partner about the clothes you like and don't like. Use **the** *and* **one / ones** *in your statements.*

Example:

A: I like the first hat.

B: I like the second one. OR I like the first one too.

7 What's Wrong with This Picture?

*Work in groups of four.
Talk about what you see.
Use* **a**, **an**, *or* **the**.

Example:

A: I see a car in the store.
The car has four people
in it.

B: I see . . .

Can / Can't

I can't understand her message.

Grammar **in Context**

🎧 *Listen and read the conversation and the phone message.*

MARK: Judy, Steve, thanks for coming.

JUDY: Hi, Mark. What's the problem?

MARK: I have a message from Kathy on my answering machine. But I can't understand all of it. Listen.

[*Phone message with lots of noise in the background*]

> Hi, Mark. It's Kathy. I can't meet you today. Please call me at 796-774 ☆ ! ⋀⋁ It's important. Call right away, please.

STEVE: I can't hear the last part of the phone number. Can you?

JUDY: No, I can't. Kathy sounds upset. Do you think she's in trouble?

MARK: I don't know. She left her cell phone here. Look, I need to take this package to *The Daily Times*. Can you do me a favor? Wait here in case Kathy calls again?

STEVE: Of course. Go! And don't worry. Judy and I can get her phone number.

MARK: You can?

STEVE: Sure. Go. Don't worry. And take it easy. I'm sure Kathy's fine.

MARK: Thanks. I'll be back soon.

Expressions

Do you know these expressions? Write new ones in your notebook.

1. **A:** Can you do me a favor? Wait here in case Kathy calls?
   B: Of course.

2. **A:** Can you do me a favor? Can you explain this to me?
   B: Sure. No problem.

3. **A:** I'm very upset. I think Kathy's in trouble.
   B: Don't worry. I'm sure she's fine.

With a Partner

A. *Practice the conversation with three partners.*

B. *Discuss the following with a partner.*

Steve says, "Judy and I can get her phone number." How can they do that?

Grammar **Presentation**
Can / Can't

Affirmative and Negative Statements

Subject	*Can / Can't*	Base Form of Verb
I You He / She / It We You They	**can** **can't**	**help**.

Yes / No Questions

Can you **do** me a favor?
Can he **understand** French?

Short Answers

Yes, I **can**.
No, he **can't**.

Wh- Questions

Where **can** she **be**?
Who **can help**?

Notes	**Examples**
1. ***Can*** is a **modal**. A modal changes the meaning of the verb that follows. *Can* has different meanings including **ability**, **possibility**, and **request**.	• I **can understand** German. *(ability)* • I **can meet** you at four. *(possibility)* • **Can** you **do** me a favor? *(request)*
2. Use the **base form** of the verb **after** *can*. ▶ **BE CAREFUL!** Do not use *to* after *can*. Do not add –*s* to verbs that follow *can*.	• I **can speak** Spanish. • We **can understand** English. • He **can write** Arabic. NOT ~~He can to write Arabic.~~ NOT ~~He can writes Arabic.~~
3. ***Cannot*** is the negative form. ***Can't*** is the contraction. Use *can't* in speaking and informal writing.	• I **cannot help** you. • I **can't help** you.
4. For **questions** (*yes / no* questions or *wh-* questions), put ***can*** before the subject (unless the subject is ***who*** or ***what***).	• **Can** she **speak** English? • How **can** we **help**? • Who **can help**?

Pronunciation Note

In a sentence, ***can*** sounds like "kn" and is hard to hear. The verb that follows is stressed:
I can SPEAK Spanish.
Can't has a longer vowel sound than *can* and is easy to hear: *I CAN'T speak French.*

Focused Practice

1 Discover the Grammar

A. *Read Grammar in Context again. Underline all sentences with* **can** *and* **can't**. *Which sentence is a request?*

 B. *Can Judy and Steve reach Kathy? Listen to their conversation. Underline* **can** *and* **can't**. *Which sentence is a request?*

    JUDY: Okay. How can we get the phone number? I can't understand Kathy. Can you?

    STEVE: Well, we know the first six numbers—796-774. Right?

JUDY: Uh-huh.

STEVE: There are only ten possibilities for the seventh.

JUDY: Good idea. Let's try them.

STEVE: 796-7740 . . . *[To Judy]* an answering machine . . . 796-7741 . . . Hello? Is Kathy White there? . . . *[To Judy]* wrong number . . . 796-7742 . . . Hello? Is Kathy White there? . . . Yes? Can I speak with Ms. White? *[To Judy]* She's at the police station. Hello, Kathy . . . Are you okay? . . . Uh-huh. Oh. Uh-huh. Okay.

JUDY: Well?

STEVE: She's okay, but she wants Mark to go there.

② At the Police Station

Grammar Notes 1–3

A. *Complete the conversation. Use the phrases in the box.*

> a. you can speak a little Chinese
> b. Can you two wait for her grandmother
> c. She can't speak
> d. Can she remember her grandma's number
> e. Can you help her

KATHY: Mark, this is Mei Liang. She was lost in the park. She was very, very upset. _____ a word of English.
1.

MARK: Oh? Poor kid!

KATHY: Mark, _____. _____?
2.   3.

MARK: Well, let me see. I hope she can understand Mandarin. *[Mark speaks with Mei Liang.]* . . . Uh . . . She lives with her grandmother.

KATHY: That's good to know. _____?
4.

MARK: *[Speaks with Mei Liang]* She can't remember the number, but her grandmother's name is Li Li Wang, and they live in Kent.

OFFICER: I'm looking it up in the phone book . . . We've got her number. Thank you. _____?
5.

MARK: Sure.

OFFICER: *[Calls Li Li Wang]* Her grandmother is on the way. She's really upset.

B. *Now listen to the conversation and check your work.*

3 Can or Can't?

A. *Listen to the sentences. Check the word you hear.*

1. can ❑ can't ❑   4. can ❑ can't ❑

2. can ❑ can't ❑   5. can ❑ can't ❑

3. can ❑ can't ❑   6. can ❑ can't ❑

B. *Complete the conversations. Use* **can** *or* **can't**.

1. **A:** We _____ hear you.
   B: Sorry. Is that better?

2. **A:** We _____ hear you.
   B: That's good.

3. **A:** I _____ believe it.
   B: It's true.

4. **A:** I _____ believe it.
   B: Me too.

5. **A:** I _____ see the board.
   B: Then change your seat.

6. **A:** I _____ see the board.
   B: Good. Please read the sentence on the board.

C. *Now choose a conversation. Read* **A**. *Your partner reads* **B**.

4 Editing

Correct these sentences. There are six mistakes. Add **can** *in two places.*

1. Li Li Wang *can* understand English, but she can't speak it well.

2. Mei Liang Wang can't speaks English. She can to speak Mandarin Chinese.

3. Mei Liang is a good ice skater. She can skates very well.

4. Mei Liang sing well, but she can't not dance.

Communication Practice

5 Drama

Complete these conversations with a partner. Read them to the class.

1. **A:** Can I please speak to _____?

   B: I'm sorry. _____.

   A: What? What happened?

   B: _____.

2. **A:** Can you do me a favor? Can you _____?

   B: I'm sorry, I can't. I just can't do it. Please understand.

   A: _____?

   B: _____.

6 Think of the Possibilities

Work in groups. You have five minutes. Make a list of all the things you can do in a car. The group with the longest list wins.

Example:

1. We can drive.
2. We can listen to the radio.

7 Tic Tac Toe

Walk around the class. Find someone who can do each thing. Write the name of the student in the box. When you have three names in any direction, you win.

Example:

MARIA: Can you water ski?

KEIKO: Yes, I can. *(Maria writes Keiko's name in the box labeled "water ski.")*

water ski	speak Mandarin	understand calculus
Keiko		
play the guitar	understand Italian	play tennis
play golf	dive	play chess

Review or SelfTest

I. *Complete the conversations. Circle the correct letter.*

1. **JESSICA:** Do we have any fruit?   A B Ⓒ D
   TIM: _____
   (A) Yes, I have.   (C) No, we don't have any.
   (B) No, we have some.   (D) Yes, they don't have any.

2. **KATHY:** _____   A B C D
   JOSH: Sure. Hold on.
   (A) Can you please speak   (C) Is Amanda your sister?
         with Amanda?   (D) Can I speak with Amanda?
   (B) Do you know Amanda?

3. **CLERK:** Do you like the dark blue jacket?   A B C D
   KEN: _____
   (A) No, but I like the   (C) No, I don't like tan
         brown one.   jackets.
   (B) Yes, I like the red one.   (D) Yes, I need a red jacket.

4. **CLERK:** _____   A B C D
   KEN: Very comfortable.
   (A) How does it look?   (C) How can I help you?
   (B) How much does it cost?   (D) How does it feel?

5. **LAURA:** Do you like John's tie?   A B C D
   KEN: _____
   (A) Yes, I like the ties.   (C) Yes, but I don't like it.
   (B) No, I'm not.   (D) No, I don't like it.

II. *Complete the conversations. Use the words in parentheses in the correct order.*

1. **ANNIE:** What can I have for breakfast?

   JESSICA: _____ How about a slice of toast? _____
                             (toast / how / of / about / a / slice / ?)

2. **KATHY:** _____
                        (look / it / does / how / ?)
   AMANDA: Really great. It's your color.

3. **CLERK:** _____
                     (shoes / the / like / do / black / you / ?)
   KEN: No, but I really like the brown ones.

4. JESSICA: Is there a message from Ben?

   TIM: _____

   (I / yes, / his / can't / but / message / understand /.)

5. KELLY: _____

   (guitar / Jeremy / the / can / play / ?)

   JESSICA: Yes. He plays very well.

III. *Annie and Ben are making breakfast for their parents. Look at the picture. Write sentences about what they have and don't have. Use* **some** *or* **any** *and the words in parentheses.*

   1. (eggs)   They have some eggs.

   2. (coffee) _____

   3. (juice) _____

   4. (fruit) _____

   5. (bagels) _____

   6. (milk) _____

IV. *Complete the paragraphs with* **a, an, the, one,** *and* **ones.**

Josh and Amanda are talking with _____*a*_____ car salesman. They need
                                    1.

_____ new car. They see a lot of cars, expensive _____ and cheap
   2.   3.

_____. Josh wants to buy _____ expensive car. Amanda wants to
   4.   5.

buy _____ cheap _____.
   6.   7.

    Right now _____ salesman is showing them two cars, _____
                      8.   9.

old red car and _____ new blue car. Josh wants _____ blue
             10.   11.

_____. Amanda wants _____ red _____.
  12.   13.   14.

V. *Write sentences with the words in parentheses. Use* **It's** *and a possessive noun with* **'s** *or* **s'**.

   1. (Jeremy / guitar)   It's Jeremy's guitar.

   2. (Annie / cat) _____

   3. (the / men / department) _____

   4. (the / women / department) _____

   5. (Jessica / parents / house) _____

▶ *To check your answers, go to the Answer Key on page 283.*

UNIT

21 Review: Imperative, Present Progressive, and Simple Present

Talk to her. We need her business.

Grammar **in Context**

🎧 *Listen and read the conversation. Herb is a new sales representative at Arthur Andrews Company.*

TIM: Herb, do you see that woman over there?

HERB: The blonde?

TIM: Uh-huh. She's talking to Sabrina.

HERB: Is she wearing a gray suit?

TIM: Yes, that's the woman. She's standing next to the water fountain. Go and talk to her. We need her business. Show her our new ads.

HERB: Me? I'm new here.

TIM: Well, you need the practice.

HERB: What do I say to her?

TIM: Introduce yourself, ask about her new muffins, and show her our new ads.

HERB: Okay. She's walking this way. . . Wait a second. I know her!

TIM: You do?

HERB: Yes. Her mom and my mom are friends. That's Rita Jonas.

TIM: You're right. Beginner's luck! Give your mom a big kiss. Don't forget.

Words and Expressions

Do you know these words and expressions? Write new ones in your notebook.

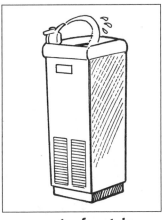

a water fountain

a muffin

an advertisement (an ad)

1. A: Tell her about our new ads.
   B: Me?

2. A: What do I do?
   B: Introduce yourself, ask about her new muffins, and show her our new ads.

With a Partner

A. *Practice the conversation with a partner.*

B. *Talk about well-known successful businesswomen. Who are they? Where do they live? What kinds of businesses do they have?*

Example:

Martha Stewart is a successful businesswoman. She lives in Connecticut. She's originally from New Jersey.

She publishes a magazine and appears on radio and TV. Her business is about the home. She often finds new uses for old things.

C. *What do you think? Is it difficult for women to be successful in business today?*

Martha Stewart

Grammar **Presentation**
Review: Imperative, Present Progressive, and Simple Present

Contrast			
Imperative	**Present Progressive**	**Simple Present**	**Simple Present (non-action verbs)**
Talk to her.	She**'s talking** to Rita.	They **talk** every week.	They **like** to talk.
Don't call her.	I**'m not calling** her now.	She **doesn't call** me.	She **doesn't have** a phone.

Non-action Verbs					
Description	**Emotions**	**Mental States**	**Needs**	**Possession**	**Senses**
be	like	agree	need	have	feel
look	love	know	prefer	own	hear
sound	hate	understand	want	belong	see

Notes

1. Use the **imperative** to:
— give **directions**
— make **suggestions**
— make **requests**

2. Use the **present progressive** to talk about **actions** that are **in progress**.

3. Use the **simple present** to talk about:
— **facts**
— **repeated actions**

4. Remember that some verbs do not talk about actions. They describe emotions, mental states, and other states. These verbs are **non-action** or **stative verbs**. They are usually in the **simple present**.

Examples

- **Bake** the muffins for fifteen minutes.
- **Don't bring** muffins to the party.
- Please **help** me.

- He**'s learning** Chinese.
- She**'s talking** about him *now*.

- The store **belongs** to Rita.
- She **talks** about him all the time.

- I **know** that woman.
  NOT ~~I am knowing that woman.~~
- I **don't own** a car.
  NOT ~~I'm not owning a car.~~

Reference Notes
1. Look at Unit 1 for more about the imperative. **2.** Look at Units 9–11 for more about the present progressive. **3.** Look at Units 12–15 for more about the simple present tense.

Focused Practice

1 Discover the Grammar

*Read each sentence. Write **N** for sentences that are talking about right **now**.
Write **F** for sentences that give **facts**. Write **RA** for sentences that describe
repeated actions. Write **R** for sentences that make **requests**.*

_F_ 1. Rita owns health food stores.

_____ 2. Please ask about her muffins.

_____ 3. She's talking to Sabrina.

_____ 4. She's coming this way.

_____ 5. Please give your mom a kiss.

_____ 6. Don't forget, please.

_____ 7. They come here often.

_____ 8. Go and talk to her, please.

2 Beginner's Luck   Grammar Notes 1–3

A. *Complete the conversation with sentences from the box.*

> a. Yes, it is. Here. Take a look at our new ads.
>
> b. Excuse me, Rita. We need your help.
>
> c. I'm working for Arthur Andrews now. I'm a sales representative.
>
> d. All you need is good advertising.
>
> e. What are you doing

RITA: Herb? Herb Okun?

HERB: Yes, it's me.

RITA: _____ here?
                                1.

HERB: _____
                                2.

RITA: That's great. Arthur Andrews is an advertising firm, right?

HERB: _____
                                3.

RITA: You know, these ads are very well done.

HERB: Thanks. So . . . your company has a new line of muffins?

RITA: That's right. Here. Try one.

HERB: Mmm. Delicious! _____
                                              4.

MAN: _____
                          5.

RITA: Okay. Herb, can you call me tomorrow morning?

HERB: Of course.

B. *Now listen and check your work.*

3 **Conversations**   Grammar Notes 1–4

Complete the sentences. Use the words in parentheses and the correct tense.

RITA: Any messages?

LIZ: Only one. Herb Okun called. <u>Do you know</u> him?
                                1. (you / know)

RITA: Yes, I do. _____ for an advertising firm.
                      2. (He / work)
_____ at these ads. What _____?
   3. (Look)   4. (you / think)

LIZ: _____ funny.
        5. (They / be)

RITA: _____.
          6. (I / agree)

[Rita calls Herb.]

HERB: Hello?

RITA: Hi, Herb. This is Rita.

HERB: Hello. Thanks for returning my call. So Rita, how _____ the ads?
                                                              7. (you / like)

RITA: _____ at them now. _____ them a lot.
        8. (I / look)   9. (I / like)

HERB: That's great.

RITA: _____ about changing advertising firms right now.
        10. (we / talk)

HERB: You know, advertising is the key to good business.

RITA: Who do I speak to at Arthur Andrews?

HERB: _____ Tim Olson at 890-0777.
        11. (Call)
He can answer all your questions.

RITA: Thanks, Herb.

HERB: Thank *you*.

4 **Editing**

Correct the sentences.
There are eight mistakes.

Woman in the News: Rita Jonas

Rita Jonas ~~has~~ thirty-three years old. She own ten health food
stores. One hundred people works for her. Her workers are
saying, "Rita is a great boss. She understand her business and
her workers. Her company is like a family. She's knowing our
names and our interests. She is helping us when we have
problems. We are being lucky to work for her."

Communication Practice

5 A Radio Interview

Jessica Olson of KZYX News is talking with Rita Jonas. Listen and complete the sentences. Use the affirmative or negative forms of the verbs in parentheses.

1. Rita _____ _____ stores.
    (have)

2. Rita _____ to open any new _____ at this time.
    (plan)

3. Rita _____ an online business.
    (start)

4. Rita _____ all over the world. Sometimes she _____ her
    (travel)   (see)
   husband or son for _____ or _____ weeks.

5. Her husband _____. He _____ too.
    (complain)   (travel)

6. Rita and Paul _____ to leave Redmond.
    (want)

6 Write about Yourself

A. *Look at the chart. Talk with a partner about Rita Jonas. How are you and your partner like Rita Jonas? How are you different?*

B. *Complete the chart for yourself. Then on a piece of paper write sentences about yourself. Don't write your name on your paper. Put all papers in a hat. Pick one and find the writer.*

	Rita Jonas	You
Occupation	businessperson	
Eyes	brown	
Hair	blond	
Likes	jazz, hiking	
Dislikes	big cities	
Favorite season	summer	
Age	33	
Favorite color	red	
At this time	She's wearing a red suit and black shoes. She's meeting three new salespeople.	

UNIT

22

The Simple Past:
Regular Verbs (Statements)

The party was fun, but we missed you.

Grammar **in Context**

🎧 *Listen and read these e-mail messages.*

Subj: Thanks
Date: 3/10   6:43 PM
From: JudyJohnson@uw.edu
To: KWhite@aal.com

Kathy,

Thanks for the chocolates. Everyone enjoyed them. My birthday
party was fun, but it wasn't the same without you. Mark looked like
a lost dog. :>(

How's Boston? How's the convention?

Judy

Subj: Boston
Date: 3/11   3:43 PM
From: KWhite@aal.com
To: JudyJohnson@uw.edu

Hi Judy,

Sorry I missed your party. Once again, Happy Birthday.

As for Boston, it's super. :) But the convention's another story.
I arrived Monday night and stayed at a big hotel. The hotel was awful!
It was noisy and dirty. Yesterday I moved in with my cousin Ted.
I didn't want to impose, but he insisted. He's really special. I want
you to meet him.

Kathy

146

Subj: Who's Ted?
Date: 3/11 6:50 PM
From: JudyJohnson@uw.edu
To: KWhite@aal.com

Hi Kathy,

Who's this secret cousin Ted? I'd love to meet him.

Judy

Words and Expressions

🎧 *Do you know these words and expressions? Write new ones in your notebook.*

a hotel

a convention

a presentation

1. **A:** Sorry I missed your party.
   B: It wasn't the same without you.

2. **A:** I want you to meet my cousin.
   B: I'd love to meet him.

3. **A:** How's the food?
   B: It's good. But the service is another story.

4. **A:** Mark seemed pretty sad.
   B: Yeah. He looked like a lost dog.

With a Partner

A. *Read the e-mail messages with a partner.*

B. *Tell about a convention or a special event you attended. Was it interesting? Did you stay at a hotel or with a friend or relative?*

Grammar **Presentation**
The Simple Past: Regular Verbs (Statements)

Statements	
Affirmative	**Negative**
I **missed** the party. You **missed** the convention. He **missed** lunch. She **missed** the party. It **arrived** yesterday.	I **didn't miss** the convention. You **didn't miss** the party. He **didn't miss** dinner. She **didn't miss** the convention. It **didn't arrive** last week.
We **missed** the presentation. You **missed** the convention. They **missed** the presentation.	We **didn't miss** the dinner. You **didn't miss** the party. They **didn't miss** the party.

Past Time Expressions		
yesterday	*ago*	*last*
yesterday morning **yesterday** evening	two days **ago** a month **ago**	**last** night **last** week

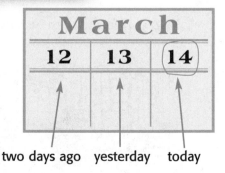

two days ago   yesterday   today

Notes

Examples

1. Use the **simple past** tense to talk about an **event** that happened in the **past**.

    Now

    Past ·······**X**···············⋮···············➤ Future

    I arrived last night.

- I **arrived** last night.
- Yesterday I **moved** in with Ted.

2. **Regular verbs** in the simple past tense **end in –ed**.

    If the base form ends in *–e*, add only *–d*.

    If the base form ends in *–y* after a consonant, change the *y* to *i* and add *–ed*.

- I stay**ed** at a hotel.
- I arriv**ed** yesterday.
- I stud**ied** all night.

base form
stay

arriv**e**

stud**y**

3. Use *did not* + the **base form** of the verb for a **negative statement** in the simple past.

Use *didn't* for speaking and informal writing.

- She **did not stay** at the hotel.

- She **didn't stay** at the hotel.

4. Time expressions come at the beginning or the end of a sentence.

- *Last night* I arrived in Boston.
- I arrived in Boston *last night*.

Pronunciation Note
The regular simple past verb ending has three sounds: **/t/**, **/d/**, and **/ɪd/**. The sound of the past tense ending depends on the last sound of the base form of the verb.
I missed you. **/t/**
She arrived at 7 P.M. **/d/**
He insisted. **/ɪd/** (= extra syllable)

Reference Notes
1. Look at Unit 7 for the past of *be*. **2.** Look at Unit 23 for irregular past tense verbs.
3. Look at Appendix 11 on page 269 for more on the spelling and pronunciation of the simple past tense of regular verbs.

Focused Practice

 Discover the Grammar

A. *Read* Grammar in Context *again. Circle the simple past verbs.*

Example:
Everyone (enjoyed) them.

B. *Read about Kathy's cousin. Circle the simple past verbs.*

Six years ago Ted Geller graduated from college. A year after graduation, Ted and four friends started an online business. For three years they worked very hard. They worked very long hours too. They started at seven and finished at eleven. They hired and fired a lot of people. They learned a lot about business. In their third year, a big company offered to buy their company. The five partners agreed. Ted ended up without a job but with $6 million. He used half his money to help poor children. Ted is an unusual person.

2 Pronunciation

A. *Read the sentences. Underline the verb. Write the base form of the verb.*

Sentence	Base Verb	/t/	/d/	/ɪd/
1. He <u>graduated</u> from college last year.	graduate			✓
2. They started a business.				
3. They worked long hours.				
4. They hired many people.				
5. They learned a lot.				
6. A company wanted to buy their business.				
7. They agreed.				

B. *Now listen and check (✓) the sound of the –ed.*

3 Last Weekend Grammar Notes 1–3

Look at the pictures. Complete the sentences. Use the affirmative or negative of the verbs in the box.

Saturday

Sunday

clean	play	rain	stay	watch

Saturday it ___rained___ all day long. Judy _____ home.
    1.   2.
She _____ her apartment. Then she _____ TV. She
        3.   4.
_____ tennis.
        5.
    Sunday it _____. It was a beautiful day. Judy _____
                    6.   7.
home. She _____ her apartment. She _____ tennis in
                8.   9.
the park.

4 Editing

Correct the mistakes in the messages. There are five mistakes.

1. I'm sorry I ~~did miss~~ 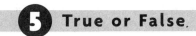 your call. Please leave your name and a short message.

2. Hi, Ted. This is Al. I am arrived this morning. I'm at the Grand Hotel. The number is 345-9090.

3. Hello, Ted. This is Melissa. I yesterday talked to Ellen. She did loved your speech.

4. Hi, Ted. This is Judy. Sorry I was missed your call. I was at the library. Call me. I have some wonderful news.

Communication Practice

5 True or False

Work in small groups. Write five true sentences and one false sentence about yourself as a child. Read your sentences to your group. Your group guesses the false sentence. Use the ideas in the box or your own ideas.

| play a sport | like a food | listen to a kind of music | travel to a place |

Example:

As a child I didn't play basketball. I played soccer. I liked pasta. I didn't like fish. I listened to rock. I didn't listen to jazz.

6 Information Gap: Famous People

Work with a partner. Student B, turn to the Information Gap on page 278 and follow the instructions there.

Student A, read the sentences below to Student B. Student B names the people.

Marie Curie   Albert Einstein

Louis Armstrong   Georgia O'Keeffe

1. She was born in Albania but lived in India. She helped the poor. *(Mother Teresa)*

2. He started the Pop Art movement. He painted celebrities. *(Andy Warhol)*

3. She married Prince Charles of England. She died in an auto crash. *(Princess Diana)*

4. He was a leader in India. He used peaceful means to reach his goals. *(Mahatma Gandhi)*

Now listen to Student B. Look at the pictures and name the people.

The Simple Past: Regular and Irregular Verbs

Well, my dear, we had an adventure!

Grammar **in Context**

🎧 *Listen and read the conversation.*

KATHY: Hi, Amanda. Say, where were you and Josh on the weekend? I called several times.

AMANDA: Well, my dear, we had an adventure!

KATHY: You did?

AMANDA: Yes. We went out of town on Saturday. We left at 3:00. About 4:00 it started to snow. In half an hour the snow was really deep.

KATHY: Oh no! Did you stop?

AMANDA: Yeah. Then it got dark. We put on all our warm clothes, so we were okay.

KATHY: Did you have anything to eat?

AMANDA: Yes, actually. We had some cookies and chocolate bars. We ate those right away. And we had some sodas. We drank them during the night.

KATHY: Was it cold?

AMANDA: Freezing! Fortunately, we had our sleeping bags. But we didn't sleep much.

KATHY: Then what happened?

AMANDA: In the morning a snowplow came along and cleared the road.

KATHY: Wow! Scary. I'm glad you're okay.

AMANDA: Thanks. Me too.

Words and Expressions

🎧 *Do you know these words and expressions? Write new ones in your notebook.*

deep snow

dark / light

put on warm clothes

during the night

1. A: Did you have anything to eat?
    B: Yes, actually.

2. A: Was it cold during the night?
    B: Freezing!

With a Partner

A. *Practice the conversation with a partner.*

B. *Last month Tim, Jessica, Jeremy, Annie, and Ben Olson went camping. Look at the picture. Each partner asks four past tense questions. Use the words and phrases in the box.*

snow	stay in a motel	sleep in sleeping bags	enjoy their breakfast
rain	sleep in beds	sleep in tents	take their dog with them

Example:

A: Did it snow?
B: No, it didn't.

B: Did they sleep in tents?
A: Yes, they did.

Grammar **Presentation**

The Simple Past: Irregular Verbs (Statements)

Statements	
Affirmative	**Negative**
I **ate** the cookies. You **had** the chocolate. She **drank** soda. We **went** camping in September.	I **did not eat** the chocolate. You **didn't have** the cookies. She **didn't drink** water. We **didn't go** in August.

The Simple Past: Regular and Irregular Verbs (*Yes / No* Questions)

Yes / No Questions			
Did	**Subject**	**Base Form**	
Did	I you	**wake** **sleep**	you up? late?
	he it we they	**stay** **snow?** **eat** **take**	home? all the cookies? warm clothes?

Short Answers	
Affirmative	**Negative**
Yes, you **did**. Yes, I **did**. Yes, we **did**. Yes, he **did**. Yes, it **did**. Yes, you **did**. Yes, they **did**.	No, you **didn't**. No, I **didn't**. No, we **didn't**. No, he **didn't**. No, it **didn't**. No, you **didn't**. No, they **didn't**.

Notes

Examples

---

1. Remember that **regular verbs** end in *–ed* in the simple past.

Irregular verbs have **different forms** in the simple past. (*See verbs in Note 5.*)

	base form
• It **started** to snow.	**start**
• I **ate** the raisins.	**eat**
• We **went** out of town.	**go**

---

2. For a **negative sentence** in the simple past, use *did not (didn't)* + the **base form** of the verb.

NOTE: Don't use *did* with the past tense form of the verb.

	did not	base form	
• He	**did not**	**sleep**	much.
• He	**didn't**	**sleep**	much.

NOT ~~He didn't slept much.~~

---

3. To make a *yes / no* question in the simple past, use *did* + the **subject** + the **base form** of the verb.

	did	subject	base form	
•	**Did**	you	**stop**?	
•	**Did**	he	**eat**	anything?

4. You can use *did* or *didn't* in the **short answer** in the simple past tense.

> **A:** Did it snow?
>
> **B:** Yes, it **did**. OR Yes.
>   No, it **didn't**. OR No.

5. Here is a list of some common **irregular verbs** and their simple past forms.

Base Form	Simple Past	Base Form	Simple Past	Base Form	Simple Past
buy	**bought**	get	**got**	put	**put**
come	**came**	go	**went**	see	**saw**
drink	**drank**	have	**had**	sleep	**slept**
eat	**ate**	leave	**left**	take	**took**

Reference Note
Look at Appendix 8 on page 267 for more irregular verbs and their simple past forms.

Focused Practice

 Discover the Grammar

Read Grammar in Context *again. Circle the irregular verbs. Write the three*
yes / no *questions in the simple past.*

_____

_____

_____

2 One of Those Days   Grammar Notes 1–2

Complete the sentences. Use the simple past of the verbs in parentheses.

Yesterday Jason _____had_____ one of those days. He _____ at 8:00.
                           1. (have)   **2. (get up)**

He _____ in a hurry, so he _____ a shower. He _____ a piece
    3. (be)   **4. (not take)**   **5. (eat)**

of toast and _____ a cup of black coffee for breakfast. Jason _____ the
              6. (drink)   **7. (leave)**

house at 8:20, but his car was in the shop, so he _____ the bus. He _____
                                                 8. (take)   **9. (arrive)**

at the office at 10:00 A.M. His boss _____ him and wasn't happy. At lunchtime,
                                      10. (see)

Jason _____ to a restaurant, but he _____ enough money to pay.
               11. (go)   **12. (not have)**

Jason _____ the office until 7:30 P.M. He _____ home at 9:00 P.M.
             13. (not leave)   **14. (get)**

It was just one of those days.

3 Questions

Complete the conversations. Write yes / no *questions with the words in the box.*

| **Verbs:** | call | get up | go | have | leave | rain |
| **Subjects:** | I | it | Jeremy | you | your parents | you and Amanda |

1. **A:** _____ Did you have _____ breakfast this morning, Ken?

   B: Yes. I had cereal, eggs, toast, and tea.

2. **A:** Josh, _____ early this morning?

   B: No, we didn't. We slept until 10 A.M. It's Saturday, remember?

3. **A:** _____ yesterday in Seattle, Mary?

   B: Yes, it did. It rained all day.

4. **A:** _____ to the movie with you?

   B: Yes, he did. Ben went too. We all really enjoyed it.

5. **A:** I'm sorry, Mark. _____ too late?

   B: No. It's only 9:45. What's up?

6. **A:** _____ for vacation, Jessica?

   B: Yes, they did. They left at 6:30 this morning for Jamaica.

4 Editing

Correct the mistakes in the postcard. There are eight mistakes.

Dear Rose,

    Greetings from beautiful Jamaica! Thanks for
taking us to the airport. Our flight ~~not leave~~ didn't leave until
1 P.M., so the plane didn't arrived until 10:30. We was
really tired when we get to the hotel. But that is two
days ago. Now the sun is shining and it's warm.

    Yesterday we go swimming at the beach. I buy
some great gifts for people. Today we sleeped
until 10!

    Hope everything is okay in Seattle. Is it cold?

Love,

    Mary

TO:
Rose Corgatelli
3677 49th Ave. SW
Seattle, WA 98116
USA

Communication Practice

5 Who's the Mystery Guest?

🎧 *Listen to the TV game show. Then listen again. Check (✓)* **Yes, No,** *or* **No Information.**

	Yes	No	No Information
1. This person was born in Texas.	❏	❏	❏
2. This person went to the University of Missouri.	❏	❏	❏
3. This person graduated from college.	❏	❏	❏
4. This person went to Hollywood.	❏	❏	❏
5. This person acted in the movie *A River Runs Through It.*	❏	❏	❏
6. This person got an academy award nomination for *Twelve Monkeys.*	❏	❏	❏
7. This person got married in 1999.	❏	❏	❏

Bonus Question: Who is the mystery guest? _____

6 Ask Other People

You have five minutes to ask your classmates seven yes / no *questions. Use the phrases in the box and a past time expression. Report interesting answers.*

eat at a fast-food restaurant	see a movie	get up after 10 A.M.
go to bed after midnight	drink tea for breakfast	buy a book or a CD

Example:

A: Did you eat at a fast-food restaurant yesterday?

B: Yes. I ate at McDonald's.

7 What's True? What's False?

A. *Work with three partners. Read about the* Titanic. *Four statements are not true. Find them. Discuss with the class.*

On April 14, 1912, the *Titanic*, a British luxury ship, left France for its first trip across the Pacific Ocean. Everyone said the *Titanic* was unsinkable. They were wrong. During the afternoon of April 15, the *Titanic* hit an iceberg. The ship started to sink. Another ship tried to help but didn't arrive in time to save everybody. When the *Titanic* went to the bottom of the ocean, 1,503 people died.

There are several movies about the *Titanic*. In *Titanic*, the 1998 version, Brad Pitt played the role of a young man who died in the disaster. This *Titanic* is the number one movie of all time.

B. *Check your answers on page 281.*

24 The Simple Past: Wh- Questions

Why did the Titanic sink?

Grammar in Context

🎧 *Listen and read the conversation and the game.*

JOSH: What's that?

AMANDA: A quiz game.

JOSH: On the Internet?

AMANDA: Uh-huh.

JOSH: Hmm. Let's see.

WHO, WHAT, WHERE, WHEN, AND WHY

Welcome to "Who, What, Where, When, and Why." Be the first to answer these questions and win a free trip. E-mail your answers to who.what@aql.com.

Here are today's questions:

1. Who directed the first *Star Wars* movie?
   a. Steven Spielberg.   **b.** George Lucas.   **c.** William Shatner.

2. What did Martin Luther King Jr. say in his famous speech?
   a. "I want to dream."   **b.** "I need a dream."   **c.** "I have a dream."

3. Where did Pablo Picasso spend most of his life?
   a. In France.   **b.** In Spain.   **c.** In Italy.

4. When did the Beatles become popular?
   a. In the 1950s.   **b.** In the 1960s.   **c.** In the 1970s.

5. Why did the *Titanic* sink?
   a. Someone started a fire.   **b.** It exploded.   **c.** It hit an iceberg.

AMANDA: Well, do you know the answers?

JOSH: I think so.

AMANDA: Then let's go for it.

Words and Expressions

🎧 *Do you know these words and expressions? Write new ones in your notebook.*

a fire

an explosion

1. A: When did Madonna become popular?
   B: In the 1980s.

2. A: Do you know the answers?
   B: Yes.
   A: Then let's go for it.

With a Partner

A. *Practice the conversation with a partner.*

B. *With your partner, answer the questions on "Who, What, Where, When, and Why."*

C. *Check your answers in the Grammar Charts below.*

Grammar **Presentation**
The Simple Past: *Wh-* Questions

Questions	Answers
Where **did** Pablo Picasso **live**?	In France.
Why **did** the *Titanic* **sink**?	It hit an iceberg.
What **did** Martin Luther King Jr. **say**?	"I have a dream."
When **did** the Beatles **become** popular?	In the 1960s.

Questions about the Subject	Answers
Who **directed** the first *Star Wars* movie?	George Lucas (did).
What **hit** the *Titanic*?	An iceberg (did).

More Irregular Verbs

Base Form	Simple Past
begin	**began**
break	**broke**
build	**built**
fly	**flew**
win	**won**
write	**wrote**

Notes

Examples

1. **Wh- questions** ask for **specific information**.

   Short answers are common, but you cannot use *yes* or *no*.

   A: Where did the *Titanic* sink?
   B: *In the Atlantic* (*Ocean*).

2. Most *wh-* questions **in the simple past** use a **wh- word + did +** the **subject +** the **base form** of the verb.

   A: When did the *Titanic* **sink**?
   B: In 1912.

3. *Wh-* questions **about the subject** use a **wh- word +** the **simple past form** of the verb. Do not use *did*.

   A: Who painted *Guernica*?
   B: Picasso.
   NOT ~~Who did paint Guernica?~~

Pronunciation Note

Wh- questions usually have rising-falling intonation: **A:** *What did he eat?*
B: *Pasta.*

To show surprise, stress the question word and use rising intonation: **A:** *He ate a snake.*
B: *What did he eat?*

Focused Practice

 1 Discover the Grammar

*Listen to these conversations. Underline the
wh- questions in the simple past. Read them aloud.*

JOSH: Amanda. It's for you. It's your brother.

AMANDA: Hi, Rob. What's up? . . . Oh, no! Are you
okay? . . . When did it happen? . . .
Where did it happen? . . . Why did you
go there? . . . What car? . . . But you don't
have a driver's license! Does Dad know? . . .
Sorry. I think Dad needs to know.

[Amanda hangs up.]

JOSH: What happened?

AMANDA: He drove Dad's car into a tree, and the body shop wants $800 to fix it.

❷ An Emergency

Complete the conversation. Use the questions in the box.

> **What did your parents say?**   **When did you do that?**
> **Why did you drive there?**   · **what happened?**

JOSH: You know, I once drove without a license.

AMANDA: _____
1.

JOSH: Oh, about ten years ago. I was fifteen, and I went to my grandmother's house.

AMANDA: _____
2.

JOSH: It was impossible to get to her home by bus. She called and said she was sick. My parents were away for the day.

AMANDA: So _____
3.

JOSH: Well, I drove to her house. She was really sick. I took her to the hospital.

AMANDA: _____
4.

JOSH: They said I did the right thing. I got my license the next month.

❸ Pronunciation

🎧 **A.** *Listen to these two conversations.*

1. **A:** I told Bill I was angry.
   B: What did you say? *(B didn't hear A. B is asking for information.)*

2. **A:** I'm getting married this afternoon.
   B: What did you say? *(B is surprised by the information.)*

🎧 **B.** *Listen to these questions. Check (✓)* **Information** *or* **Surprise**.

	Information	Surprise
1. When did they arrive?	❑	❑
2. When did they arrive?	❑	☒
3. How did she get there?	❑	☒
4. How did she get there?	☒	❑
5. What did you say?	❑	☒
6. What did you say?	☒	❑
7. Who came to your house?	❑	☒
8. Who came to your house?	☒	❑

C. *Read one of the questions in Part B. Your partner gives the number of the question you read.*

4 **In the Past** Grammar Notes 1–3

Read the answer. Write the question about the underlined words.

1. **A:** _____

   B: Jesse Owens won four Olympic gold medals <u>in Berlin</u>.

2. **A:** _____

   B: Two men built the first personal computer <u>in a garage</u>.

3. **A:** _____

   B: The Soviet Union broke up <u>in 1991</u>.

4. **A:** _____

   B: <u>Louis Braille</u> invented a way for blind people to read.

5. **A:** _____

   B: <u>World War I</u> began in 1914.

5 **Editing**

Correct the questions. There are nine mistakes.

did Amelia Earhart do
1. What ~~Amelia Earhart did~~ in 1932?

2. Where began the first Olympic Games?

3. Who did write *Don Quixote*?

4. When the Korean War began?

5. Who walk on the moon in 1969?

6. Who Lucille Ball?

7. Why Christopher Columbus sail west?

8. Where the Internet start?

9. Who paints the Sistine Chapel in Rome?

Communication Practice

6 **What's the Answer?**

A. *Work with a partner. Complete the statements. Choose from the items below.*

1. Amelia Earhart was the first woman to fly alone across the _____.
   a. Atlantic Ocean   **b.** Pacific Ocean   **c.** United States

2. The first Olympic Games began in _____.
   a. Rome   **b.** Greece   **c.** Turkey

3. _____ wrote *Don Quixote*.
   a. William Shakespeare   **b.** Jorge Luis Borges   **c.** Miguel de Cervantes

4. The Korean War began in _____.
   a. 1951   **b.** 1953   **c.** 1955

5. _____ walked on the moon in 1969.
   a. John Glenn   **b.** Yuri Gagarin   **c.** Neil Armstrong

6. Lucille Ball was _____.
   a. a writer   **b.** a scientist   **c.** an actress

7. Christopher Columbus wanted to get to _____.
   a. Africa   **b.** North America   **c.** Asia

8. The Internet first started in _____.
   a. the US Army   **b.** the Olympics   **c.** the Soviet Army

9. _____ painted the Sistine Chapel.
   a. Michelangelo   **b.** Leonardo da Vinci   **c.** El Greco

B. *Check your answers on page 281.*

7 Same and Different

Work with a partner. Interview your partner about his or her past.

You write five things that were the same in the past. Your partner writes five things that were different.

Examples:

1.   **YOU:** What sports did you play in high school?
   PARTNER: I played soccer.
   YOU: I played soccer too.

     We both played soccer in high school.

2. **PARTNER:** Where did you go on your last vacation?
   YOU: I went to the beach.
   PARTNER: I went to the mountains.

     On my last vacation, I went to the beach. Juan went to the mountains.

8 Information Gap: A Quiz Show

One student is the host. The host turns to page 279. The class works in groups of five.

Listen to the question. Talk to your partners. Raise your hands when you agree on the answer. The first group to raise hands answers first. A correct answer wins one point. A wrong answer loses one point.

Example:

   HOST: Who flew across the Atlantic in 1927?
  GROUP 1: Amelia Earhart.
   HOST: Incorrect. You lose one point.
  GROUP 2: Charles Lindbergh.
   HOST: Correct. You win one point.

PART

7 Review or SelfTest

I. *Complete the conversations. Circle the correct letter.*

1. HERB: Sorry I'm late. _____

    TIM: That's okay.

    (A) I miss the train.   (C) I missed the train.

    (B) Do I miss the train?   (D) I do miss the train.

A B Ⓒ D

2. AMANDA: _____

    JOSH: Yes, I got up after nine.

    (A) Do you get up late?   (C) When did you get up?

    (B) Did you get up late?   (D) Who got up late?

A B C D

3. TIM: How was the movie?

    STEVE: Great. _____

    (A) Everyone really   (C) Everyone really is

        enjoyed it.   enjoying it.

    (B) Everyone really   (D) What was the movie

        enjoys it.   about?

A B C D

4. TIM: _____

    STEVE: At my house.

    (A) Why did your friends   (C) Where did your

        stay there?   friends stay?

    (B) Did your friends stay   (D) Did your friends

        at your house?   stay at a hotel?

A B C D

5. TIM: _____

    STEVE: Last night about nine.

    (A) Why did they leave?   (C) When do they leave?

    (B) Who left last night?   (D) When did they leave?

A B C D

II. *Complete the paragraph. Use the simple present or the simple past of the verbs in parentheses.*

    Steven Spielberg ____is____ a very popular movie director. As a boy,
                 1. (be)

Spielberg always _____ movies. At twelve, he _____ his first
             2. (like)   3. (complete)

film. At thirteen, he _____ a prize for a forty-minute war movie.
                 4. (receive)

In college, he _____ film. At twenty, he _____ a job as a TV
           5. (study)   6. (get)

director with Universal MCA. In the next several years, he _____ many
                                         7. (direct)

successful movies including *Jaws, Star Wars, E.T., Raiders of the Lost Ark,*

Jurassic Park, and *Schindler's List.* Today people all over the world

_____ his movies.
    8. (watch)

III. *Complete the conversation. Use the simple present, present progressive, or simple past of the verbs in parentheses.*

HERB: _____Did_____ you _____get_____ the new ad for muffins?
                           1. (get)

TIM: Yes, here it _____. Sabrina _____ it to me a few minutes ago.
                     2. (be)   3. (give)

HERB: It'_____ good. I _____ it a lot.
        4. (be)   5. (like)

TIM: Yes, it is. The team _____ on it until nine o'clock last night.
                        6. (work)

HERB: _____ Rita _____ a copy?
                7. (have)

TIM: Someone _____ it to her right now.
            8. (show)

IV. *Complete the ad. Use the imperative or the simple present of the verbs in the box.*

be   ~~eat~~   hurry   save   try

🍐 🍌 🍓 Rita's Healthy Muffins 🍅 🥕 🍎

_____Do_____ you _____eat_____ muffins for breakfast?
                                1.

For lunch? For dinner? Muffins _____ delicious
                                   2.

any time of the day. _____ Rita's new fruit and
                       3.

vegetable muffins. _____. This week only,
                    4.

_____ 25 cents on any muffin.
     5.

V. *Write questions about the underlined words.*

1. MARY: _____Where did you go?_____

   JESSICA: We went <u>to the country</u>.

2. MARY: _____

   JESSICA: We left <u>at ten in the morning</u>. The drive took five hours.

3. MARY: _____

   JESSICA: It took five hours <u>because we had a flat tire on the way</u>.

4. MARY: _____

   JESSICA: <u>Jeremy</u> changed the tire.

5. MARY: _____

   JESSICA: We got home <u>at midnight</u>.

▶ **To check your answers, go to the Answer Key on page 284.**

UNIT

Subject and Object Pronouns

Why don't you give them chocolates?

Grammar **in Context**

🎧 *Listen and read the conversation.*

CARLOS: Well, Kathy, you're an American. What's a good gift?

KATHY: For what?

CARLOS: For the party at Bill's house on Saturday. I want to get him a gift.

KATHY: Right. Let me think.

CARLOS: How about flowers?

KATHY: Well, I suppose so. But you don't usually give flowers to a man.

CARLOS: He has a wife. Can I give them to her?

KATHY: Hmm. I'm not sure.

CARLOS: What about a CD of some cool Latin music? I know he likes music.

KATHY: No. Not appropriate. You don't give your boss a CD.

CARLOS: Well, what do you suggest?

KATHY: Why don't you give them chocolates? He always eats them at his desk.

CARLOS: Okay, good idea. A box of chocolates. Now, another question.

KATHY: What?

CARLOS: Tomiko and I need a ride to the party. Can you take us?

KATHY: For a price.

CARLOS: For a price? What do you mean?

KATHY: Get me a box of chocolates too.

CARLOS: I don't believe you. You're not serious, are you?

KATHY: No, just kidding! See you at 6:30 on Saturday.

Words and Expressions

🎧 *Do you know these words and expressions? Write new ones in your notebook.*

flowers

chocolates

give a ride

1. **A:** Does he like flowers?
   B: Well, I suppose so.

2. **A:** How about some flowers?
   B: I don't think so.

3. **A:** Why don't you give them chocolates?
   B: Good idea.

4. We need a ride. Can you take us?

With a Partner

A. *Practice the conversation with a partner.*

B. *Look at the pictures of the homes of famous people. Say two sentences about each of them.*

Example:

Windsor Castle belongs to Queen Elizabeth.
It belongs to her.

Windsor Castle
Queen Elizabeth

The Imperial Palace
Emperor Akihito and
Empress Michiko

The Gates Mansion
Bill Gates

Grammar **Presentation**
Subject and Object Pronouns

Subject Pronouns			
Subject	Verb	Object	
I You He She We You They	gave	them	chocolates.

Object Pronouns			
Subject	Verb	Object	
They	gave	me you him her us you them	a CD.

Notes

Examples

1. *I*, *you*, *he*, *she*, *it*, *we*, and *they* are **subject pronouns**. They replace a subject noun.

- *The boys* need a ride to the party. **They** don't have a car.

2. *Me*, *you*, *him*, *her*, *it*, *us*, and *them* are **object pronouns**. They replace an object noun.

- subject noun / object noun
  Bill loves *chocolates*.

- subject pronoun / object noun
- **He** loves **them**.

Object pronouns often come **after prepositions** like *for* or *to*.

- The chocolates are *for* him.
- Give them *to* him.

3. NOTE: *You* and *it* are both subject and object pronouns.

- subject / object
- **You**'re kidding. I don't believe **you**.

- subject / object
- **It**'s Latin music. He likes **it**.

4. The pronoun *you* is the same for singular and plural.

- I don't believe **you**. *(you = Kathy)*
- See **you** at 6:30. *(you = you and Tom)*

When *you* is **plural**, we sometimes add the word *both* to make the sentence clearer.

- See **you both** at 6:30.

Focused Practice

1 Discover the Grammar

Read the conversation. Underline the subject pronouns. Circle the object pronouns.

STEVE: Amanda, do you like parties?

AMANDA: I love them. Why?

STEVE: Well, we're having a party on Sunday at my apartment.
You and Josh are both invited. Are you free?

AMANDA: I think so. What time?

STEVE: About two o'clock.

AMANDA: What's the occasion?

STEVE: It's Jessica's birthday. Now, another question: What's a good gift?

AMANDA: Does she like music?

STEVE: Yes. She listens to it all the time.

AMANDA: Good. Get her some CDs. Now, tell me again. Where do you live?

STEVE: On Vine Street—14 Vine Street, Apartment 202.

AMANDA: Okay. See you then. Thanks.

2 How about a Book?   Grammar Notes 1–2

Complete the conversations with subject and object pronouns.

1. **A:** It's Jessica's birthday on Sunday. What's a good gift for ____her____?

   B: How about a book? _____ loves to read.

2. **A:** It's Mark's birthday next week. What's a good gift?

   B: Well, _____ likes CDs. Get _____ a CD.

3. **A:** Our car is in the shop. Can _____ give _____ a ride to the party?

   B: Sure. I'll pick _____ up at 5:00.

4. **A:** The Johnsons are having a party on Saturday. What's a good gift for _____?

   B: _____ love flowers.

5. **A:** Hello? Steve? Is _____ raining there? Do I need my umbrella?

   B: Yes, bring _____. It's raining hard.

6. **A:** My friends are visiting from Portland. _____ love parties.

   B: Well, bring _____ on Saturday. We have plenty of food.

7. **A:** How do you feel about steak for the barbecue? Do you like _____?

   B: Of course I do! _____'s delicious.

3 **Why Don't You Get Them a Travel Book?** Grammar Notes 2, 5

Write a suggestion for each picture. Start with **Why don't you get . . . ?**

a travel book

a tennis racquet

1. ___Why don't you get them a travel book?___   2. _____

a vest

a video

3. _____   4. _____

4 **Editing**

Correct the invitation. There are six mistakes.

> Dear Sarah,
>
> Jim and ~~me~~ ^I are having a party on Saturday, June 10, at 3:00. Is for our
> son, Bob, and our daughter, Sally. They birthdays are both in June. You and
> Stan are invited. Please don't bring they any presents. Are just having a band
> and lots of food, but no gifts. Please come! Give Jim and I a call at 934-6678 if
> you can come.
>
> See you soon,
> Anne

Communication Practice

5 Who Are They for?

🎧 *Listen to Tim and Jessica's conversation. Listen again and complete the chart. Use the words in the boxes.*

red	something special
orange	a game
white	a CD
green	a tennis racquet
blue	a video

Color of Box	Who is it for?	Gift
red	Cousin Martha	a tennis racquet
	Jessica	
	Jeremy	
	Ben and Annie	
	Mom and Dad	

6 What's a Good Gift?

Write down the names of five friends or relatives. Work with a partner. Talk about a good gift for each person. Then tell the class.

Example:

A: It's my brother's birthday tomorrow. What's a good gift for him?

B: Hmm. How old is he?

A: Ten.

B: Why don't you get him a soccer ball?

OR

A: It's my brother's birthday tomorrow. What's a good gift for him?

B: What does he like?

A: He loves sports.

B: How about a soccer ball?

How much / How many

How many days were you away?

Grammar in Context

🎧 *Listen and read the conversation.*

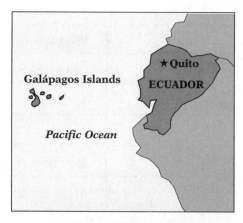

Galápagos Islands

ECUADOR

★Quito

Pacific Ocean

Quito

JUDY: Welcome back.

AMANDA: Thanks.

MARK: How was Ecuador?

JOSH: Great.

JUDY: How many days were you away?

AMANDA: Ten. We were in Quito and the Galápagos Islands.

JUDY: The Galápagos Islands? Sounds exciting. How much time did you spend there?

JOSH: Not much. Only four days. But it was great. We took about a hundred photos. And we ate and slept on a boat.

MARK: Really? How many people were on the boat?

AMANDA: Twelve including us. All very interesting people.

JUDY: I'll bet. How much did the trip cost?

The Galápagos Islands

AMANDA: Almost nothing. We won it on that Internet quiz show, "Who, What, Where, When, and Why."

JUDY: You're kidding!

AMANDA: No.

JUDY: Well, that's the way to go.

Words and Expressions

🎧 *Do you know these words and expressions? Write new ones in your notebook.*

a quiz show

win / lose

1. A: How much time did you spend there?
   B: Not much. Only ten days.

2. A: They were very interesting people.
   B: I'll bet.

3. A: How much did it cost?
   B: Almost nothing.
   A: That's the way to go.

With a Partner

A. *Practice the conversation with a partner.*

B. *Tell your partner about a wonderful vacation you took. Answer your partner's questions, but don't name the place.*

Where did you go? (to a city, to a beach, . . .)

With whom?

How much time did you spend there?

What did you see and do?

Can your partner guess the place?

Grammar **Presentation**

How much / How many

Count Nouns	
A: How many photos did you take?	
B: A lot.	(I took a lot of photos.)
Not many.	(I didn't take many photos.)
A few.	(I took a few photos.)
Sixty.	(I took sixty photos.)

Non-count Nouns	
A: How much time did you spend there?	
B: A lot.	(We spent a lot of time there.)
Not much.	(We didn't spend much time there.)
A little.	(We spent a little time there.)
Six days.	(We spent six days there.)

Notes

Examples

1. Use *how many* + a **plural count noun** to ask about a quantity of something. Use *how much* + a **non-count noun** to ask about an amount.	**A: How many days** were you there? **B:** Fifteen. *(exact quantity)* **A: How much time** did you spend there? **B:** A lot. *(large amount)*
2. Words such as *a lot*, *a few*, *a little*, *not many*, and *not much* are **general** quantity expressions. They tell only if the amount is large or small.	**A:** How many people were on the boat? **B: Not many.** *(small quantity)* **A:** How much time did you spend in Quito? **B: Not much.** *(small amount)*
3. Numbers answer questions with *how many*. Numbers give an **exact** amount.	**A:** How many days were you there? **B: Ten** days.
4. Use *how much* to ask about the **cost** of something. In this case, use *how much* **without a noun**.	• **How much** was the trip? • **How much** did the trip cost? • **How much (money)** did it cost?

> **Reference Note**
> Look at Unit 18 for more information about count and non-count nouns.

Focused Practice

1 Discover the Grammar

Read Grammar in Context *again. Underline* **how much** *and* **how many**.
Circle the nouns after them. Which sentence doesn't have a noun after how much
or how many? *Write it below.*

_____

2 A Student Trip   Grammar Notes 1–4

Read about this trip from Seattle to Washington, D.C. Match the questions and answers below.

COME TO WASHINGTON, D.C.!
See the beautiful cherry blossoms.
Visit the White House. See the Capitol.

INCLUDES:
- round-trip airfare from Seattle
- 2 nights, 3 days at the Best Eastern
- lunch and dinner for 3 days
- double rooms
- sightseeing tour of Washington, D.C.

All this for only $650!

_____ **1.** How many days is the trip?   **a.** Two.

_____ **2.** How many meals does the trip include?   **b.** Three.

_____ **3.** How much does the trip cost?   **c.** Six.

_____ **4.** How many people share a room?   **d.** $650.

3 A Radio Broadcast   Grammar Notes 1–4

A. *Complete the questions. Use* **how much** *or* **how many**.

1. ____How many____ travel books did John Phillips write?   _____

2. _____ money did John Phillips have?   _____

3. _____ children did he have?   _____

4. _____ grandchildren did he have?   _____

5. _____ time did his children spend with him? _____

6. _____ people did he leave his money to?   _____

B. *Now listen to the radio broadcast and answer the questions.*

4 A Short Vacation

Read this ad for a trip to Boston. Then write questions with **how much** *or* **how many** *to complete the conversation below.*

Visit Boston!

Only $800!

Includes:
- round-trip airfare from Seattle
- 5 days and 4 nights at Motel 9
- 4 to a room
- delicious breakfast every day
- 3-hour sightseeing tour of Boston

Visit the Freedom Trail, Faneuil Hall, Quincy Market, and Old North Church

JUDY: I need a break.

MARK: Good idea. Where do you want to go?

JUDY: I'm not sure. Maybe New York or Boston.

MARK: Well, here's an ad for a trip to Boston.

JUDY: _____?
1.

MARK: $800.

JUDY: _____?
2.

MARK: Five days.

JUDY: Do they provide meals?

MARK: Only breakfast.

JUDY: _____?
3.

MARK: Five breakfasts.

JUDY: Do you have your own room?

MARK: Uh, no.

JUDY: _____?
4.

MARK: Four people to a room.

JUDY: That's not for me.

MARK: Oh, well. It's a good price.

5 Editing

Correct the mistakes in this questionnaire. There are five mistakes.

1. **A:** How ~~much~~ many people are there in your family?

   B: Five.

2. **A:** How many book do you read in a month?

   B: Not much.

3. **A:** How much time do you spend online?

   B: Not many time.

4. **A:** How much trips do you take in a year?

   B: Two or three.

Communication Practice

6 I Ate a Lot of Ice Cream Last Night

Write four sentences with **a lot of**. *Use the verbs in the box. Your partner asks for an exact amount.*

| buy | drink | eat | find | see | spend | visit | write |

Example:

A: I drank a lot of coffee yesterday.
B: How much did you drink?
A: Eight cups.

7 Habits

A. *Work in groups. Ask your classmates four questions with* **how much** *and* **how many**. *Your classmates answer with* **a lot, a little, a few, not much, not many, some,** *or* **none**. *Or give an exact amount. Use the ideas in Exercise 5, the ideas in the box below, or your own ideas.*

time / spend on the telephone	money / give to charity in a year
e-mail messages / get in a week	people / help in a week
movies / watch in a month	clothes / buy in a month

Example:

A: How much time do you spend online?
B: Not much. About ten minutes a day.

B. *Write your questions and your classmates' answers. Report the results.*

Question	Student 1	Student 2	Student 3	Student 4
How much time do you spend online?	Not much—about 10 min. a day.			
1.				
2.				
3.				
4.				

Example:

Juan doesn't spend much time online: about ten minutes a day.

There is / There are, There was / There were

Were there cars back then, Grandpa?

Grammar **in Context**

🎧 *Listen and read the conversation.*

MARY: Bill, is there any salt?

BILL: Sure. Just a second . . . Here it is.

BEN: Grandpa, did you go camping when you were a kid?

BILL: Sure we did, Ben. We went camping a lot.

ANNIE: How did you get there?

BILL: What do you mean, Annie?

ANNIE: Well, did you walk or ride a horse or what?

BILL: No, we drove to the camping areas.

ANNIE: Were there cars back then, Grandpa?

BILL: Annie! Of course there were. I'm not *that* old!

BEN: What was it like when you were a kid, Grandma? Was there television?

MARY: Yes, there was, Ben. But TV was pretty new. There was only one channel at first.

ANNIE: Only one channel? Really? How did you live?

MARY: It wasn't hard. There were a lot of good programs on that channel.

ANNIE: Grandpa, are things better now than when you were a kid?

BILL: Well, there wasn't much stress. People didn't worry so much.

MARY: And there were fun things to do.

BILL: Like free concerts and baseball games.

BEN: Grandma, are there any more hot dogs?

MARY: Yes, there are. They're in the cooler.

Words and Expressions

🎧 *Do you know these words and expressions? Write new ones in your notebook.*

go camping

a cooler

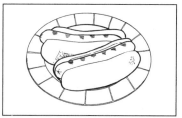

hot dogs and buns

1. A: Is there any salt?
   B: Sure. Just a second.

2. A: Grandpa, did you go camping when you were a kid?
   B: Sure we did.

3. A: Were there cars back then?
   B: Of course there were. I'm not *that* old!

4. A: What was it like when you were a kid, Grandma?
   B: TV was pretty new.

With a Partner

A. *Practice the conversation with three partners.*

B. *Look at the pictures. Did these things exist in 1925? Ask your partner.*

Example:

A: Were there photographs in 1925?

B: Yes, there were.

photographs: 1834

television sets: 1927

radios: 1913

talking movies: 1927

cars: 1889

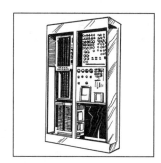

computers: 1944

Grammar **Presentation**
There is / There are, There was / There were

Statements	
Singular	**Plural**
There is some **salt** on the table. **There isn't** any **pepper**.	**There are** some **hot dogs** in the cooler. **There aren't** any **buns**.
There was only one **channel**. **There wasn't** a TV **station** in our city.	**There were** talking **movies** in 1927. **There weren't** many TV **channels** then.

Questions and Answers	
Singular	**Plural**
A: **Is there** any **salt**? B: Yes, **there is**. OR No, **there isn't**.	A: **Are there** any more **hot dogs**? B: Yes, **there are**. OR No, **there aren't**.
A: **Was there television** then? B: Yes, **there was**. OR No, **there wasn't**.	A: **Were there cars** then? B: Yes, **there were**. OR No, **there weren't**.

Notes

Examples

1. Use *there is* and *there are* to describe something in the **present**. Use *there is* if the noun is singular. Use *there are* if the noun is plural.	sing. noun • **There is** some *salt* on the table. plur. noun • **There are** some *hot dogs* in the cooler.
2. Use *there was* and *there were* to describe something in the **past**. Use *there was* if the noun is singular. Use *there were* if the noun is plural.	sing. noun • **There was** only one *channel*. plur. noun • **There were** *cars* then.
3. To state a **negative fact**, use *there isn't*, *there aren't*, *there wasn't*, or *there weren't*.	• **There isn't** any soda. **There aren't** any muffins. • **There weren't** any computers in 1925.
4. To make a **question**, put *is*, *are*, *was*, or *were* before *there*.	• **Was there** television in 1925? • **Were there** many channels?

5. Use *there* both in **questions** and in **short answers**.

A: Was **there** television then?

B: Yes, **there** was. OR No, **there** wasn't.

---

6. Use *there's* in speaking and informal writing. (*There's = There is*)

• **There's** some salt on the table.

---

7. Use *there* the **first time** you mention something. Use *it* or *they* after that.

A: Is **there** any salt?

B: Yes, **there** is. **It**'s on the table.

A: Are **there** any hot dogs?

B: Yes, **there** are. **They**'re in the cooler.

Focused Practice

 Discover the Grammar

Read Grammar in Context *again. Underline all the uses of* **there** *in the present. Circle all the uses of* **there** *in the past. Draw an arrow between* **there** *and the noun.*

Example:

Bill, is there any salt?

2 Redmond Then and Now   **Grammar Notes 1–3**

Complete the article about Redmond. Use **there is**, **there are**, **there was**, *and* **there were***. Use the affirmative and the negative.*

   Tim Olson's parents lived in Redmond in 1950. Today Tim and Jessica and their

children live in Redmond. What a change between then and now! In 1950, Redmond

was a very small town. _____There were_____ only 573 people in it. Today
                              1.

Redmond is a small city. _____ about 45,300 people in the city
                                      2.

limits. In 1950, _____ many stores in Redmond. Today
                         3.

_____ a lot. _____ any big companies in
          4.   **5.**

1950, but today _____ many. And _____
                        6.   **7.**

one very big company: Redmond is the headquarters of Microsoft.

3 Annie's Report

Annie is writing a report about Seattle. She is calling the Public Library Quick Information line. Write her questions. Use **how many** *and* **are there** *or* **were there**.

LIBRARIAN: Quick Information. May I help you?

ANNIE: Yes. I'm writing a report about Seattle, and I need some information.

LIBRARIAN: Okay. What do you need to know?

ANNIE: *How many people are there in Seattle today?*
                                          1.

LIBRARIAN: Let's see . . . there are 563,374 people in Seattle today, according to the 2000 census.

ANNIE: Thanks. And _____
                                            2.

LIBRARIAN: In 1950? There were 467,591 people in Seattle in 1950.

ANNIE: Okay. _____
                                            3.

LIBRARIAN: Let's see . . . there were three TV stations in 1950.

ANNIE: Three stations. Thank you. _____
                                            4.

LIBRARIAN: There are seven TV stations today.

ANNIE: Okay. Just two more questions. First, _____
                                            5.

LIBRARIAN: Hmm. There are six professional sports teams today.

ANNIE: Thank you. And _____

LIBRARIAN: Let me just check . . . There was only one professional sports team in 1950.

ANNIE: Thanks very much.

LIBRARIAN: You're welcome. Glad to help.

4 An Accident Report

Complete Jessica Olson's TV report about an accident. Use **there**, **it**, *or* **they**.

Good afternoon. This is Jessica Olson reporting. About an hour ago ___*there*___
                                            1.

was a serious accident on the Evergreen Freeway. _____ happened near
                                            2.

downtown Seattle. A truck that was carrying oranges hit a milk truck. Fortunately,

no one was hurt. But right now _____'s milk all over the highway.
                                            3.

_____ is causing traffic problems. _____ are also oranges everywhere.
   4.   **5.**

_____ are about ten police officers at the scene. _____ are directing
   6.   **7.**

traffic. Stay tuned for more information.

This is Jessica Olson reporting, KZYX News.

5 Editing

Correct Ben's composition. There are eight mistakes.

Ben Olson

Redmond

Redmond is a city now, but in 1950 it was a tiny town. There ~~are~~ were
only about five or six hundred people here then, but now there is almost
50,000 people. There wasn't many stores in 1950, but it's a lot of stores
now in the Redmond Town Center. There are no big companies in 1950,
but now they are a lot. It's one really big and important company. Do you
know what it is? There is Microsoft, of course.

Communication Practice

6 There Was Heavy Fog This Morning

Read the statements. Then listen to the weather report. Check (✓) **True, False,** *or* **No Information.**

	True	False	No Information
1. It was foggy this morning in Seattle.	❏	❏	❏
2. It's raining now in Seattle.	❏	❏	❏
3. There are some clouds now in Seattle.	❏	❏	❏
4. It's hot in the mountains near Seattle.	❏	❏	❏
5. There's rain in San Francisco.	❏	❏	❏
6. It's hot in Los Angeles.	❏	❏	❏
7. There are clouds in Los Angeles.	❏	❏	❏
8. It's hot in Hawaii.	❏	❏	❏

7 Write about the Past

Write sentences about a city in the past and today. Use these topics or your own. Then read your sentences to a partner. Discuss: Is life better today or in the past?

traffic problems	stores	big companies
sports teams	TV stations	stress

Example:

Fifty years ago there weren't many traffic problems in Bangkok.
Today there are a lot of traffic problems.

Review or SelfTest

I. *Complete the conversations. Circle the correct letter.*

1. **ANDREA:** _____   A   B   C   Ⓓ
   KATHY: There were a lot of people—about twenty.
   (A) How many people are there at the party?
   (C) Do you have many parties?
   (B) How much food was there at the party?
   (D) How many people were there at the party?

2. **BEN:** Dad, were there cameras when you were young?   A   B   C   D
   TIM: _____
   (A) Sure we did. I'm not that old.
   (C) Sure there was. I'm not that old.
   (B) Sure there are. I'm not that old.
   (D) Sure there were. I'm not that old.

3. **JUDY:** _____   A   B   C   D
   MARK: Sorry. My car's in the shop.
   (A) Can you give me a ride to the party?
   (C) What time does the party start?
   (B) Are you going to the party?
   (D) Can I go to the party?

4. **JEREMY:** Dad, I don't know what to get you and Mom for your anniversary.   A   B   C   D
   TIM: _____
   (A) Why don't you get her some flowers?
   (C) Why don't you get me some flowers?
   (B) Why don't you get us some flowers?
   (D) Why don't you get them some flowers?

II. *Write questions about the underlined expressions. Use* **how much** *or* **how many**.

1. **A:** _____ How many days were you away? _____

   B: We were away <u>ten days</u>.

2. **A:** _____

   B: We drove <u>about a thousand miles</u>.

3. **A:** _____

   B: <u>Four people</u> went on the trip.

4. **A:** _____

   B: The trip cost <u>about $1,000</u>.

III. *Look at the picture. Complete the paragraph with* **a few**, **a little**, **a lot**, **many**, *and* **much**.

It's Jeremy's seventeenth birthday party. There are ___a lot___ of Jeremy's

friends at the party, and everyone is having a good time. _____ of the kids are
                                                                          2.

singing songs. _____ of them are dancing. There's a video playing on TV, but
                    3.

not _____ of the kids are watching it. There's not _____ pizza left,
        4.   5.

but there is _____ cake.
                  6.

IV. *Complete the paragraphs. Use the words in the box. Some words can be used twice.*

there is	there was	it was	they were
there are	there were	they are	

In downtown Madison today, ___there are___ a lot of stores.
                                      1.

_____ large and modern. _____ a movie complex.
     2.   3.

_____ six theaters in it. Fifty years ago _____ only a few
     4.   5.

stores here. _____ very small. _____ no movie complexes.
                  6.   7.

Today _____ two high schools in Madison. _____
          8.   9.

both very modern. Fifty years ago _____ only one high school in
                                        10.

Madison. _____ very small. _____ only forty-four
              11.   12.

students in the school.

▶ *To check your answers, go to the Answer Key on page 284.*

UNIT

Descriptive Adjectives

I like romantic music.

Grammar **in Context**

🎧 *Listen and read these personal ads from* The Seattle Daily.

The Seattle Daily

 Love Lines

❤❤❤❤❤❤❤❤❤❤❤❤❤❤❤❤❤❤❤❤❤❤❤❤❤❤

— MEN —

A. Am I for you? Are you interested in a 35-year-old, fun-loving man? I'm easy-going. I like romantic music and long walks on the beach. I'm looking for a kind, sensitive woman.

B. Rich 80-year-old, active, healthy, young-at-heart man. Wants to enjoy life with a lively, middle-aged woman.

C. Tall, slim, 25-year-old scientist. Enjoys hiking and biking. Looking for woman with similar interests.

— WOMEN —

A. Let's get together. Artistic 20-year-old woman looking for sensitive, artistic man.

B. 23-year-old athletic engineer. Enjoys tennis, mysteries, and fast cars. Looking for an intelligent man with similar interests.

C. 75-year-old woman. Rich, funny, warm, and honest. Enjoys movies, travel, and art. Looking for a man with similar interests. Must be over 55.

Words and Expressions

🎧 *Do you know these words and expressions? Write new ones in your notebook.*

athletic

artistic

fun-loving

romantic

1. A: Are you interested in mysteries?
   B: Yes, I like them a lot.

2. A: Let's get together.
   B: Okay. When?

With a Partner

A. *Read the personal ads with a partner.*

B. *Discuss with a partner:*

What's important in love?

1. age (young, middle-aged, old)

2. looks (tall, dark, good-looking)

3. personality (kind, friendly, romantic)

4. profession (an athlete, an engineer, a teacher)

5. likes and dislikes (romantic music, mysteries, tennis)

6. money

7. race or religion

Grammar **Presentation**
Descriptive Adjectives

	Noun	*Be*	Adjective
This	**woman**	is	**artistic**.
These	**women**	are	

	Be		Adjective	Noun
She	is	an	**artistic**	**woman**.
They	are			**women**.

Notes	**Examples**

1. Adjectives **describe nouns**.

- noun   adjective
- This *music* is **romantic**.
- adjective   noun
- I like **romantic** *music*.

2. Adjectives can come:
— **after the verb** *be*
— **before a noun**

- The woman *is* **artistic**.
- She's an **artistic** *woman*.

3. Do not add *–s* to an adjective.

- He's looking for a **fast** car.
- They like **fast** cars.
  NOT ~~They like fasts cars.~~

4. For **adjective + noun**:
— Use *a* before the adjective if the adjective begins with a **consonant sound**.
— Use *an* before the adjective if it begins with a **vowel sound**.

- She's **a** young woman.
- She's **an** artistic woman.

5. BE CAREFUL! Adjectives can end in *–ing*, *–ly*, and *–ed*.

Some adjectives contain **two or more words**.

- She's an **interesting** woman.
- She's **lively** and **friendly**.
- She's never **bored**.
- She's **easy-going** and **young-at-heart**.

6. Colors can be **nouns** or **adjectives**.

- noun
- **Red** is his favorite color.
- adjective
- He has a **red** car.

Focused Practice

1 Discover the Grammar

Read Grammar in Context *again. Find a descriptive adjective for each noun.*

1. _____ music
2. _____ walks
3. _____ scientist
4. _____ man
5. _____ woman
6. _____ interests

2 The Johnsons   Grammar Notes 1–3

Ken Johnson is showing pictures of his family to his friend Brian. Complete the sentences. Use the words in parentheses. Add an adjective from the box.

artistic	easy-going	red	young-at-heart	athletic

1. My dad and I are similar. We don't worry about most things.

__We're easy-going men_____.
         (men / we're)

2. This is my sister Judy. She's good at all sports.

_____.
         (an / she's / woman)

3. My mom loves to garden, sing, and paint.

_____.
         (have / I / an / mother)

(continued on next page)

4. My granddad acts like a kid.

_____ .
(he's)

5. This is my dream:

_____ .
(a / sports car)

③ A Description of Mia
Grammar Notes 1–5

🎧 *Listen to the conversation between Ken and his friend Brian. Then find Brian's friend Mia in the picture. Circle Mia.*

④ Editing

Correct this letter to advice columnist Dahlia. There are six mistakes.

Dear Dahlia,

My boyfriend, Joe, is wonderful. He's ⅄ kind, honest, and intelligent. He has an job good and a heart kind. There's only one problem. He doesn't like to spend money. He's stingy. We always watch TV or go to frees concerts and picnics. I have fun with Joe, but I want to do differents things. Do you have any suggestions?

Sincerely,

Rosa

Communication Practice

5 Opposites

Work with a partner. Look at the following words. Write the opposite. Use the words in the box.

| cold | dishonest | serious | mean | stingy | unfriendly |

a. friendly _____

b. kind _____

c. generous _____

d. honest _____

e. funny _____

f. warm _____

6 Important Qualities

Work in small groups. Look at the words in Exercise 5.

- What quality do you look for in a friend?
  Complete the sentence: I want a _____ friend.

- List these qualities from 1 to 6. 1 is the most important.
  1. _____   3. _____   5. _____
  2. _____   4. _____   6. _____

- What other qualities are important in a relationship?
  _____

7 Physical Qualities

Work with a partner. Add more adjectives to this list of physical qualities. Use your dictionary.

Age: young, _____   **Weight:** thin, _____

Height: short, _____   **Other qualities:** strong, _____

8 Personal Ads

Answer one of the personal ads on page 186. Post your answer on the wall. Read other answers.

Example:

> Dear Am I for You,
>
> I think you are for me. I'm easy-going, and I love long walks on the beach.
>
> I'm an artist. I love to read and write and talk. I'm twenty-six years old. There's one other thing. I love cats. I have ten cats. Is that okay? Please write or e-mail me at catlover@aw.com.
>
> Sincerely,
> You're for Me

Comparative Adjectives

Rock is better than rap.

Grammar **in Context**

🎧 *Listen and read the conversation.*

KEN: So when's the party?

LAURA: Saturday night. It starts about eight.

MARTY: How many people are coming?

LAURA: I've got fifteen on the list.

MARTY: What about music? I can bring my rap and metal CDs.

KEN: Get real! We want to dance, right? Rap is bad for dancing, and metal is worse.

CELINE: Let's have rock. It's a lot better for dancing.

LAURA: Okay. My older brother has a lot of rock CDs. Now, what about food?

KEN: How about steak? We can barbecue some steak.

CELINE: Pizza's easier and quicker than steak. And it's cheaper.

KEN: Okay, sounds good. And what about entertainment? Besides dancing, I mean.

MARTY: How about watching some videos?

LAURA: Well . . . I'm tired of them. Games are more interesting than videos.

KEN: Hey, I know a really funny new game. We can play that.

CELINE: Sounds good.

Expressions

🎧 *Do you know these expressions? Write new ones in your notebook.*

1. **A:** How many people?
   B: I've got fifteen on the list.

2. **A:** I can bring my rap and metal CDs.
   B: Get real! Rock is better for dancing.

3. **A:** How about watching videos?
   B: I'm tired of them. Games are more interesting.

With a Partner

A. *Practice the conversation with three partners.*

B. *Write the names of two movies. Which is better? Which is more interesting? Tell your partners your opinion.*

Example:

In my opinion, *Titanic* was better than *Cast Away*. It was a lot more interesting.

Grammar **Presentation**
Comparative Adjectives

Comparative Adjectives with -*er*				
		Comparative Adjective	*than*	
Pizza	is	**quicker**	**than**	steak.
It	's	**cheaper.**		

Comparative Adjectives with *more*				
		Comparative Adjective	*than*	
Movies	are	**more interesting**	**than**	television.
They	're	**more expensive.**		

Notes	Examples
1. Use the **comparative form** of an adjective **+ *than*** to compare **two** people, places, or things. We **can omit *than*** when the context is clear.	• Ken is **taller than** Laura. • Pizza is **quicker than** steak. • And it's **cheaper**. *(cheaper than steak)*
2. To form the comparative of **short (one-syllable)** adjectives, **add –er** to the adjective. If the adjective **ends in –e**, just **add –r**.	young → young**er** • Laura is **younger than** Ken. large → larg**er** • New York is **larger than** Chicago.
3. To form the comparative of **two-syllable** adjectives that **end in –y**, change the **y to i** and **add –er**.	easy → eas**ier** • Pizza is **easier than** steak.
4. To form the comparative of most adjectives of **two or more syllables**, use **more** before the adjective.	crowded → **more** crowded • New York is **more crowded than** Chicago. interesting → **more** interesting • *Titanic* is **more interesting than** *Cast Away*.
5. The adjectives *good* and *bad* have **irregular** comparative forms.	good → **better** • Rock is **better than** metal for dancing. bad → **worse** • Rap is **worse than** metal for dancing.
6. Use *which* to ask about a comparison of things or places.	**A:** *Which* is **better**, rock or rap? **B:** I think rock is **better** (**than** rap).

Focused Practice

1 Discover the Grammar

Ken's younger cousin Jerry is writing a composition. Read his possible topics.
Circle the comparatives. Then check (✓) **Agree** *or* **Disagree**.

Composition Topics	Agree	Disagree
1. Television is usually (more interesting) than movies.	❏	❏
2. Science is more important than art.	❏	❏
3. City life is healthier than country life.	❏	❏
4. History is easier than math.	❏	❏
5. Skiing is more difficult than snowboarding.	❏	❏
6. Dogs are better pets than cats.	❏	❏
7. Heavy metal is more exciting than rock.	❏	❏
8. Chemistry is harder than biology.	❏	❏

2 Compare the People

Grammar Notes 2–5

Look at the picture. Compare the people. Use the words in parentheses.

1. (Marty / tall / Ken) _____   Ken is taller than Marty.

2. (Marty / old / Ken) _____

3. (Celine / short / Laura) _____

4. (Lisa / good / David) _____ at dancing.

5. (Maia / bad / Jason) _____ at singing.

6. (Mike's clothes / colorful / Ryan's clothes) _____

7. (Elena's hair / dark / Kelly's hair) _____

3 **Make Conversations**

Complete the conversations. Put the words in the right order.

1. A: worse, / cafeteria food / is / Which / restaurant food / or / ?

   Which is worse, cafeteria food or restaurant food?

   B: is / worse / cafeteria food / think / I / .

   _____

2. A: father / you / taller / Are / your / than / ?

   _____

   B: heavier / he's / but / Yes, / .

   _____

3. A: Paris / than / Is / interesting / more / Marseilles / ?

   _____

   B: expensive / Yes, / more / but / it's / .

   _____

4. A: *Titanic* / better, / *Cast Away* / is / or / Which / ?

   _____

   B: think / *Cast Away* / better / I / is / .

   _____

4 **Editing**

Correct Jerry's composition. There are eight mistakes in comparatives.

Jerry Johnson

Dogs Rule

In my opinion, a dog is a ~~gooder~~ *better* pet than a cat. I know because we have a dog and a cat. Here are my reasons. First, a dog is friendly than a cat. My dog is more happy to see me when I come home. My cat just doesn't care. Second, a dog is activer. I always take my dog for a walk. I can't do that with my cat. She only wants to sleep. Third, a dog is interestinger than a cat. My dog is a lot more playful that my cat. He knows a lot of tricks. The cat doesn't know any tricks at all. She's a lot boringer. Last, a dog is more protectiver than a cat. My dog barks if anyone comes to the house. The cat just runs and hides. I think dogs rule.

Communication Practice

5 A Discussion

Work with a partner. Look again at Discover the Grammar *on page 195.*
Discuss your answers to **Agree** *and* **Disagree**. *Then tell the class.*

Example:

Television is usually more interesting than movies.

A: I disagree. Television is usually a lot more boring.

B: I disagree too. A lot of movies are more exciting than TV programs.

6 Ken's New Job

Listen to Ken's conversation with his grandmother. Read the statements.
Then listen again. Check (✓) **True**, **False**, *or* **No Information**.

	True	False	No Information
1. Ken's new job is harder than his old one.	❏	❏	❏
2. Ken's new job is more interesting than his old one.	❏	❏	❏
3. Ken's salary is better than before.	❏	❏	❏
4. Ken is happier than before.	❏	❏	❏
5. Grandma thinks Ken is healthier than before.	❏	❏	❏
6. Grandma says 10:30 is better than 12:00 or 1:00.	❏	❏	❏
7. Ken's classes are harder than before.	❏	❏	❏

7 A Class Survey

Work in groups of four. On the chart, write down the names of two types of music,
two TV programs, two school subjects, two activities, and two people. Ask members of
other groups their opinions. Use **which** *for the things and* **who** *for the people. Fill in*
the chart with the number of people who like each thing. Discuss with the class.

Example:

Which is better for dancing, salsa or rock?

Music / good for dancing	salsa (8)	rock (10)
TV program / funny		
School subject / difficult		
Activity / interesting		
Person / important		

30

Superlative Adjectives

I had the strangest dream . . .

Grammar **in Context**

🎧 *Listen and read the conversation.*

JUDY: I had a really strange dream last night.

MARK: You always have strange dreams.

JUDY: Yes, but this one was the strangest dream of all.

MARK: Tell me about it.

THE COLDEST DAY OF THE YEAR

JUDY: Okay. I was in New York City on a very cold day. The paper said it was the coldest day of the year. I was late for a concert. I asked a guy, "What's the quickest way to get to 33rd Street and Seventh Avenue?" He said, "The quickest way isn't the best way. The best way is with me."

MARK: So did you go with him?

JUDY: Uh-huh. We rode together on his scooter. At times the scooter went up in the air. It was the most wonderful ride in the world. We laughed the whole way there.

MARK: And then?

JUDY: Well, then I woke up. But that's not all.

MARK: Listen, it's getting late. Tell me the rest on the way to class.

JUDY: Oops! You're right. Come on. Let's go.

Words and Expressions

🎧 *Do you know these words and expressions? Write new ones in your notebook.*

a guy

a scooter

1. **A:** Excuse me. What's the quickest way to get to 33rd Street?
   B: Take the number 1 train.

2. **A:** It's getting late.
   B: You're right. Come on. Let's go.

With a Partner

A. *Practice the conversation with a partner.*

B. *Tell your partner your most interesting dream.*

Grammar **Presentation**
Superlative Adjectives

Superlative Adjectives with *–est*			
		Superlative Adjective	
It	was	**the coldest**	day of the year.

Superlative Adjectives with *the most*			
		Superlative Adjective	
It	was	**the most wonderful**	ride in the world.

Notes

Examples

Notes	Examples
1. Use the **superlative form** of an adjective to **compare three or more** people, places, or things.	• He is **the greatest** singer in the world. • It was **the coldest** day of the year.
2. To form the superlative of **short (one-syllable)** adjectives, use *the* before the adjective and **add** *–est* to the adjective. If the adjective **ends in** *–e*, add *–st*.	quick → **the** quick**est** • It's **the quickest** way to school. strange → **the** strang**est** • I had **the strangest** dream.

3. To form the superlative of **two-syllable** adjectives that **end in –y**, change the **y to i** and **add –est**.

funny → **the funniest**
- I had **the funniest** dream last night.

4. To form the superlative of **longer** adjectives, use **the most** before the adjective.

wonderful → **the most** wonderful
- It was **the most wonderful** ride in the world.

5. The adjectives **good** and **bad** have **irregular** superlative forms.

good → **the best**
- It was **the best** day of my life.

bad → **the worst**
- It was **the worst** day of my life.

6. We sometimes use a **possessive** adjective (**my**, **his**, **her**, **your**, **our**, **their**) in place of **the**.

- It was **my longest** dream.
- It's **her best** composition.

Reference Note
Look at Unit 29 for the comparative form of adjectives.

Focused Practice

Discover the Grammar

A. *Read the rest of Judy and Mark's conversation. Underline the three superlatives.*

MARK: Okay. What happened next?

JUDY: Well later, on my way to the cafeteria, I saw a large crowd in front of the gym. It was the largest crowd since the last basketball game. And everyone was looking up at a tightrope walker. I looked up and I saw the man in my dream. It was the most amazing thing. I think I have special powers.

MARK: Sorry, Judy. I don't think so. I was at the gym too. It was Alonzo Bonzo—one of the best tightrope walkers ever. He was on TV on "The Jessica Olson Show" last week. You probably saw him there, and *that's* why you dreamed about him.

JUDY: Oh. Well, it was a very exciting dream.

B. *Complete the chart.*

Adjective	Comparative Adjective	Superlative Adjective
strange	stranger	the strangest
cold		
	quicker	
		the most wonderful
		the most amazing
	better	

2 Alonzo's Scarves

Grammar Notes 1–4

Alonzo Bonzo is giving away his handmade scarves. Complete the conversation. Use the superlative form of the words in parentheses.

ALONZO: Here's _____.
1. (my / long / scarf)
Who would like it?

STUDENT: Give it to Bob. He's

_____ here.
2. (the / tall / guy)
He's the captain of our basketball team. He likes bright clothes.

ALONZO: Good idea. Here, Bob. This scarf is nice and bright.

BOB: Thanks, Alonzo. It's cool. And I need a warm scarf.

ALONZO: And this is _____. It's 100% wool.
3. (my / heavy / scarf)

STUDENT: Give it to Sally. She's from one of

_____ in the
4. (the / cold / place)
world—Alaska.

ALONZO: Enjoy it, Sally. Now this one here is

_____ of all.
5. (the / colorful)

MARK: That's for Judy. She loves bright colors.

3 Editing

*Correct the thank-you note.
There are five mistakes. Then
label the people in the photo.*

Dear Alonzo,

    Thanks again for the scarf. I'm home for vacation and your scarf is perfect for Alaska. Here's a photo of me in my scarf. I'm with my brother and sisters. Kate, my ~~most old~~ ^{oldest} sister, is next to me. Ann, my the youngest sister, is sitting in front of Kate. Ruth is next to Ann. She's the talkative of all of us. She's always on the phone. I'm holding my brother, Sam. He's the baby—the younger one in the family. He's also the most funniest, the quickest, and the cutest.

    Well, I hope you're enjoying the holiday.

            Sincerely yours,

            Sally Pawa

Communication Practice

4 A Stamp Collection

🎧 *Listen to a man talk about his stamps. Write his description of each stamp.
Use the superlatives in the box.*

the oldest	the biggest	the most colorful
the most artistic	the most valuable	the newest

1. the Italian stamp   _____
2. the Brazilian stamp   _____
3. the Austrian stamp   _____
4. the Korean stamp   _____
5. the Swiss stamp   _____
6. the Egyptian stamp   _____

5 Sports

Work with a partner. Look at the boxes. Circle three sports. Then compare them. Use the superlative form of the adjectives.

Sports	
baseball	skiing
basketball	soccer
football	swimming
golf	tennis

Adjectives	
boring	exciting
dangerous	expensive
difficult	interesting
easy	popular

Example:

A: Which sport do you think is the most boring?

B: I think golf is the most boring. What do you think?

6 Discussion

A. *Work in small groups. List five cities, five holidays, and five actors or actresses.*

Cities	Holidays	Actors
_____	_____	_____
_____	_____	_____
_____	_____	_____
_____	_____	_____
_____	_____	_____

B. *Compare them. Use superlatives. For example, discuss:*

1. Which city is the most beautiful? the oldest? the most international? the most crowded?

2. Which holiday is the most important? the longest holiday? the oldest?

3. Who's the best actor? the best actress? the most popular? the oldest? the youngest? the funniest?

   Example:

   A: I think Rio de Janeiro is the most beautiful city of all.

   B: Really? I don't agree. I think . . .

C. *Tell the class about your discussion.*

31 Prepositions of Time: In, On, At

See you on Saturday at 2:30.

Grammar **in Context**

🎧 *Listen and read the conversation.*

TIM: Tim Olson.

FELIX: Hello, Tim! This is Felix Maxa calling. Do you remember me? We met in August on the train to Seattle.

TIM: Felix! Of course! It's great to hear from you. How are you doing?

FELIX: Wonderful. Say, I called to invite you and your wife to our house for a barbecue.

TIM: Hey, that sounds like fun. We'd really like that. When is it?

FELIX: On Saturday, the 20th. In the afternoon.

TIM: I think we're free. But I need to check with Jessica. Can I call you back?

FELIX: Sure.

[Later]

FELIX: Hello?

TIM: Hi, Felix. This is Tim. We're free on the 20th. We can come to the barbecue.

FELIX: Great!

TIM: What's the address?

FELIX: We're at 819 Fortieth Avenue. From Forty-fifth, turn left on Stone Way and then right on Fortieth. It's the third house on the right, a light blue two-story.

TIM: Okay. What time?

FELIX: About 2:30.

TIM: Great. Can we bring anything?

FELIX: Just yourselves.

TIM: Okay, thanks a lot. I'm looking forward to it. See you on Saturday at 2:30. 'Bye.

Words and Expressions

Do you know these words and expressions? Write new ones in your notebook.

a two-story house

OH, BOY. VACATION TOMORROW.

look forward to

1. A: I called to invite you to a barbecue.
   B: That sounds great. When?

2. A: Can I call you back?
   B: Sure.

3. A: We're free on the 20th.
   B: Great!

4. A: Can we bring anything?
   B: Just yourselves.

With a Partner

A. *Practice the conversation with a partner.*

B. *Look at the bulletin board. Say when each event is.*

Example:

The Chess Club barbecue is on Saturday, the twentieth of May, at 2:30 P.M.

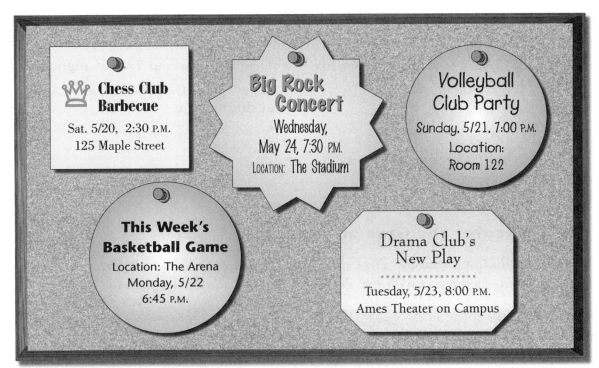

♛ **Chess Club Barbecue**
Sat. 5/20, 2:30 P.M.
125 Maple Street

Big Rock Concert
Wednesday,
May 24, 7:30 P.M.
LOCATION: The Stadium

Volleyball Club Party
Sunday, 5/21, 7:00 P.M.
Location:
Room 122

This Week's Basketball Game
Location: The Arena
Monday, 5/22
6:45 P.M.

Drama Club's New Play
Tuesday, 5/23, 8:00 P.M.
Ames Theater on Campus

Grammar **Presentation**

Prepositions of Time: *In, On, At*

In	*On*	*At*
in 2001	**on** Saturday	**at** 2:30 P.M.
in January	**on** January 20th	**at** dinnertime
in the morning	**on** weekends	**at** night
in the afternoon	**on** holidays	
in the evening	**on** weekdays	

Notes	Examples

1. Use *in* with **years, months, parts of the day**, and in expressions like *in a few minutes*.

- I was born **in 1982**.
- We were in Spain **in August**.
- The barbecue is **in the afternoon**.
- Can I call you back **in a few minutes**?

▶ **BE CAREFUL!** Don't use *in* with **night**. Use *at*.

- The game is **at night**.
  NOT ~~The game is in the night.~~

2. Use *on* with **days** of the week, **dates**, and in expressions like *on weekdays* or *on weekends*.

- The barbecue is **on Saturday**.
- It's **on January 21st**.
- I often go to the movies **on weekends**.

3. Use *at* with **times** and in expressions like *at night* and *at dinnertime*.

- The party starts **at 7:00 at night**.
- We always have good conversations **at dinnertime**.

Focused Practice

 Discover the Grammar

Read Grammar in Context again. Find all the time expressions. Circle all phrases with **in**. *Underline all phrases with* **on**. *Put a check above all phrases with* **at**.

Example:

We met in August on the train to Seattle.

② At the Barbecue

Complete the conversation. Use **in**, **on**, *and* **at**.

TIM: This is a nice big meal. Is lunch the biggest meal in Romania?

FELIX: Yes, it is, actually. We don't eat very much for dinner.

JESSICA: Are mealtimes the same as here? I mean, for example, do you eat lunch ___at___ noon like we do?
1.

DANIELA: No, we usually have lunch later _____ the afternoon— _____ 2:00 or 2:30—
2.   3.
or even later.

TIM: What about breakfast? I usually have breakfast _____ 6:45 or 7:00.
4.
Is it similar in Romania?

FELIX: Well, we usually have breakfast a bit later— _____ 7:30 or so.
5.

JESSICA: So it's a long time between breakfast and lunch. You must get hungry.

DANIELA: Well, people usually have a snack, like a sandwich, _____ the late morning—
6.
_____ 11:30 or so.
7.

FELIX: It's different _____ weekends, of course. We get up later.
8.

TIM: I'd like to visit Romania sometime.

DANIELA: Well, Felix and I are going back to Romania _____ a few days—on separate
9.
flights, unfortunately. But we'll send you a postcard.

JESSICA: Great.

③ More Questions for Felix and Daniela

Complete the questions and answers. Use the correct forms of the words given.
Add **at**, **on**, *and* **in the** *where necessary.*

1. A: What time / be / dinner/ ?

B: Dinner / be / usually / 7:00 or 7:30.

2. A: What time / people / start work / morning / ?

B: People / usually / start work / 8:00 / .

3. A: What time / people / leave work / evening / ?

B: They / usually / leave work / 5:00 / .

4. A: What / people / do / evenings / ?

B: They / often / watch TV / evenings / .

5. A: What / people / do / weekends / ?

B: They / often / visit friends / weekends / .

A: _____What time is dinner?_____

B: _____

A: _____

B: _____

A: _____

B: _____

A: _____

B: _____

A: _____

B: _____

4 Editing

Correct the statements below. There are ten mistakes.

1. Daniela is leaving Seattle ~~in~~ *on* Monday, January 25th, on 12:00 noon.
2. Her flight arrives in Chicago in 6:00 P.M. at the evening.
3. Her flight to London leaves at 7:30 P.M. in the night.
4. Flight 774 arrives in London in 11:30 A.M. on the morning.
5. Her flight to Bucharest leaves in 2:00 P.M. in January 26th.
6. It arrives in Bucharest at 6:05 P.M. at evening.

Communication Practice

5 Felix's Flights

*Listen to the telephone conversation. Then complete the chart. Use **on** or **at**.*

Day and date Felix leaves Seattle	Time first flight leaves Seattle	Time second flight leaves Seattle	Day and date Felix returns to Seattle
on Thursday, January 30th			

6 Find Out

Work with three partners. Ask questions. Complete the chart. Tell the other groups.

Example:

A: What time do you get up on weekdays?
B: I usually get up at 7:00 on weekdays.

	You	Student 1	Student 2	Student 3
get up / weekdays				
get up / weekends				
have dinner / weeknights				
have breakfast / weekends				

Information Gap: When in the World?

Work in pairs.

Student B, look at the Information Gap on page 279. Follow the instructions there.

Student A, get information from Student B. Ask questions with **when** *or* **what time***. Then answer Student B's questions. Choose an answer from the box below. Use* **in, on,** *or* **at** *in each answer.*

Example:

A: When do Americans usually vote?

B: Americans usually vote on a Tuesday. When do the French usually vote?

A: The French usually vote on a Sunday.

Student A's questions

1. Americans / usually vote / ?

2. summer normally begin / in the Southern Hemisphere / ?

3. afternoon / begin / ?

4. Brazilians / celebrate / Carnaval / ?

5. fall normally begin / in the Southern Hemisphere / ?

Student A's Answers

12:00 midnight	December 21st	July 6th
September	a Sunday	

8 Game: *In, On, At*

Write down the time of a big event in your life.

Examples:

I got married on June 3, 1992, at night.

I graduated from college on May 15, 1999, in the afternoon.

Then tell your classmates the event. Do not tell them the time. Your classmates ask yes / no *questions and guess the date and the time of the event.*

Example:

A: I got married.

B: Did you get married in July?

A: No, I didn't.

C: Did you get married in June?

A: Yes, I did.

PART 9 Review or SelfTest

I. *Complete the conversations. Circle the correct letter.*

1. JUDY: Is the meeting in the morning?   A B Ⓒ D
    MARK: _____

    (A) Yes. It's in the afternoon.   (C) No. It's at night.
    (B) When?   (D) It wasn't in the morning.

2. TIM: When are you free?   A B C D
    AL: _____

    (A) On the tenth at 2:00 P.M.   (C) Yes, I am.
    (B) Are you free too?   (D) No, I'm not free.

3. ANNIE: Was it cold?   A B C D
    MARY: _____

    (A) It was the coldest day   (C) Yes. I was sick
         of the year.   all weekend.
    (B) Yes. It was cool.   (D) No. It was cold.

4. BEN: Is New York larger than Chicago?   A B C D
    BILL: _____

    (A) Yes, it's large.   (C) Yes, it is.
    (B) Chicago is large.   (D) No. New York is larger.

II. *Compare the following movies. Write the name of the movie and the comparative or superlative form of the adjective in parentheses.*

Meet the Parents	The Thing	Erin Brockovich
☆ ☆ ☆ ☆	☆ ☆ ☆	☆ ☆ ☆ ☆ ☆
starring Robert DeNiro		*starring Julia Roberts*
Hilarious! A laugh a minute!	Scary. Bring someone to hold on to. Good special effects.	Based on a true story. Excellent acting. Entertaining and inspiring. Don't miss it.
Time: 1 hour, 48 minutes	Time: 1 hour, 49 minutes	Time: 2 hours, 12 minutes

1. (long) ___Erin Brockovich___ is ___longer than___ *The Thing*.

2. (scary) _____ is _____ *Meet the Parents*.

3. (serious) _____ is _____ *Meet the Parents*.

4. (funny) _____ is _____ *Erin Brockovich*.

5. (long) _____ is _____ of the three movies.

6. (good) This reviewer thinks _____ is _____ of the three movies.

III. *Complete these telephone conversations. Use* **in**, **on**, *or* **at**.

BRIAN: Hello?

JEREMY: Hi, Brian. It's Jeremy.

BRIAN: Oh, hi, Jeremy. Listen, I'm having dinner right now. Can I call you back
_____in_____ a few minutes?
      1.

JEREMY: Sure.

[Ten minutes later]

JEREMY: Hello.

BRIAN: Hi, Jeremy.

JEREMY: Oh, hi. *Star Trek VII* is playing at the Cineplex. Are you free _____ Saturday?
                                        2.

BRIAN: What time?

JEREMY: The first show is _____ noon. Is that okay?
                     3.

BRIAN: Noon? No way. _____ weekends I sleep until 1:00. How about a later show?
                  4.

JEREMY: Well, I can't make it later. But there's a show _____ Sunday _____ 6:00.
                                        5.   6.

BRIAN: Sounds good to me. We can meet at the bus stop _____ 5:30.
                                                7.

JEREMY: Okay. See you Sunday.

BRIAN: 'Bye.

IV. *Correct the conversation. There are six mistakes.*

JUDY: How was your party?

KEN: Cool. We had lots of ~~goods~~ *good* CDs and pizzas great. It ended on 3:00 at the morning. Did you have a nice weekend?

JUDY: No. I just studied and watched a video bad.

KEN: What video?

JUDY: *The Thing*. It was the boring movie in the world.

KEN: You're kidding! My friends and I saw it. We loved it.

▶ *To check your answers, go to the Answer Key on page 284.*

UNIT

32 The Future with *Be going to*: Statements

Hurry up! We're going to be late!

Grammar **in Context**

🎧 *Listen and read the conversations.*

LAURA: Ken, hurry up! We're going to be late!

KEN: What's the hurry? It's just a silly little soccer game!

LAURA: It's not silly, and it's not little. Sam's on the team! It's a big game. I think they're going to win.

KEN: I know. That's what you told me. Is your brother a pretty good player?

LAURA: He's really good.

KEN: Do I need an umbrella?

LAURA: No. It's not going to rain . . . Come on.

[Later]

LAURA: Can't you drive any faster?

KEN: I'm already doing the speed limit. But how come you like soccer so much?

LAURA: It's a great game. A lot of people can play it. You don't have to be a giant.

KEN: But is it a real sport? Take basketball or baseball. Those are sports.

LAURA: Soccer is the most popular sport in the world.

KEN: Well, it's not the most popular sport in *my* world.

LAURA: Oh, no! A traffic jam! The game's going to start soon.

KEN: Laura, chill out! We're going to make it on time.

A traffic jam

Words and Expressions

🎧 *Do you know these words and expressions? Write new ones in your notebook.*

basketball

baseball

football

soccer

a giant

a speed limit

1. A: Can't you drive any faster?
   B: I'm already doing the speed limit.

2. A: How come you like soccer so much?
   B: It's a great game.

3. A: Oh, no! Look at this traffic!
   B: Laura, chill out. We're going to make it on time.

4. You don't have to be a giant to play soccer.

With a Partner

A. *Practice the conversations with a partner.*

B. *Think of three sporting events. Tell your partner who you think is going to win.*

Example:

I think Brazil is going to win the next World Cup.

Grammar **Presentation**
The Future with *Be going to*: Statements

Affirmative Statements		
am going to	*is going to*	*are going to*
I **am going to have** a party next weekend.	He **is going to graduate** in June. She **is going to be** an Olympic athlete. It **is going to rain** today.	We **are going to see** a movie tonight. You **are going to enjoy** the party. They **are going to bring** pizza to the party.

Negative Statements		
am not going to	*is not going to*	*are not going to*
I **am not going to drive** fast.	It **is not going to rain**.	We **are not going to be** late.
I'**m not going to drive** fast.	It'**s not going to rain**. It **isn't going to rain**.	We'**re not going to be** late. We **aren't going to be** late.

Future Time Expressions		
this afternoon	*tonight*	*tomorrow*
He's going to study **this afternoon**.	He's going to play soccer **tonight**.	**Tomorrow** he's going to visit his parents.

Notes

Examples

1. We can use *be going to* to talk about the **future**.	• We'**re going to be** late. • It'**s going to rain**.

2. To form the future with *be going to*, use *am*, *is*, or *are* + *going to* + the **base form** of the verb.	*be* *going to* base form • They **are** **going to** **win**.

3. To make a **negative sentence**, place *not* before *going to*.	• They are **not going to** lose. • It's **not going to** snow.

4. Use **contractions** in speaking and informal writing.

- The game**'s going to start** soon.
- It **isn't going to rain**. Don't worry.

Pronunciation Note
In conversation, we sometimes pronounce *going to* as "gonna." But we write "going to."

Focused Practice

1 Discover the Grammar

A. *Look at* Grammar in Context *again. Underline all the examples of* **be going to**.

Example:

We're going to be late.

B. *Match the questions and answers.*

___d___ **1.** Josh, do I need my heavy coat?   **a.** Yes. He's going to see her tonight.

_____ **2.** Mom, what's for dinner?   **b.** The Rams. They're going to win.

_____ **3.** Which team is the best?   **c.** Judy's going to graduate.

_____ **4.** What's happening next June?   **d.** Yes. It's going to snow.

_____ **5.** Does Mark have a serious girlfriend?   **e.** We're going to have steak.

2 Annie's Volleyball Game   Grammar Notes 1–2

Complete the sentences. Use the correct form of **be going to** *and the verbs in parentheses.*

It's Saturday. Annie Olson is on a volleyball team. Her team __is going to play__
                                                            1. (play)

for the championship this afternoon. The weather _____ warm
                                                    2. (be)

and sunny. Everybody in the family _____ the game. Ben
                                      3. (attend)

_____ four friends, and Jeremy _____ his
   4. (invite)   **5. (take)**

girlfriend. Tim and Jessica _____ the game. Mary and Bill Beck
                               6. (videotape)

_____ with their friends, Mr. and Mrs. Corgatelli. Everyone thinks
   7. (go)

Annie's team _____—everyone except Annie, that is. She's very
                8. (win)

nervous. She doesn't think she _____ very well.
                                  9. (play)

3 **Who's Going to Win?**   Grammar Notes 1–2

Look at the pictures. Complete each sentence with an affirmative or negative form of **be going to** *and the verb in parentheses.*

1. Skier 34 _____is going to win_____.
   (win)

2. Skier 21 _____second.
   (finish)

3. The Porpoises _____.
   (win)

4. The Dolphins _____.
   (win)

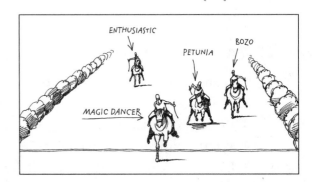

5. Runner 81 _____.
   (lose)

6. Runner 14 _____.
   (win)

7. Magic Dancer _____.
   (win)

8. Petunia _____ last.
   (finish)

4 **Editing**

Correct Amanda's note. There are six mistakes.

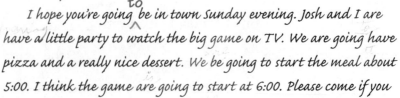

Dear Kathy,
     I hope you're going ^{to} be in town Sunday evening. Josh and I are have a little party to watch the big game on TV. We are going have pizza and a really nice dessert. We be going to start the meal about 5:00. I think the game are going to start at 6:00. Please come if you can. But can you let us know? We going to be out of town until Tuesday. Call after that, okay?
     Amanda

Communication Practice

5 Laura's Brother's Game

🎧 *Read the sentences. Listen to the conversation. Then listen again and check (✓)* **True**, **False**, *or* **No Information**.

	True	False	No Information
1. Ken thinks the game is boring.	❏	❏	❏
2. Ken thinks it's going to rain.	❏	❏	❏
3. Laura thinks it's going to rain.	❏	❏	❏
4. The score is two to one.	❏	❏	❏
5. Laura thinks Sam's team is going to win.	❏	❏	❏
6. Laura has another brother besides Sam.	❏	❏	❏
7. Sam kicks a goal.	❏	❏	❏
8. Ken wants to go to another game sometime.	❏	❏	❏

6 Game: We're Going to Attend the Next Olympics

Play in groups of eight. Your group is going to take a trip to the next Olympics. Each person says one thing he or she is going to take on the trip. The person who can remember everything is the winner.

Example:

ELENA: I'm going to take my skis.

AHMED: Elena is going to take her skis. I'm going to take my camera.

ANNA: Elena is going to take her skis. Ahmed is going to take his camera. I'm going to take my diary. . . .

UNIT

33 The Future with *Be going to*: *Yes / No* Questions

Are you going to have a big part?

Grammar **in Context**

🎧 *Listen and read the conversation.*

JESSICA: How was work, Tim?

TIM: Same old, same old. How was your day?

JESSICA: Actually, I had an interesting call.

TIM: Oh?

JESSICA: You know Dan Evans, the TV producer? Well, he has an idea for a new show.

TIM: What kind?

JESSICA: Another news program.

TIM: Really?

JESSICA: Uh-huh. It's going to be on national TV, and he wants me to be in it.

JEREMY: Awesome! Are you going to have a big part?

JESSICA: Yes, I am. I'm going to be the main reporter.

JEREMY: That's so cool.

TIM: Hmm . . . Is it going to mean a lot of travel?

JESSICA: I think so.

ANNIE: Don't take it, Mom. I don't want you to travel.

BEN: Yeah. Who's going to help me with my homework?

TIM: Hey, guys. *I'm* still going to be here.

JESSICA: Anyway, kids, don't worry . . . The show isn't going to air for a long time.

Words and Expressions

🎧 *Do you know these words and expressions? Write new ones in your notebook.*

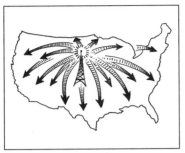

national TV

a producer

a big part

1. A: How was work?
   B: Same old, same old.

3. A: Is it going to mean a lot of travel?
   B: I think so.

2. A: How was your day?
   B: Actually, I have some interesting news.

With a Partner

A. *Practice the conversation with four partners.*

B. *People say changes cause stress. Is your partner going to make more than three of these life changes this year? Ask your partner.*

Example:

A: Are you going to graduate this year?

B: Yes, I am. I'm going to graduate in June.

graduate

get a job

move

get married

become a parent

buy a house

C. *How many classmates are going to make more than three life changes this year?*

Grammar **Presentation**

The Future with *Be going to*: Yes / No Questions

Yes / No Questions	Short Answers	
Am I going to get the job? **Is it** going to mean a lot of travel? **Are we** going to move?	Yes, **you are.** Yes, **it is.** Yes, **we are.**	No, **you're not.** OR No, **you aren't.** No, **it's not.** OR No, **it isn't.** No, **we're not.** OR No, **we aren't.**

Notes

Examples

1. For *yes / no* questions with *be going to*, put *am*, *is*, or *are* **before the subject**.	• **Am I** going to watch TV tonight? • **Is he** going to change jobs? • **Are they** going to buy a house?
2. Use **contractions** in negative short answers.	**A:** Is he going to change jobs? **B:** No, he**'s not.** OR No, he **isn't.**

Focused Practice

1 Discover the Grammar

Match the questions and answers.

____ **1.** Is it going to rain?

____ **2.** Are we going to be late?

____ **3.** Is the soccer game going to be in the park?

____ **4.** Are you going to have pizza?

____ **5.** Are they going to win?

a. No, it's going to be at the school.

b. I think so. Those clouds are very dark.

c. No, it's early. We have a lot of time.

d. Yes, they are.

e. No, I'm not.

2 Jessica's and Tim's Thoughts   Grammar Note 1

Write yes / no questions with **be going to** *and the words in parentheses.*

A. Jessica's thoughts about the new job:

1. (I / get the job) _____ *Am I going to get the job?* _____

2. (it / mean a lot of work) _____

3. (the children / be okay) _____

4. (Tim / want to spend more time at home) _____

B. Tim's thoughts about the new job:

5. (Jessica / change) _____

6. (Jessica / work all the time) _____

7. (we / have time together) _____

8. (Jessica / earn more than me) _____

3 Not Again! Grammar Note 1

Complete the conversations. Use the simple past, the simple present, the present progressive, or **be going to** *for the future. Use the verbs in parentheses.*

1. (rain)

TIM: It _____rained_____ yesterday. It _____ now. _____
it _____ tomorrow?

JESSICA: I'm afraid so. That's what the weatherman says.

2. (have)

JEREMY: I'm tired of tofu. We _____ tofu last night. We _____
tofu now. _____ we _____ tofu tomorrow?

TIM: Oh, no. Tomorrow we _____ veggie burgers.

3. (wear)

JESSICA: I know you like that sweater, but you always _____ it. You
_____ it every day last week. You _____ it now.
_____ you _____ it tomorrow?

JEREMY: Probably. Michelle likes the color.

4. (watch)

JESSICA: You _____ that movie last night. Why _____ you
_____ it again now?

JEREMY: I love it. I _____ probably _____ it tomorrow too.

5. (cook)

JEREMY: Mom, _____ dinner tonight?

JESSICA: Yes, I am.

TIM: No, I _____ tonight. You _____ dinner last night
and the night before. It's my turn.

JESSICA: Oh, that's right.

JEREMY: That's good. No more tofu.

4 What's the Story?

Grammar Note 1

🎧 *Josh gets a phone call from Amanda. Listen to their conversation. Then listen to the conversation between Josh and Jason. Check (✓)* **Yes**, **No**, *or* **No Information**.

	Yes	No	No Information
1. Are Amanda and Josh going to have a baby in six months?	☐	☒	☐
2. Are Amanda and Josh going to move before the baby is born?	☐	☒	☐
3. Is Amanda going to stay home for three months?	☒	☐	☐
4. Is Josh going to change jobs?	☐	☐	☒
5. Is Josh's mother going to take care of the baby?	☐	☒	☐
6. Is it going to cost over $100,000 to raise a child?	☐	☒	☐

5 Editing

Correct Jessica's phone messages. There are four mistakes.

>   *to be*

1. Hi, Jessica. This is Maria. Are you going ~~being~~ in San Francisco for the conference? I need to know. Please call me at 931-8878.

2. Hi, honey. I forgot my date book. Is Fred and Janet going to meet us at eight or eight-thirty? Please call.

3. This message is for Jessica Olson. This is George Selig. Is the conference going start on the sixth or the seventh?

4. Hi, Mom. I'm not going to be home until nine. Al and I am going to study together.

Communication Practice

6 Ask the Fortune Teller

You can ask the fortune teller three questions. Which three questions are you going to ask? Work in small groups. Compare your choices.

_____ **1.** Am I going to be rich?

_____ **2.** Am I going to be famous?

_____ **3.** Am I going to find true love?

_____ **4.** Am I going to make a difference in the world?

_____ **5.** Are scientists going to find a cure for AIDS? cancer? heart disease?

_____ **6.** Are people going to travel to the moon on vacations?

_____ **7.** Are most people going to live to be 120 years old?

_____ **8.** _____?

7 Leaders

Work with a partner. Student A, pretend you are the mayor of your city. Student B, pretend you are the director of your English school. Ask your partner four questions about his or her job. Use **be going to** *and the ideas in the box or your own ideas.*

For the mayor	For the English school director
build inexpensive homes	have smaller classes
lower taxes	lower tuition
fight crime	have more free clubs and activities
build more schools	have better food in the cafeteria

Example:

B: Are you going to build inexpensive homes?

A: Yes, I am. People need inexpensive places to live. I'm going to build 3,000 inexpensive homes.

8 Game: What Are They Going To Do?

Work with a partner. Look at the picture. Write as many sentences as you can with **be going to***. The pair of partners with the most correct sentences wins.*

The Future with *Be going to*: *Wh-* Questions

What are you going to do on Sunday?

Grammar **in Context**

🎧 *Listen and read the conversations.*

KATHY: Mark, what's bothering you? You look pretty nervous.

MARK: I *am* nervous. How am I going to say this?

KATHY: Say what?

MARK: Well, I have something important to say.

KATHY: Let me guess . . . You're going to move away. Or . . . maybe you're going to visit your grandmother in Nashville.

MARK: No. This is about us . . . Will you marry me?

KATHY: Well . . . I only have one thing to say.

MARK: Oh, no. What?

KATHY: What took you so long to ask?

[Later]

MARK: Hello?

JOSH: Hey, Mark. This is Josh. What are you going to do on Sunday?

MARK: No plans. Why?

JOSH: A bunch of us are going to watch the big game. Do you want to come?

MARK: Well, yeah, I think so. By the way, Kathy and I have some big news.

JOSH: Oh yeah? What?

MARK: We're engaged.

JOSH: What? That's great, man! Congratulations!

MARK: Thanks. Tell you about it on Sunday. So what time is the party going to start?

Words and Expressions

🎧 *Do you know these words and expressions? Write new ones in your notebook.*

engaged

a bunch of flowers

a bunch of people

1. **A:** What's bothering you? You look nervous.
   B: I *am* nervous.

2. **A:** Will you marry me?
   B: Yes, I will.

3. What took you so long to ask?

4. **A:** By the way, we have some news.
   B: Oh yeah? What?

5. **A:** Kathy and I are engaged.
   B: That's great! Congratulations!

With a Partner

A. *Practice the conversations with two partners.*

B. *Look at the pictures. Ask and answer questions with your partner. First ask a yes / no question. Then ask a question with* **what**, **where**, **when**, *or* **why**.

watch TV

go shopping

read a novel

go skiing

Example:

A: Are you going to watch TV tonight?
B: Yes, I am.
A: What are you going to watch?
B: I'm going to watch *Star Trek*.

Grammar **Presentation**

The Future with *Be going to*: *Wh-* Questions

Wh- Questions	**Answers**
***How* am I** going to say this? ***When* is he** going to ask? ***What* are you** going to do on Sunday?	Say what? Probably tonight. Watch the big game.

Wh- Questions about the Subject	**Answers**
Who* is** going to win the game? ***What's going to happen?	The Titans (are). They're going to kick a goal.

Notes

Examples

1. To ask a *wh-* **question** in the future with *be going to*, start with the *wh-* **word**. Use the correct form of *be* + a **subject** + *going to* + the **base form** of the verb.

Wh- word	*be*	subject	*going to*	base form
A: What	**are**	**you**	**going to**	**do**

  on Sunday?

B: Watch the game.

2. For a *wh-* **question about the subject**, use *who* or *what* + *is* + *going to* + the **base form** of the verb.

Wh- word	*be*	*going to*	base form
A: Who	**is**	**going to**	**win** the game?

B: The Titans (are).

Focused Practice

 Discover the Grammar

A. *Read* Grammar in Context *again. Circle the* **be going to** *questions. Underline the* **be going to** *statements.*

Example:

(How am I going to say this?) You're going to move away.

B. *Match the questions and answers.*

__d__	**1.** Mom, what time are we going to have dinner?	**a.** Jeremy is, Dad. I did them last night.
_____	**2.** When are you guys going to get married?	**b.** Because it's always in the shop.
_____	**3.** What are you going to do tonight, Steve?	**c.** Next summer—probably in June.
_____	**4.** Why are you going to sell your car, Judy?	**d.** At six o'clock sharp.
_____	**5.** Who's going to do the dishes tonight, kids?	**e.** I'm probably going to watch a video.

2 The Engagement

Complete the conversation with wh- *questions. Use the words in parentheses.*

AMANDA: This is fantastic! So _____when are you going to have_____ the wedding?
1. (when / you / have)

KATHY: Next summer, we think—probably in June.

JUDY: A June wedding! Perfect. _____?
2. (where / it / be)

MARK: Right here in Seattle.

JOSH: What about your honeymoon? _____?
3. (where / you / go)

MARK: Well, we're thinking about India.

STEVE: India? Wow! _____? Big bucks?
4. (how much / that / cost)

MARK: Well, quite a bit. But Kathy works at a travel agency, you know. It doesn't cost her much to travel. And our parents are going to help—as a wedding present.

JOSH: _____ there? In India, I mean.
5. (how long / you / be)

KATHY: At least two weeks.

STEVE: _____?
6. (what places / you / visit)

MARK: Well, the Taj Mahal, Bombay, and Calcutta for sure. And we have to see the Ganges River. Hopefully we can go to some other places.

AMANDA: Awesome. And when you come back, _____?
7. (where / you / live)

KATHY: In an apartment, at first. Eventually we're going to look for a house.

MARK: Okay, enough questions about us. Now *I've* got a question.

_____ this game?
8. (who / win)

3 Editing

Correct the conversations. There are seven mistakes.

1. **A:** Who $\overset{is}{\wedge}$ going to do the dishes tonight, kids?
   B: Jeremy going to do them, Mom. I did them last night.

2. **A:** Amanda, how many people we are going to invite?
   B: I think about eight.

3. **A:** Where Mark and Kathy are going to go on their honeymoon?
   B: They're going to go to India.

4. **A:** What time is going to start the party?
   B: It's going to start at about 5:30.

5. **A:** How the weather is going to be on Saturday?
   B: The weatherman says is going to be sunny and warm.

Communication Practice

4 What Are We Going to Eat?

Listen to Josh and Amanda's conversation before their party. Write the five wh- *questions with* **be going to**.

1. _____
2. _____
3. _____
4. _____
5. _____

5 Consider the Future

Work in groups of three. Ask questions using the words in the box. Then tell the class.

who / next president	what / job / have in the next five years
where / live / in ten years	what / important thing / buy soon

Example:

A: Who's going to be the next president?
B: I think . . . is going to be the next president.
C: B thinks . . . is going to be the next president.

6 Vacation Time for the Olsons

Talk about the picture with a partner. Ask your partner questions with **be going to**.
Use **where**, **who**, **how long**, **what**, **what time**, *and* **when**. *Take turns.*

SEATTLE / ORLANDO: April 1, Flight 610,
departs Seattle, Washington, 10:30 A.M.,
arrives Orlando, Florida, 8:00 P.M.

....

ORLANDO / SEATTLE: April 15, Flight 224,
departs Orlando, Florida, 9:00 A.M.,
arrives Seattle, Washington, 4:30 P.M.

The Olsons' itinerary

Example:

A: Where are the Olsons going to go?
B: Orlando, Florida.

Review or SelfTest

I. *Complete the conversations. Circle the correct letter.*

1. JOSH: What are you going to do tonight?   A Ⓑ C D
   MARK: _____

   (A) We're going out
       tomorrow night.
   (B) We're going to watch
       a video.
   (C) What are you doing
       tonight at 9:30?
   (D) Are you going to stay
       home tonight?

2. FELIX: Is it going to rain?   A B C D
   TIM: _____

   (A) Why is it always raining?
   (B) It isn't raining.
   (C) It's not snowing.
   (D) I think so.

3. KATHY: What's bothering you?   A B C D
   MARK: _____

   (A) I'm here.
   (B) We're late.
   (C) We're happy.
   (D) I'm interested.

4. BILL: When are we going to go shopping?   A B C D
   MARY: _____

   (A) We're out of food.
   (B) We're going to go
       shopping.
   (C) At two o'clock.
   (D) Rose is going to
       come with us.

5. KEN: _____   A B C D
   LAURA: It's a really exciting game.

   (A) How come you like
       soccer?
   (B) Where does your
       brother play soccer?
   (C) When is the
       soccer game?
   (D) How do you play
       soccer?

II. *Look at the pictures. Write sentences about what is going to happen.*
Use the verbs in the box.

cook	get	go	~~watch~~

1. <u>He's going to watch TV.</u>   **2.** _____

3. _____   4. _____

III. *Write a question for each answer. Use* **be going to** *in each question.*

1. **ROSE:** _____ When is Jeremy going to graduate? _____

    MARY: Jeremy's going to graduate a year from now.

2. **FELIX:** _____

    TIM: Yes, it is. Actually, it's going to snow a lot.

3. **STEVE:** _____

    AMANDA: Mark and Kathy are going to go to India on their honeymoon.

4. **MARK:** _____

    JUDY: Yes, Ken's going to go to college.

5. **MARY:** _____

    ROSE: Don't you remember? *You're* going to drive us to the airport.

IV. *Correct the letter. There are five mistakes.*

᪉᪉ ᪉᪉ ᪉᪉ ᪉᪉ ᪉᪉ ᪉᪉ ᪉᪉ ᪉᪉ ᪉᪉ ᪉᪉ ᪉᪉ ᪉᪉ ᪉᪉ ᪉᪉ ᪉᪉ ᪉᪉ ᪉᪉

Sunday, May 20

Dear Mary,

    Thanks for driving us to the airport. We arrived in Acapulco at 1:00 p.m. and went right to the hotel. The weather is beautiful so far, but it looks like ^it^ is going to rain. Tomorrow we going to go swimming in the morning. In the afternoon are we going to go fishing out in the ocean.

    When you and Bill are going to come with us on a trip? We always have such a good time when we travel.

    The only thing I miss about Seattle is baseball. Our team is going to win?

    I'll write again soon.

Love,

Rose

▶ *To check your answers, go to the Answer Key on page 285.*

UNIT

Suggestions: *Let's . . . ,*
Why don't we . . . ?

Let's do something for him.

Grammar **in Context**

🎧 *Listen and read the newspaper article and the conversation.*

MARK: Take a look at this article.

The Seattle Daily

FIRE DESTROYS HOME

After a five-day camping trip, the Somers returned home. To their horror, their home was destroyed. Firefighters worked for hours last night but were unable to save anything. Mr. Somers said, "We have no insurance and very little money in the bank. But," he added, "we're strong, and we can start again."

KATHY: How awful! They lost everything!

MARK: It's terrible, and I know Jon Somers. He drives a truck for *The Seattle Daily*. A terrific guy! He's always there for others.

KATHY: Well, now let's do something for *him*.

MARK: Like what? He needs money. We don't have money.

KATHY: No, but you're a journalist. Your words are powerful. And I can write too. Why don't we write an article about him for the paper? The paper can ask readers for contributions.

MARK: You know, that's a wonderful idea.

KATHY: Let's ask Steve to help.

MARK: Let's not ask Steve right away. First let's write the article.

KATHY: Okay. So let's get started.

MARK: Now?

KATHY: Sure. There's no time like the present.

Words and Expressions

🎧 *Do you know these words and expressions? Write new ones in your notebook.*

a truck

a contribution

terrific

terrible

1. **A:** How awful! They lost everything!
   B: It's terrible.

2. **A:** Let's do something for him.
   B: Like what?

3. **A:** Let's get started.
   B: Now?
   A: There's no time like the present.

With a Partner

A. *Practice the conversation with a partner.*

B. *Imagine that a classmate is sick. You and your partner make suggestions for the class.*

Example:

A: Let's send him letters.
B: Great idea.
A: Why don't we visit him?
B: Okay.

Grammar **Presentation**
Suggestions: *Let's . . . , Why don't we . . . ?*

Suggestions with *Let's . . .*					
Affirmative			**Negative**		
Let's	ask call	Steve.	Let's not	ask call	him right away.

Suggestions with *Why don't we . . . ?*		
Why don't we	write send	an article? an e-mail message?

Responses	
Agree	**Disagree**
1. A: Let's ask Steve. **B: Good idea.**	**1. A:** Let's ask Bob. **B: Let's not ask Bob. Let's ask Sam.**
2. A: Why don't we take a break? **B: Okay.**	**2. A:** Let's have dinner at India Garden. **B: Why don't we go to China Grill instead?**
3. A: Let's have a party. **B: That's a good / great / wonderful idea. I'd love to.**	**3. A:** Why don't we go to a soccer game? **B: I'd rather not. Why don't we . . . ?**

Notes

Examples

Notes	Examples
1. Use *Let's* or *Why don't we* to make **suggestions**. Use *Let's* or *Why don't we* + the **base form** of the verb. NOTE: Use a **question mark** at the end of suggestions with *Why don't we*.	• **Let's write** an article. • **Why don't we buy** Jon a book? • **Why don't we** get him a mystery**?**
2. The **negative** of *Let's* is *Let's not*.	• **Let's not** write a newsletter.
3. *Let's* is short for *Let us*. We almost always use the short form.	• **Let's** have lunch.

Focused Practice

1 Discover the Grammar

Read Grammar in Context *again. Write the suggestions in the conversation.*

Well, now let's do something for him.
_____

_____

_____

_____

_____

2 Let's Get Something to Eat   Grammar Notes 1–3

Complete the conversation. Use the suggestions in the box.

> **a.** Let's not have pizza.
>
> **b.** Let's share.
>
> **c.** That's a good idea, but let's call first.
>
> **d.** Let's get something to eat.
>
> **e.** Let's ask his coworkers.
>
> **f.** Why don't we order Thai food for a change?

MARK: How can we get more information about Jon Somers?

KATHY: _____ We can go to the *Seattle Daily* office tomorrow.
  _{1.}

MARK: _____
  _{2.}

KATHY: Okay.

MARK: It's almost nine. I'm hungry. _____
  _{3.}

KATHY: Do you want to order a pizza?

MARK: Pizza? Hmm. I like pizza, but I'm tired of it. _____
  _{4.}

_____
  _{5.}

KATHY: Okay.

MARK: Thai Palace isn't expensive, and they deliver.

KATHY: Okay. I'd like the noodle dish, *pad thai*.

MARK: Good choice. I want *tom kha gai*. That's spicy coconut milk and chicken soup.

KATHY: Mmm. _____
  _{6.}

3 A Meeting

Mark calls Kathy. She can't hear him and gets the wrong message. Listen and change her three mistakes.

KATHY: Hello.

MARK: Hi, Kathy. It's Mark. Listen, Kathy. I'm still at the *Seattle Daily*. I can't meet you at five. Let's meet at five-thirty.

KATHY: Okay. Where?

MARK: Why don't we meet in front of the photo shop on 14th Street?

KATHY: That's pretty far away.

MARK: It's not so far, and it's a nice place to meet.

KATHY: Okay. Bye. See you later.

4 Editing

Correct the conversations. There are four mistakes.

1. **A:** I'm hungry. Let's to stop for lunch.

   B: There are no restaurants on this road.

2. **A:** Why we don't take a walk?

   B: Okay. That's a good idea.

3. **A:** Is Route 1 the best way to get to the restaurant?

   B: Let's don't take Route 1. There's always traffic on that road.

4. **A:** Maria was absent again. Let's us visit her.

   B: Why don't we call before we visit?

Communication Practice

5 Make Suggestions

Work with a partner. Read the situations. For each one make suggestions with **Let's** *and* **Why don't we.**

Situations

1. A friend has a birthday soon.
2. A friend is going to have a baby.
3. Your classroom is very noisy.
4. Your classroom is very hot.

Example:

A: Bob's birthday is next week. Let's call him.

B: Why don't we send him a card?

A: I have a better idea. Let's . . .

6 Role Play

Work with a partner. Read the situations. Choose one and have a discussion. Include suggestions with **Let's** *and* **Why don't we**.

Situations

1. You and a friend find a gold watch. Nobody is nearby.
2. You are hungry. Suggest a restaurant. Your friend agrees or suggests a different restaurant. Give reasons for your suggestions.

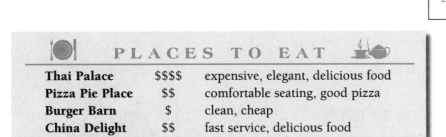

PLACES TO EAT		
Thai Palace	$$$$	expensive, elegant, delicious food
Pizza Pie Place	$$	comfortable seating, good pizza
Burger Barn	$	clean, cheap
China Delight	$$	fast service, delicious food

7 Expressions with *Let's*

A. *Work with a partner. Match the letter that explains the expression.*

_____ 1. Let's hit the road.   **a.** Let's meet.
_____ 2. Let's make a deal.   **b.** Let's stop what we're doing.
_____ 3. Let's get together.   **c.** Let's leave.
_____ 4. Let's take a break.   **d.** Let's agree.

B. *Complete the conversations with expressions 1 to 4 above. Then practice the conversations with a partner.*

1. **A:** I really hate cooking.
   B: And I hate cleaning.
   A: _____. I clean and you cook.

2. **A:** It's late. We can finish this job tomorrow. _____
   B: You're right. We have a long drive home.

3. **A:** This job is taking a long time.
   B: I know. What time is it?
   A: Almost one-thirty. _____
   B: Good idea.

4. **A:** Do you live around here?
   B: Yes. I live in this building. How about you?
   A: I live in the next building.
   B: Well, _____. Are you free for lunch tomorrow?
   A: Yes, I am.

Requests: *I would like . . . ;*
Invitations: *Would you like . . . ?*

Would you like a cheese pizza?

Grammar **in Context**

🎧 *Listen and read the conversations.*

MICHELLE: Hello?

JEREMY: Hi, Michelle. This is Jeremy.

MICHELLE: Oh, hi, Jeremy!

JEREMY: Uh, . . . I was wondering . . . Would you like to go out for pizza and then go ice skating? Kevin and Maria are going.

MICHELLE: Oh, I'd love to. When?

JEREMY: Saturday afternoon, about 4:30?

MICHELLE: Good. Do you want to meet somewhere?

JEREMY: Yeah. Let's meet in front of the pizza place at 4:15.

MICHELLE: Sure. See you at 4:15 on Saturday. 'Bye.

JEREMY: 'Bye.

[Saturday]

WAITER: All right. What would you all like?

JEREMY: A large pizza. A supreme.

WAITER: And what would you like on the pizza?

KEVIN: We'd like pepperoni and cheese. Okay, you guys?

MARIA: Sure. But let's have anchovies, too.

KEVIN: Maria! Give me a break! You're not serious, are you?

MARIA: No! Just kidding. Actually, I hate anchovies.

Ice skating

MICHELLE: How about half pepperoni and cheese, and half peppers and mushrooms?

JEREMY: Sounds fine.

WAITER: Would you all like something to drink? We have a special on root beers today.

MARIA: Sounds good. Okay, everyone?

EVERYONE: Yeah, great.

Words and Expressions

🎧 *Do you know these words and expressions? Write new ones in your notebook.*

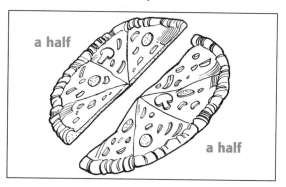

1. A: Would you like to go out for pizza?

    B: I'd love to. When?

2. A: We'd like pepperoni and cheese. Okay, you guys?

    B: Sure. But let's have anchovies, too.

3. A: How about half pepperoni and half cheese?

    B: Sounds fine.

4. A: Give me a break! You're not serious, are you?

    B: No. Just kidding.

With a Partner

A. *Practice the conversations with four partners.*

B. *You and your partner are at a restaurant. Look at the pictures. Ask and answer.*

soup / salad

potatoes / rice

pie / cake

coffee / tea

Example:

A: Would you like soup or salad?

B: I'd like salad. Would you like . . . or . . . ?

A: I'd like . . .

Grammar **Presentation**
Requests: *I would like . . .*; Invitations: *Would you like . . . ?*

Affirmative Statements

I He She We They	**would like** **'d like**	a pizza. to go out.

Questions

Would you **like** a pizza?
Would you **like** to go out?
What would you **like** to drink?

Short Answers

Yes, please. OR No, thank you.
Yes. I'd love to. OR Sorry, I can't.
Iced tea, please.

Notes

Examples

---

1. Use *would like* to ask for what you want.
   It is more **polite** than *want*.

   NOTE: Use **contractions** in conversation
   or informal writing.

   ▶ BE CAREFUL! *Like* is different from
   would like.

   - I **would like** a cheese pizza.

   - I**'d like** a cheese pizza.

   - I **like** pizza a lot. *(in general)*
   - But today I**'d like** a hamburger. *(today)*

---

2. *Would like* can be followed by:
   — a **noun**
   OR
   — an **infinitive** (*to* + the **base form**
   of the verb)

   - He would like **a steak**. *(noun)*

   - She would like **to have** a salad. *(infinitive)*

---

3. Use *Would you like . . . ?* for polite
   invitations. Then add a noun or an
   infinitive.

   - **Would you like** a soda? *(noun)*

   - **Would you like** to go out? *(infinitive)*

---

4. **Short answers** to polite invitations vary
   depending on what the invitation is
   about.

   NOTE: We don't usually use *Yes, I would*
   or *No, I wouldn't* in these short answers.

   A: Would you like *pizza*?

   B: **Yes, please.** OR **No, thank you.**

   A: Would you like *to go out* with us?

   B: **Yes, I'd love to.** OR **Sorry, I can't.**

Focused Practice

1 Discover the Grammar

A. *Read* Grammar in Context *again. Circle* **would like** *in questions and answers.*

B. *Match the questions and answers.*

   c   **1.** What would you like to drink, Amanda?   **a.** New Zealand. But it's expensive.

_____ **2.** Steve, what would you like to eat?   **b.** No, thanks. Just pizza.

_____ **3.** What video would you like to see, Annie?   **c.** Tea with lemon, please.

_____ **4.** Would you like a hamburger, Ben?   **d.** *Titanic.*

_____ **5.** Where would you like to go on vacation?   **e.** I'd like a steak.

2 What Would They Like?   Grammar Notes 1–3

Complete the conversation with **would like**. *Use pronouns and contractions in Jessica's answers.*

WAITRESS: Okay, ma'am. What _____would the children like_____ to drink?
                                        1. (the children)

JESSICA: _____. Oh, wait a minute.
                            2. (root beers)
My daughter doesn't like root beer.

WAITRESS: How about a lemonade?

JESSICA: Yes, that's good. _____.
                                3. (a lemonade with ice)

WAITRESS: And for your husband?

JESSICA: _____.
                        4. (coffee)

WAITRESS: And for you, ma'am?

JESSICA: _____.
                        5. (iced tea)

WAITRESS: All right. Does everyone want today's special?

JESSICA: Everyone except my daughter. _____.
                                        6. (a turkey sandwich)

3 You like or You'd like?

A. *Listen to the sentences. Circle the letter of the sentence you hear.*

1. **a.** I'd like a hamburger, Mom.
   b. I like hamburgers, Mom.
2. **a.** Tim, they'd like soup, not salad.
   b. Tim, they like soup, not salad.
3. **a.** Dad, we'd like chicken.
   b. Dad, we like chicken.
4. **a.** Josh? He'd like steak.
   b. Josh? He likes steak.
5. **a.** Annie, you'd like ice cream, right?
   b. Annie, you like ice cream, right?
6. **a.** She'd like chocolate.
   b. She likes chocolate.

B. *Work with a partner. Say the sentences to each other. Your partner tells you which sentence you said.*

4 Editing

Correct the conversations. There are six mistakes.

1. **WAITER:** ~~Do~~ Would you like coffee, sir?

   MARK: Yes, please.

   WAITER: And for you, ma'am?

   KATHY: I like tea with lemon.

2. **MICHELLE:** Would you like vanilla ice cream, Jeremy?

   JEREMY: No. Vanilla is boring. I'd liked chocolate chip.

3. **JOSH:** How many children do you like to have, Amanda?

   AMANDA: About six, I think.

   JOSH: Oh, no! You're kidding, aren't you?

   AMANDA: Yes, of course. I like two or three.

4. **KEN:** Do you like to come with us to Mexico?

   LAURA: Thanks, but I'm going to the Caribbean.

Communication Practice

5 I'd Really Like a Piece of Apple Pie

🎧 *Read these statements. Then listen to Steve, Judy, and Mark in a restaurant.*
Check **True** *or* **False**.

	True	False
1. Judy likes hamburgers.	❏	❏
2. Judy would like a hamburger today.	❏	❏
3. Mark would like a hamburger today.	❏	❏
4. Steve would like onions on his hamburger.	❏	❏
5. Mark likes tea.	❏	❏
6. Steve and Mark would like coffee.	❏	❏
7. Mark and Judy want pie for dessert.	❏	❏
8. Steve wants chocolate cake.	❏	❏

6 I'd like . . .

Write six sentences about what you would like for your birthday. Then tell a partner.

Example:

A: What would you like for your birthday?

B: I'd like a new car. I'd also like . . .

7 Role Play: After the Game

A. *Work with a partner. You and a friend come home to your house after a soccer*
game. Offer your friend something to eat and drink. Use the following
conversation as a model, but change the foods and drinks.

Example:

A: What would you like to drink? I've got (orange juice) and (root beer).

B: (Root beer), please. I don't like (orange juice).

A: OK. Here you go. So, what would you like to eat? (Pizza)?

B: No, thanks. I like (pizza), but I don't feel like it now.

A: Okay. Then how about a (turkey sandwich)?

B: Great! I'd love a (turkey sandwich).

B. *Now switch roles.*

Necessity: *Must* and *Have to*

Students must pass a test.

Grammar **in Context**

🎧 *Listen to the conversation between Josh and Amanda. Then read the advertisements.*

AMANDA: Josh, look at these ads for high schools. Some of these schools are like night and day.

JOSH: *[Laughing]* High schools? The baby isn't born yet!

AMANDA: True, but high school is so important. We have to make sure the school we choose is right.

ACADEMIC ACADEMY

A high school must prepare a student for life. Students at Academic Academy have to work hard. From Monday through Friday our students attend school from eight to five. They have three hours of homework every night. They study English, mathematics, computers, science, and social studies. Every three months they must pass a written test in each subject. Parents must sign all homework and tests. The school year starts in September and goes until June. Every June our students get top scores on statewide tests. Then they enjoy a long summer vacation.

Graduates of Academic Academy go on to the best colleges. We are proud of our graduates.

Body and Mind Center

Students at Body and Mind Center love school! And when they graduate, they are well-rounded teens. Students study and do physical activity every day. We understand that some people don't do well on tests. Here, students don't have to take tests. They can write papers instead. However, we believe that everyone must learn to work with others and give to others. Our students work in teams and do volunteer work. They learn to draw, play an instrument, and speak a second language. Our school day goes from nine to two. Students attend school eleven months of the year.

Students at Body and Mind Center don't say "I *have to* go to school." They *want to*.

Words and Expressions

Do you know these words and expressions? Write new ones in your notebook.

a uniform

play an instrument

1. A: Are they alike?
   B: No. They're completely different. They're like night and day.

2. A: How long is your school day?
   B: It's from nine to two.

3. A: Do you have to take a test?
   B: No, we can write a paper instead.

With a Partner

A. *Read* Grammar in Context *with a partner.*

B. *Compare Academic Academy and Body and Mind Center. Which school do you like? Why?*

Grammar **Presentation**
Necessity: *Must*

Affirmative and Negative Statements			
I You He / She / It We You They	**must** **must not**	**arrive** **be**	late.

Necessity: *Have to*

Affirmative Statements			
I You We You They	**have to**	**take**	a test.
He She It	**has to**	**be**	on time.

Negative Statements				
I You We You They	**don't**	**have to**	**take**	a test.
He She It	**doesn't**		**be**	on time.

Yes / No Questions				
Do	I you we they	**have to**	**take**	a test?
Does	he she it		**be**	on time?

Short Answers					
Affirmative			Negative		
Yes,	you I we they	**do.**	**No,**	you I we they	**don't.**
Yes,	he she it	**does.**	**No,**	he she it	**doesn't.**

Wh- Questions
What do I **have to** study? ***Where*** does she **have to** go?

Notes	Examples
1. Use *must* and *have to* to talk about **necessity**. They both mean "it is necessary," but *must* is **stronger** and **more formal** than *have to*. ▶ **BE CAREFUL!** Do not add an *–s* to *must* in the third-person singular. Do not use *to* after *must*. Do not add *–s* to the base form of the verb.	• Students **must attend** class from eight to five. • We **have to be** in school by eight. • **He must** take that test. NOT ~~He musts take that test.~~ NOT ~~He must to take that test.~~ NOT ~~He must takes that test.~~
2. Use *must not* to talk about **prohibition**. It means "it is not allowed." It is very strong. Use *mustn't* in speaking and informal writing.	• You **must not drink and drive**. It's too dangerous. • You **mustn't smoke** here. It's against the law.
3. Use *don't have to* to talk about **lack of necessity**. It means "it's not necessary; you have a choice."	• We **don't have to go** to computer lab. *(We can go to computer lab, but we don't need to.)* • He **doesn't have to take** a test. He can write a paper instead.
4. The **base form** of the verb **follows** *must* and *have to*.	• I **must** *leave* now. • She **has to** *buy* another book.
5. **Don't confuse** the expression *have to* with the verb *have*.	• We **have to do** a lot of homework. • We **have** homework every day.
6. We usually use *have to*, not *must*, for **questions**.	• **Do** we **have to** leave? • When **does** he **have to** take the test?

Focused Practice

① Discover the Grammar

What do the underlined words mean? Match the underlined words on the left with their meaning on the right.

_____ **1.** You <u>mustn't</u> wear jeans to school.

_____ **2.** You <u>must</u> be in school at 8:00 A.M.

_____ **3.** You <u>don't have to</u> wear a suit.

a. You have a choice.

b. You have to.

c. You can't.

② Rules of the Schools
Grammar Notes 1–5

Complete the sentences. Choose from the words in parentheses.

1. Students _____ take tests. They can write papers.
                (mustn't / don't have to)

2. The rule is: Parents _____ sign homework.
                   (have to / don't have to)

3. Students _____ learn to use computers. Computers are a part of
           (have to / don't have to)
today's world. The Internet is basic to all their work.

4. Students _____ come late. They must learn to be on time.
              (must / mustn't)

5. Students _____ class for five hours a day.
              (have to / have)

③ Homework
Grammar Notes 1, 3, 4, 5

🎧 *Listen to the conversation between Ken and Laura. Write **T** (True), **F** (False), or **NI** (No Information) next to each statement. Correct the false ones.*

_____ **1.** Laura has to do a lot of homework.

_____ **2.** Laura is going to go to Ray's party.

_____ **3.** Laura has to write a journal.

_____ **4.** Ken and Laura have the same English teacher.

_____ **5.** Ken has to learn to plan his time better.

④ Editing

Correct the conversation. There are five mistakes.

A: What's wrong?

B: I have ^to^ do homework for every class: English, math, science, and history.

A: Is it all for tomorrow?

B: Well, I must to do English and history homework for tomorrow.

A: What about your science and math homework?

B: I mustn't to do my science homework for tomorrow, but I have to a science test the day after tomorrow. I must starts studying today.

Communication Practice

5 What's Your English Class Like?

Work with a partner. Think about your English class. What do you have to do?
What don't you have to do? Check (✓) the box.

	Have to	Don't have to	Must not
1. do homework every day	❏	❏	❏
2. sit in the same seat every class	❏	❏	❏
3. memorize grammar rules	❏	❏	❏
4. stand when the teacher speaks	❏	❏	❏
5. always speak English in class	❏	❏	❏
6. work in pairs or groups	❏	❏	❏
7. use a dictionary in class	❏	❏	❏
8. smoke in class	❏	❏	❏
9. eat in class	❏	❏	❏

6 Talk about Athletes

Work in small groups. Talk about these athletes. Use **must** *and* **have to** *in the*
affirmative and negative.

a sumo wrestler

a basketball player

jockeys

a football player

a climber

a surfer

Example:

A sumo wrestler must be very heavy. He has to eat a lot.
He must not let his opponent push him out of the wrestling area.

Advice: *Should / Shouldn't*

Should I go to college next fall?

Grammar **in Context**

🎧 *Listen and read the conversation.*

JUDY: Ken, here's someone you should meet.

KEN: Okay.

JUDY: Steve, I'd like to introduce you to someone special.

STEVE: Sure, Judy.

JUDY: This is my brother, Ken. He's visiting from Michigan. He's on spring break now.

STEVE: It's good to meet you, Ken.

KEN: Good to meet you too.

JUDY: Steve, Ken has a question. You're a professor, so you're a good person to ask.

STEVE: Sure. What's on your mind?

KEN: I'm wondering about school. I'm going to graduate in a couple of months. Should I go to college next fall or wait a year?

STEVE: Hmm. Big question. What do you want to study?

KEN: Well, that's just it. I don't know. I guess I should go to college, but . . .

STEVE: But?

KEN: I want to do something else for a while. Actually, I'd like to travel.

STEVE: Well, a lot of people don't agree with this, but here's my opinion. I think kids should go to college when they're ready. So why don't you wait a year?

KEN: Hmm. I need to think about it. Thanks a lot, Steve.

Words and Expressions

🎧 *Do you know these words and expressions? Write new ones in your notebook.*

graduate

go to college

wonder

agree

1. A: What's on your mind?
   B: Well, I'm wondering about school.

2. I'm going to graduate in a couple of months.

With a Partner

A. *Practice the conversations with two partners.*

B. *Look at the pictures. Give advice. Say what each person should do.*

Example:

He should get up.

Grammar **Presentation**
Advice: *Should / Shouldn't*

Affirmative and Negative Statements

I You He She We You They	**should** **shouldn't**	**buy**	a new car. a used car.

Questions

Should I buy a new car?
Should teenagers drive before they're eighteen?

Short Answers

Yes, **you should.** OR No, **you shouldn't.**
Yes, **they should.** OR No, **they shouldn't.**

Notes

Examples

---

1. Use *should* to give **advice** or talk about a good thing to do. Use *should* + the **base form** of the verb.

▶ **BE CAREFUL!** Don't add an *–s* to *should* in the third-person singular.

Don't use *to* after *should*.

Don't add *–s* to the verb following *should*.

- I **should practice** the piano every day.
- Kids **should go** to college when they're ready.
- She **should take** an umbrella.
  NOT ~~She shoulds take an umbrella.~~
  NOT ~~She should to take an umbrella.~~
  NOT ~~She should takes an umbrella.~~

---

2. To make **negative statements** with *should*, put *not* after *should*.

Use **contractions** in speaking and informal writing.

- You **should not** eat a big meal before bedtime.
- I **shouldn't** eat so much at night.

---

3. To ask *yes / no* questions with *should*, put *should* before the subject.

A: **Should I** go to college?
B: Yes, you should. You need a college degree to get a good job.

4. ***Should*** is **different** from ***must*** and ***have to***. ***Should*** gives advice.

Must and ***have to*** show necessity.

- Children **should** eat a good breakfast every day. *(advice)*

- Drivers **must** have a driver's license to drive legally. *(necessity)*

- In many countries, people **have to** be eighteen years old to vote. *(necessity)*

Focused Practice

1 Discover the Grammar

A. *Read* Grammar in Context *again. Underline all the uses of* **should** + *the base form of the verb.*

Example:

Ken, here's someone you <u>should meet</u>.

B. *Match the conversations.*

  d   **1.** Should I give Amanda a call?

_____ **2.** What time should we leave for the concert?

_____ **3.** I'm really tired, Mom.

_____ **4.** Should we take an umbrella, Mark?

_____ **5.** The car is really dirty.

_____ **6.** What should I get Jeremy for his birthday?

a. How about a sweater?

b. Yeah. I should wash it.

c. Yes. It looks like rain.

d. Yes. Find out why she's not here yet.

e. Let's leave about 6:30.

f. Maybe you should go to bed early tonight.

2 Should We Move Next to Her Parents?   Grammar Notes 1–3

Complete the conversation between Mark, Kathy, Amanda, and Josh. Use **should** *and the verbs in parentheses.*

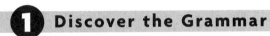

MARK: So . . . any advice from you old married folks?

AMANDA: About what?

MARK: Well . . . For example, ____should we move____
                             1. (we / move)
next to Kathy's parents?

AMANDA: Hmm. I don't think _____
                                  2. (married couples / live)
next to their parents.

KATHY: What about the wedding? _____ a lot of people?
                                     3. (we / invite)

(continued on next page)

AMANDA: Well, that's up to you. But a big wedding is always nice.

MARK: _____ to India on our honeymoon?
   4. (we / still go)

JOSH: What do you mean?

KATHY: Well, we want to, but it's expensive. _____ someplace cheaper?
   5. (we / try)

JOSH: This is a great opportunity! I think _____ to India.
   6. (you / go)

---

3 Advice to Travelers   Grammar Note 4

Read about traveling to India. Complete the paragraph with **should** *or* **must** *and the verbs in parentheses.*

a passport

a visa

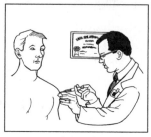

an immunization

a credit card

a traveler's check

cash

✈ **Advice To Travelers** 🧑‍💼

If you are traveling to India, you _____ a valid passport.
   1. (have)

You _____ a visa also. Immunizations are not necessary.
   2. (have)

You _____ your doctor what he or she advises. You
   3. (ask)

_____ a credit card for emergencies, and you _____
   4. (carry)   5. (carry)

most of your money in traveler's checks. You _____
   6. (not / carry)

too much money in cash.

4 Editing

Correct the conversations. There are four mistakes.

1. **JOSH:** What about dinner tonight?

    AMANDA: I think we should ~~to~~ go out for dinner.

2. **JESSICA:** How is Jeremy doing in math, Mrs. Gómez?

    TEACHER: Pretty well, but he should studies more.

3. **TIM:** We should buy Jeremy a new guitar?

    JESSICA: Well, I think Jeremy should earn the money himself.

4. **JEREMY:** Should I buy a used car?

    TIM: No, you shouldn't. Should you buy a new car.

Communication Practice

5 Give Me a Break!

Listen to the conversation. Complete the statements.

1. Jeremy thinks they should go _____.

2. Michelle thinks they should go _____.

3. Kevin thinks they should go _____.

4. Maria thinks they should go _____.

5. Michelle thinks they should wear _____.

6 An Opinion Poll

*Read the statements. Check **Agree** or **Disagree**. Then discuss your answers with the class.*

	Agree	Disagree
1. Teenagers shouldn't drive before they're 18.	❑	❑
2. People over seventy shouldn't drive.	❑	❑
3. Everyone should go to college.	❑	❑
4. Smoking should be illegal.	❑	❑
5. Everyone should study music and art.	❑	❑
6. High school students shouldn't work.	❑	❑

7 What Should I Do?

Write three sentences about things you should do and three about things you shouldn't do. Talk with a partner. Compare your lists.

Example:

I should get more sleep. I shouldn't stay up so late.

Review or SelfTest

I. *Complete the conversations. Circle the correct letter.*

1. KATHY: Wow! Look at those dark clouds!   A Ⓑ C D
   MARK: Yeah. _____ take an umbrella.
   (A) You must   (C) You don't have to
   (B) You should   (D) You're going to

2. TIM: What would you like, Ben?   A B C D
   BEN: _____
   (A) I like hamburgers.   (C) Let's not have
   (B) Why don't you get   hamburgers.
       a hamburger?   (D) I'd like a hamburger.

3. AMANDA: Where should we eat?
   JOSH: _____   A B C D
   (A) Why don't we go to Spiro's? (C) Let's not.
   (B) I'd really like to. No time (D) Let's meet there.
       like the present.

4. MICHELLE: Would you like to see a video?   A B C D
   MARIA: _____
   (A) Why don't we go there?   (C) How about a video?
   (B) Sure, I'd love to.   (D) Same old, same old.

5. KEN: _____   A B C D
   STEVE: I think you should. Students should go to
           college when they're ready.
   (A) Should I wait a year to   (C) Would you like to go
       go to college?   to college next fall?
   (B) How about going to   (D) Am I going to wait a
       college next fall?   year to go to college?

II. *Complete the sentences. Use* **should**, **shouldn't**, *or the correct form of* **have to** *and* **don't have to** *with the verbs in parentheses.*

1. To drive legally, a person _____ a driver's license.
                                    (have)

2. Drivers _____ to check their tires before a long trip.
                 (remember)

3. Drivers _____ too fast, but many of them do.
                 (drive)

4. Tourists _____ a camera on a trip, but it's a good idea.
                  (take)

III. *Write questions for these answers.*

1. **A:** _____ Would you like to go ice skating? _____

   B: Great idea! Yeah, let's go ice skating.

2. **A:** _____

   B: Yes, you should. A new car is much better than a used car.

3. **A:** _____

   B: Yes, I do. I like pizza a lot.

4. **A:** _____

   B: No, thank you. I had two cups of coffee for breakfast.

5. **A:** _____

   B: Yes, he should. Jeremy should definitely study more.

IV. *Correct the* Five Rules for Travelers. *There are five mistakes.*

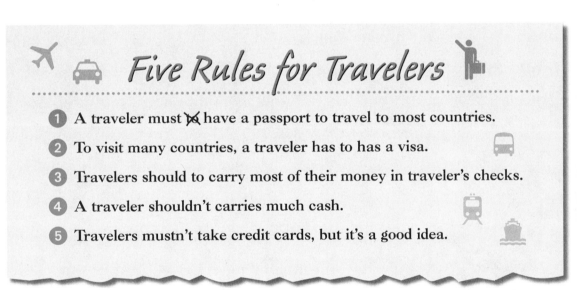

Five Rules for Travelers

1. A traveler must ⨯ have a passport to travel to most countries.
2. To visit many countries, a traveler has to has a visa.
3. Travelers should to carry most of their money in traveler's checks.
4. A traveler shouldn't carries much cash.
5. Travelers mustn't take credit cards, but it's a good idea.

▶ *To check your answers, go to the Answer Key on page 285.*

APPENDICES

Map of the World

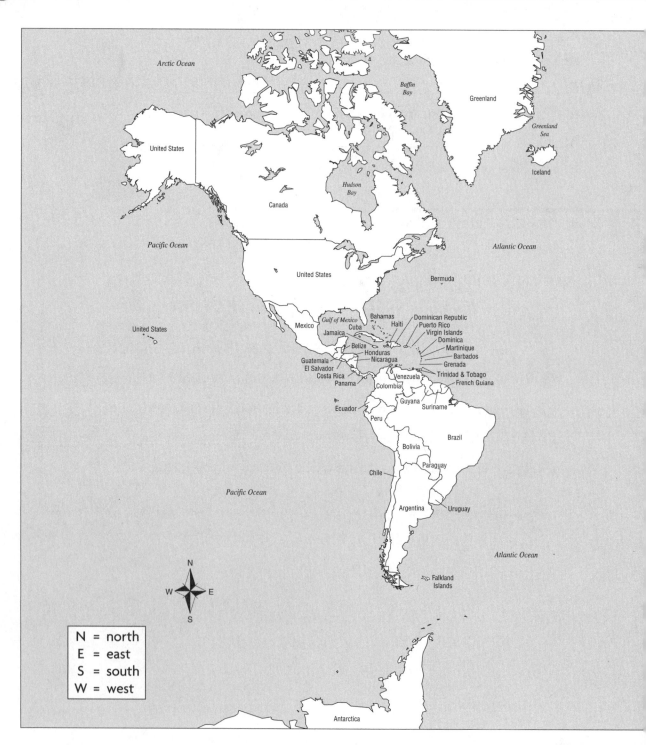

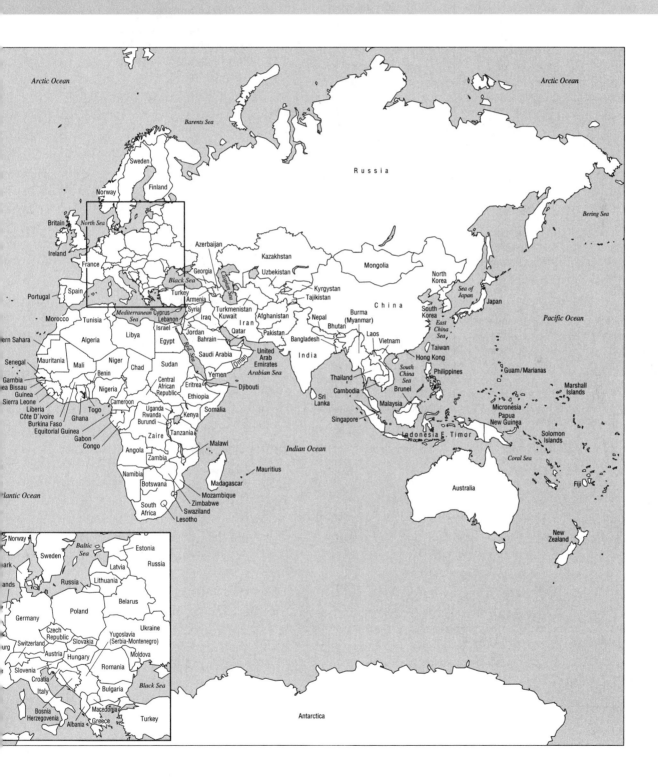

Arctic Ocean

Arctic Ocean

Barents Sea

Bering Sea

Russia

Sweden

Norway

Finland

North Sea

Britain

Ireland

France

Azerbaijan

Kazakhstan

Mongolia

North Korea

Sea of Japan

Japan

Portugal

Spain

Georgia

Black Sea

Caspian Sea

Turkey

Armenia

Kyrgystan

Tajikistan

China

South Korea

East China Sea

Pacific Ocean

Morocco

Tunisia

Mediterranean Sea

Cyprus

Lebanon

Syria

Iraq

Turkmenistan

Kuwait

Iran

Afghanistan

Nepal

Burma (Myanmar)

Taiwan

Hong Kong

ern Sahara

Algeria

Libya

Israel

Jordan

Egypt

Bahrain

Qatar

Pakistan

Bhutan

Laos

Vietnam

Saudi Arabia

United Arab Emirates

India

Bangladesh

South China Sea

Philippines

Guam/Marianas

Senegal

Mauritania

Mali

Niger

Chad

Sudan

Yemen

Oman

Arabian Sea

Thailand

Cambodia

Brunei

Marshall Islands

Gambia

ea Bissau

Guinea

Sierra Leone

Liberia

Côte D'Ivoire

Burkina Faso

Equitorial Guinea

Benin

Nigeria

Cameroon

Togo

Ghana

Central African Republic

Eritrea

Ethiopia

Djibouti

Sri Lanka

Malaysia

Singapore

Micronesia

Papua New Guinea

Gabon

Congo

Uganda

Rwanda

Burundi

Zaire

Kenya

Tanzania

Somalia

Indonesia E. Timor

Solomon Islands

Angola

Zambia

Malawi

Indian Ocean

Coral Sea

Namibia

Botswana

Madagascar

Mauritius

Fiji

South Africa

Zimbabwe

Mozambique

Swaziland

Lesotho

Australia

lantic Ocean

New Zealand

Antarctica

Norway

Sweden

Baltic Sea

Estonia

Russia

ark

ands

Russia

Latvia

Lithuania

Belarus

Germany

Poland

urg

Switzerland

Czech Republic

Slovakia

Ukraine

Austria

Hungary

Moldova

Slovenia

Croatia

Romania

Italy

Bulgaria

Black Sea

Bosnia Herzegovenia

Macedonia

Albania

Greece

Turkey

Yugoslavia (Serbia-Montenegro)

259

CARDINAL NUMBERS

1 = one	11 = eleven	21 = twenty-one
2 = two	12 = twelve	30 = thirty
3 = three	13 = thirteen	40 = forty
4 = four	14 = fourteen	50 = fifty
5 = five	15 = fifteen	60 = sixty
6 = six	16 = sixteen	70 = seventy
7 = seven	17 = seventeen	80 = eighty
8 = eight	18 = eighteen	90 = ninety
9 = nine	19 = nineteen	100 = one hundred
10 = ten	20 = twenty	200 = two hundred
		1,000 = one thousand
		1,000,000 = one million
		10,000,000 = ten million

EXAMPLES

That book has **eighty-nine** pages.
There are **thirty** days in September.
There are **five** rows in the room.
She is **eleven** years old.
He has **three** children.

ORDINAL NUMBERS

1st = first	11th = eleventh	21st = twenty-first
2nd = second	12th = twelfth	30th = thirtieth
3rd = third	13th = thirteenth	40th = fortieth
4th = fourth	14th = fourteenth	50th = fiftieth
5th = fifth	15th = fifteenth	60th = sixtieth
6th = sixth	16th = sixteenth	70th = seventieth
7th = seventh	17th = seventeenth	80th = eightieth
8th = eighth	18th = eighteenth	90th = ninetieth
9th = ninth	19th = nineteenth	100th = one hundredth
10th = tenth	20th = twentieth	200th = two hundredth
		1,000th = one thousandth
		1,000,000th = one millionth
		10,000,000th = ten millionth

EXAMPLES

It's his **fifty-first** birthday.
It's September **thirtieth.**
He's in the **fourth** row.
It's her **eleventh** birthday.
Jeremy is their **first** child.
Annie is their **second** child.
Ben is their **third** child.

TEMPERATURE

We measure the temperature in degrees (°).

Changing from degrees Fahrenheit to degrees Celsius:

$$(°F − 32) \times 5/9 = °C$$

Changing from degrees Celsius to degrees Fahrenheit:

$$(9/5 \times °C) + 32 = °F$$

DAYS OF THE WEEK

Weekdays	Weekend
Monday	Saturday
Tuesday	Sunday
Wednesday	
Thursday	
Friday	

MONTHS OF THE YEAR

Month	Abbreviation	Number of Days
January	Jan.	31
February	Feb.	28*
March	Mar.	31
April	Apr.	30
May	May	31
June	Jun.	30
July	Jul.	31
August	Aug.	31
September	Sept.	30
October	Oct.	31
November	Nov.	30
December	Dec.	31

*February has 29 days in a leap year, every four years.

THE SEASONS

Spring—March 21–June 20

Summer—June 21–September 20

Autumn or Fall—September 21–December 20

Winter—December 21–March 20

TITLES

Mr. (Mister) / mɪstər /unmarried or married man

Ms. / mɪz /   unmarried or married woman

Miss / mɪs /   unmarried woman

Mrs. / mɪsɪz/   married woman

Dr. (Doctor) / daktər / doctor (medical doctor or Ph.D.)

③ Parts of the Body

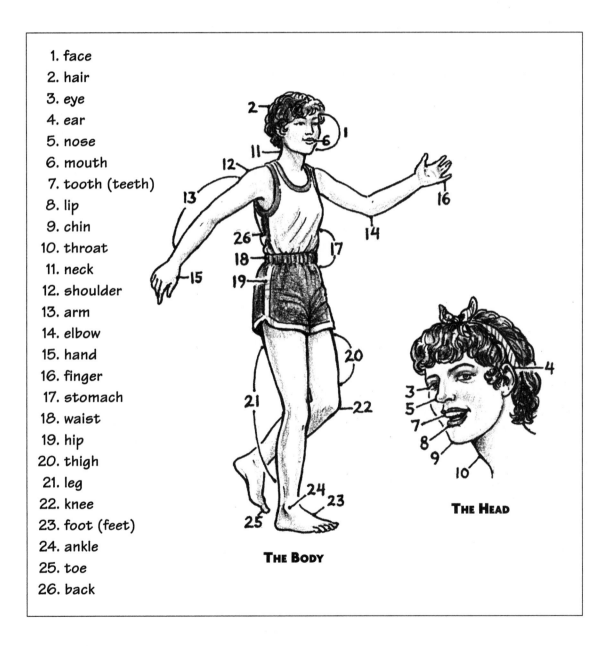

1. face
2. hair
3. eye
4. ear
5. nose
6. mouth
7. tooth (teeth)
8. lip
9. chin
10. throat
11. neck
12. shoulder
13. arm
14. elbow
15. hand
16. finger
17. stomach
18. waist
19. hip
20. thigh
21. leg
22. knee
23. foot (feet)
24. ankle
25. toe
26. back

THE BODY

THE HEAD

SPELLING RULES

1. Add *-s* to form the plural of most nouns.	car book video photograph	car**s** book**s** video**s** photograph**s**
2. Add *-es* to form the plural of nouns that end in *ss*, *ch*, *sh*, and *x*. (This ending adds another syllable.)	cla**ss** sandwi**ch** di**sh** bo**x**	clas**ses** sandwich**es** dish**es** box**es**
3. To form the plural of nouns that end in a **consonant** + *y*, change the *y* to *i* and add *-es*.	par**ty** strawber**ry**	par**ties** strawber**ries**
4. To form the plural of nouns that end in a **vowel** + *y*, add *-s*.	b**oy** k**ey**	b**oys** k**eys**
5. Some plural nouns are **irregular**.	man woman child person	**men** **women** **children** **people**
6. Some nouns **do not have a singular form**.		**clothes** **(eye)glasses** **pants**

PRONUNCIATION RULES

1. The **final sounds** for regular plural nouns are / s /, / z /, and /ɪz /.		
2. The plural is pronounced / s / **after** the **voiceless sounds** / p /, / t /, / k /, / f /, and / ɵ /.	cup**s** cat**s** book**s**	puff**s** brea**ths**
3. The plural is pronounced / z / **after** the **voiced sounds** / b /, / d /, / g /, / v /, / m /, / n /, / ŋ /, / l /, / r /, and / ð /.	ca**bs** car**ds** do**gs** wi**ves** roo**ms**	pa**ns** son**gs** ba**lls** car**s** pa**ths**
4. The plural is pronounced / z / **after** all **vowel sounds**. Vowels are voiced.	k**eys** tomat**oes**	mov**ies**
5. The plural is pronounced / ɪz / **after** the sounds / s /, / z /, / ʃ /, / ʒ /, / ʧ /, and / ʤ /. (This adds another syllable to the word.)	kis**ses** buz**zes** di**shes**	gara**ges** mat**ches** a**ges**

Common Non-count Nouns*

Food	Liquids	School Subjects	Abstract Ideas
bread	coffee	algebra	advice
broccoli	juice	biology	beauty
butter	milk	chemistry	energy
cake	soda	English	existence
cheese	tea	geography	happiness
chicken	water	history	help
ice cream		music	love
fish		psychology	noise
lemonade		science	sleep
meat		Spanish	stress
pasta			time
pepper			
pie			
pizza	**Weather**	**Sports**	**Others**
rice			
salad	fog	baseball	dessert
salsa	ice	basketball	furniture
salt	rain	football	homework
soup	snow	soccer	information
spaghetti		swimming	mail
sugar		tennis	medicine
		volleyball	money
			news
			paper

*Some nouns can be either count or non-count nouns.

Do you want some pizza? *(non-count)*   I don't want salad tonight. *(non-count)*
Let's order a pizza. *(count—an entire pizza)*   Mom is making a salad. *(count)*

Quantifiers

a bottle of *(juice, milk, soda, water)*   a liter of *(juice, milk, soda, water)*
a bowl of *(cereal, soup)*   a loaf of *(bread)*
a can of *(soda, tuna)*   a pair of *(gloves, pants, skis, socks, shoes)*
a cup of *(hot chocolate, coffee, tea)*   a piece of *(cake, meat, paper, pie)*
a foot of *(snow, water)*   a quart of *(milk)*
a gallon of *(juice, gas, milk)*   a slice of *(cake, cheese, pie, pizza, toast)*
a glass of *(juice, milk, water)*

1. *A* and *an* are the **indefinite articles**. We use them before **singular count nouns**.

- My sister has **a truck**.
- She has **an old car** too.

2. Use *a* before a word that begins with a **consonant sound**.

   Use *an* before a word that begins with a **vowel sound**.

   BE CAREFUL! It is the **sound**, not the letter, that matters.

- I ate **a sandwich** for lunch.

- My brother drives **an orange car**.

- Sally is attending **a university** in Montreal. (*The word* university *begins with the consonant sound / y /—not with a vowel sound.*)

3. *The* is the **definite article**. You can use *the* before singular count nouns, plural count nouns, and non-count nouns.

- **The cat** is sleeping. (*singular count noun*)
- **The students** are studying. (*plural count noun*)
- **The coffee** is delicious. (*non-count noun*)

4. Use *the* for **specific things** that the listener and speaker know about.

A: How was **the movie**?
B: It was really exciting.

5. Use *the* when the speaker and listener know there is **only one** of the item.

A: **The weather** is beautiful.
B: Yes. **The sun** is really bright.

6. Use *the* when you are talking about **part of a group**.

- There are a lot of houses in my neighborhood. **The houses** on Elm Street are all beautiful. **The houses** on Maple Street are all ugly.

7. Use *the* when you are talking about something for the **second time**.

A: Do you have any pets?
B: Yes, I have a parrot and a cat. **The parrot** can talk. **The cat** just sleeps all the time.

8. Use *the* before the **plural name** of a whole family.

- **The Becks** live in Seattle. **The Olsons** live in Redmond.

9. Use *the* with **phrases with *of*** when there is only one of the item that follows *the*.

- Ankara is **the capital of Turkey**.
- Sally attends **the University of Montreal**.
  BUT I'd like **a** cup of coffee.

10. Use *the* with the **names of a few countries**.

- We live in **the United States**.
  BUT We live in America.
- Colin is from **the United Kingdom**.
  BUT Colin is from Britain.
- Jan is from **the Netherlands**.
  BUT Jan is from Holland.

The Present Tense of *Be*

Singular		
Subject	*Be*	
I	**am**	a student.
You	**are**	
He She	**is**	
It	**is**	in the United States.

Plural		
Subject	*Be*	
We You They	**are**	in the United States.

The Past Tense of *Be*

Singular			
Subject	*Be*		**Time Marker**
I	**was**	at a restaurant	last night.
You	**were**		
He She It	**was**		

Plural			
Subject	*Be*		**Time Marker**
We You They	**were**	at a restaurant	last night.

The Present Progressive

Subject	*Be*	**Base Form of Verb + *-ing***
I	**am**	working.
You	**are**	
He She It	**is**	
We You They	**are**	

The Simple Present Tense

Subject	Verb
I You We They	**work.**
He She It	**works.**

The Simple Past Tense

Subject	Base Form of Verb + *-ed* / *-d* / *-ied*
I You He She It We You They	**worked. arrived. cried.**

Be Going to for the Future

Subject	*Be*	*Going to*	Base Form of Verb	
I	**am**			
You	**are**			
He She	**is**	**going to**	**study**	tomorrow.
You We They	**are**			
It	**is**	**going to**	**rain**	

8 Base Forms and Past-Tense Forms of Common Irregular Verbs

Base Form	Past-tense Form	Base Form	Past-tense Form	Base Form	Past-tense Form
be	was, were	give	gave	say	said
begin	began	go	went	see	saw
break	broke	grow	grew	sing	sang
bring	brought	have	had	sit	sat
build	built	hear	heard	sleep	slept
buy	bought	hit	hit	speak	spoke
come	came	know	knew	spend	spent
do	did	leave	left	stand	stood
drink	drank	lose	lost	swim	swam
drive	drove	make	made	take	took
eat	ate	mean	meant	tell	told
fall	fell	meet	met	think	thought
find	found	put	put	understand	understood
fly	flew	read / rid /	read / rɛd /	wake	woke
forget	forgot	ride	rode	win	won
get	got	run	ran	write	wrote

9 The Present Progressive: Spelling Rules

1. Add *-ing* to **base form** of the verb.	bring	bring**ing**
	cook	cook**ing**
	see	see**ing**
2. If a verb **ends in a silent** *e*, drop the final *e* and add *-ing*.	writ**e**	writ**ing**
3. If a **one-syllable verb** ends in a consonant, a vowel, and a consonant (**CVC**), double the last consonant before adding *-ing*.	**CVC** run hit	run**n**ing hit**t**ing
However, do not double the last consonant if it is a *w*, *x*, or *y*.	gro**w** fi**x** pla**y**	gro**w**ing fi**x**ing pla**y**ing
4. In **longer verbs** (two or more syllables) that end in a consonant, a vowel, and a consonant (**CVC**), double the last consonant only if the last syllable is stressed.	**CVC** permít *(The last syllable is stressed.)* devélop *(The last syllable is not stressed.)*	permi**tt**ing developing

SPELLING RULES FOR THE THIRD-PERSON SINGULAR AFFIRMATIVE

1. **Add -s** to form the third-person singular form of most verbs.

   - Jessica works. I work too.
   - Jeremy wears T-shirts. I wear blouses.

   Add -es to verbs that end in **ch, s, sh, x**, or **z**.

   - I teach Mandarin. Steve teaches journalism.
   - I fix my mountain bike. Tim fixes his own car.

2. If the verb ends in a **consonant + y**, change the **y** to **i** and add **-es**.

   - I study in the library. Judy studies at home.

   If the verb ends in a **vowel + y**, do not change the **y** to **i**. Add **-s**.

   - I play volleyball. Annie plays soccer.

3. Some verbs have **irregular forms** for the third-person singular.

   - I have
   - I do.
   - I go.

   - He **has**.
   - She **does**.
   - It **goes**.

PRONUNCIATION RULES FOR THE THIRD-PERSON SINGULAR AFFIRMATIVE

1. The **final sound** for the third-person singular form of the simple present tense is pronounced **/ s /, / z /**, or **/ ɪz /**. The final sounds of the third-person singular are the same as the final sounds of plural nouns. (See Appendix 4 on page 262.)

/ s /	**/ z /**	**/ ɪz /**
walks	rides	dances

2. **Do** and **say** have a change in the vowel sound.

   - I do. **/ du /**
   - I say. **/ seɪ /**

   - She does. **/ dʌz /**
   - He says. **/ sɛz /**

SPELLING RULES

1. If the verb **ends in an** *e*, add *-d*.

move	moved

2. If the verb **ends in a consonant**, add *-ed*.

cover	covered
dream	dreamed

3. If a **one-syllable verb** ends in a consonant, a vowel, and a consonant (**CVC**), double the last consonant and add *-ed*.

CVC

hug	hugged
rub	rubbed

However, do not double the last consonant if it is a *w*, *x*, or *y*.

row	rowed
mix	mixed
stay	stayed

4. If a **two-syllable verb** ends in a consonant, a vowel, and a consonant (**CVC**), double the last consonant only if the last syllable is stressed.

CVC

refér	referred *(stressed)*
énter	entered *(not stressed)*

5. If the verb ends in a **consonant** + *y*, change the *y* to *i* and add *-ed*.

marry	married
study	studied

6. If the verb ends in a **vowel** + *y*, do not change the *y* to *i*. Add *-ed*.

enjoy	enjoyed
play	played

There are **exceptions** to this rule. These verbs are **irregular verbs**.

pay	**paid**
lay	**laid**
say	**said**

PRONUNCIATION RULES

1. The **final sounds** for regular verbs in the past tense are **/ t /, / d /**, and **/ ɪd /**.

2. The final sound is pronounced **/ t /** **after** the **voiceless sounds / f /, / k /, / p /, / s /, / ʃ /** and **/ tʃ /**.

laughed	developed	washed
liked	crossed	watched

3. The final sound is pronounced **/ d /** **after** the **voiced sounds / b /, / g /, /dʒ /, / l /, / m /, / n /, / r /, / ŋ /, / ð /, / ʒ /, / v /**, and **/ z /**.

rubbed	hummed	bathed
hugged	cleaned	massaged
judged	hired	moved
called	banged	used

4. The final sound is pronounced **/ d /** **after vowel sounds**.

stayed	died	snowed
agreed	argued	

5. The final sound is pronounced **/ ɪd /** **after / t /** and **/ d /. / ɪd /** adds a syllable.

act	acted
end	ended

269

12 Modals

Function	Modals	Examples
to make **polite requests**	**would like** **Can you . . .**	• I**'d like** pepperoni. • **Can you** do me a favor?
to express **ability**	**can**	• I **can** speak Spanish.
to express **possibility**	**can**	• I **can** meet you at 4:00.
to express **necessity**	**must** **have to**	• Students **must** pass a written test. • They **have to** be in school by 8:00.
to express **advisability**	**should**	• I **should** practice the piano every day. • She **should** take an umbrella.
to express **prohibition**	**mustn't**	• You **mustn't** drink and drive. • You **mustn't** smoke here.
to indicate that something is **not a requirement**	**don't / doesn't have to**	• Students **don't have to** take tests at this school. • Josh **doesn't have to** work tomorrow.

13 Comparisons with Adjectives

Comparative Form				
(To Compare Two People, Places, or Things)				
Seattle	is	older busier more exciting	than	Redmond.
Redmond	is	smaller prettier more peaceful	than	Seattle.

Superlative Form				
(To Compare Three or More People, Places, or Things)				
Jim	is	**the**	oldest happiest most successful	of my three brothers.
Nancy	is	**the**	youngest prettiest most interesting	of my four sisters.

GLOSSARY OF GRAMMAR TERMS

Adjective

An adjective describes a noun or pronoun.

- I have a **blue** car. *(The adjective* blue *describes the car.)*
- Mary is **happy** today. *(The adjective* happy *describes Mary.)*

Adverb

An adverb describes a verb.

- Steve **often** skips breakfast. *(The adverb* often *describes when Steve skips breakfast.)*
- We're going to leave **tomorrow**. *(The adverb* tomorrow *shows when we're going to leave.)*

Article

An article comes before a noun. There are three articles in English: *a, an*, and **the**.

- I ate **a** banana and **an** apple. *(indefinite articles)*
- **The** banana tasted good, but **the** apple tasted terrible. *(definite article)*

Auxiliary (Helping) Verb

An auxiliary verb occurs with and "helps" a main verb.

- Tim **is** fixing his car. *(The auxiliary verb* is *helps the main verb* fixing.)
- **Does** Annie play soccer? *(The auxiliary verb* does *forms the question.)*
- **Did** Mark and Kathy get married? *(The auxiliary verb* did *forms the question.)*
- Mark **can** speak Mandarin. *(The modal auxiliary* can *helps the main verb* speak.)

Base Form

The base form of a verb is the form you find in a dictionary. It has no endings.

- **Listen** to the tape and **follow** the instructions.
- Do they **like** to play soccer?
- You should **eat** fruits and vegetables every day.

Comparative

Comparative forms make comparisons between two people, places, or things.

- Jeremy is **older than** Annie.
- Redmond is **more peaceful than** Seattle.

Imperative

The imperative form of the verb gives a command. It tells someone what to do. The imperative is the same as the base form.

- Students, please **write** your name on your paper.
- **Add** the eggs and the sugar. **Bake** the cookies for fifteen minutes.

Modal

A modal is a kind of auxiliary. It comes before a main verb. Four common modal auxiliaries are **can**, **should**, **would**, and **must**.

- **Can** you swim?
- Students **should** go to college when they're ready.
- **Would** you like tea or coffee?
- Travelers **must** have a valid passport.

Noun

A noun is the name of a person, place, animal, or thing.

- **Ken** is seventeen years old. *(the name of a person)*
- Steve lives in **Seattle**. *(the name of a place)*
- Amanda has a **cat**. *(the name of an animal)*
- She also has an old **car**. *(the name of a thing)*
- **Skiing** is enjoyable. *(the name of a thing)*

Object

An object usually shows who receives the action in a sentence.

- Tim loves **Jessica.** He loves **her**.
  (Jessica *and* her *receive the action. They are objects.)*
- Jessica loves **Tim.** She loves **him**.
  (Tim *and* him *receive the action. They are objects.)*

Preposition

A preposition is a connecting word. It is usually short. It is always followed by a noun or a pronoun.

- Ken went **to** the soccer game **with** Laura.
- Annie is **at** school now.

Progressive

A progressive verb form shows that an action is in progress. The action is not finished. We show that a verb is progressive by adding **-ing** to the base form.

- Tim is **taking** a shower.
- Judy and Mark are **studying** at the University of Washington.

Pronoun

A pronoun replaces a noun. We often use a pronoun when we don't want to repeat a noun.

- Annie is Jeremy's sister. **She** is eleven years old. (She *refers to the noun* Annie.)
- Mary and Bill Beck are landing at the airport at 6:00 P.M. Can **you** pick **them** up?
  (You *refers to the person spoken to.* Them *refers to* Mary and Bill Beck.)

Sentence

A sentence is a group of words with a subject and a verb. It can stand by itself.

- Mark is traveling in India. *(Sentence: subject* Mark; *verb* is traveling.
  This group of words can stand by itself.)
- Is traveling in India. *(Not a sentence: no subject)*

Stative Verb

A stative verb is a non-action verb. Stative verbs show states, not actions. We do not often use them in the progressive form.

- Jeremy **has** a brother and a sister.
- I **know** Mr. and Mrs. Olson.

Subject

A subject usually shows who performs the action in a sentence. A sentence makes a statement about the subject.

- **Daniela Maxa** teaches literature at the University of Washington. *(makes a statement about Daniela Maxa)*
- **She** is from Romania. *(makes another statement about Daniela Maxa)*

Superlative

Superlative forms make comparisons among three or more things or people.

- Of all the cities in North America, I think New York is **the most exciting**, Toronto is **the most interesting**, and Vancouver is **the prettiest**. But Seattle is **the best**.

Tense

Tense means time. We often speak of the **past** and **present** tenses.

- The Olsons **took** a vacation last year. *(past tense)*
- They usually **take** a vacation every August. *(present tense)*

Verb

A verb describes an action, a fact, or a state.

- Tim **is fixing** his car. *(action)*
- New York **has** more than 8 million people. *(fact)*
- Josh **hates** most sports, but I **love** them. *(states)*

Wh- Question

A *wh-* question is a question that asks for information. It begins with *what*, *when*, *where*, *why*, *which*, *who* or *how*.

- **What's** your name?
- **Where** are you from?
- **How** are you?

Yes/No Question

A *yes/no* question has a *yes* or *no* answer.

- **Are** you from here? (Yes, I am. OR No, I'm not.)
- **Do** you speak Spanish? (Yes, I do. OR No, I don't.)
- **Did** their plane arrive? (Yes, it did. OR No, it didn't.)
- **Were** they late? (Yes, they were. OR No, they weren't.)

INFORMATION GAPS

Student B, answer Student A's questions about business cards 1 and 2. Then look at 3 and 4. Ask Student A questions and complete the cards.

1.

China Palace
30 Main Street
Ann Arbor, Michigan 48104
U.S.A.

2.

Turkish Delights
213 East 79th Street
New York, New York 10021
U.S.A.

3.
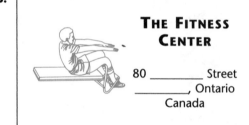
THE FITNESS CENTER
80 _____ Street
_____, Ontario
Canada

4.

Jim's Gym
_____
Vancouver, British Colombia
_____

Example:

B: Where's the Fitness Center?

A: It's in Ottawa, Ontario.

B: What street is it on?

A: . . .

Unit 8, Exercise 6

Student B, answer Student A's questions about the weather in Tokyo. Then complete this chart. Ask Student A questions about the weather in Rio.

Example:

B: How was the weather in Rio last Sunday?

A: It was sunny and warm.

	Tokyo		Rio de Janeiro
Sunday			
Monday			
Tuesday			

Student B, answer Student A's questions. Then complete the story below. Ask Student A wh- questions in the present progressive.

Example:

B: Where is Alonzo Bonzo walking on a tightrope?

A: Across the park.

Good afternoon. This is KZYX News and I'm Jessica Olson. I'm speaking to you from the park. Tightrope walker Alonzo Bonzo is walking _____*across the park*_____ on a tightrope! The tightrope is a hundred feet above the park. Alonzo is wearing a red shirt, black pants, and a yellow hat. There is a net under the tightrope.

_____ are waiting by the net. His wife is in the park watching him. Why is Alonzo doing this? For money? No, says his wife. He's doing it because

_____. Alonzo is walking very slowly. He's halfway across! Now he's three-quarters of the way across! Now he's on the other side! Congratulations to Alonzo Bonzo! Everybody is _____.

This is Jessica Olson, KZYX News.

Student B, answer Student A's questions. Choose an answer from the box below. Then ask Student A about the meaning of a word from your list. Write the answer. Take turns.

Example:

B: "Tiny" means "very small". What does "large" mean?

A: "Large" means "big".

Student B's Answers	
12:00 A.M.	not interesting
12:00 P.M.	very bad
great	good
very small	sad

Student B's Words

1. large   _big_____
2. relatives _____
3. opposites _____
4. smart _____

5. cousins _____
6. cute _____
7. single _____
8. second _____

Student B, listen to Student A. Look at the pictures and name the people.

Andy Warhol   **Princess Diana**   **Mahatma Gandhi**   **Mother Teresa**

Now read your sentences to Student A. Student A names the people.

1. She painted close-up pictures of flowers and pictures of the American Southwest. She painted until she was in her eighties. She died at the age of 99. *(Georgia O'Keeffe)*

2. He was a famous American musician. People called him "Satchmo." He played the trumpet. He helped make jazz famous. *(Louis Armstrong)*

3. This German-born American developed the theory of relativity. He received a Nobel Prize in 1921. *(Albert Einstein)*

4. She lived in France. She discovered radium. She worked with her husband. They were both scientists. *(Marie Curie)*

Unit 24, Exercise 8

Host, ask the following questions.

Example:

HOST: Who flew across the Atlantic in 1927?
GROUP 1: Amelia Earhart.
HOST: Incorrect. you lose one point.
GROUP 2: Charles Lindbergh.
HOST: Correct. You win one point.

1. Who wrote *One Hundred Years of Solitude*?   *(Gabriel García Márquez)*
2. Who was the king of rock and roll?   *(Elvis Presley)*
3. When did the United Nations begin?   *(1945)*
4. In what century did Mozart live?   *(The 18th century: 1756–1791)*
5. Where did Marie Antoinette live?   *(In Austria and in France)*

INFORMATION GAP FOR STUDENT B

Unit 31, Exercise 7

*Student B, first answer Student A's questions. Use **in, on,** or **at** in each answer. Choose from the items in the box. Then ask questions with **when** or **what time**.*

Example:

A: When do Americans usually vote?
B: Americans usually vote on a Tuesday. When do the French usually vote?
A: The French usually vote on a Sunday.

Student B's Answers

12:00 noon	a Tuesday
March	February or March
December 21	

Student B's questions

1. the French / usually vote / ?
2. winter normally begin / in the Northern Hemisphere / ?
3. each day / begin / ?
4. Canadians / celebrate / Canada Day / ?
5. fall normally begin / in the Northern Hemisphere / ?

PUZZLES AND GAMES
ANSWER KEY

UNIT 2
With a Partner
(in order of the pictures)
New York, Quebec, Bangkok, Istanbul

UNIT 3
With a Partner
Lima—capital of Peru
Taipei—capital of Taiwan
Canberra—capital of Australia

Caracas—capital of Venezuela
Brasília—capital of Brazil

UNIT 12
9. True or False?

1. True.

2. False. Most people in Thailand don't use chopsticks.

3. True.

7. True.

4. False. People in Britain drive on the left.

5. False. People don't live at the North Pole.

6. False. Penguins live in Antarctica.

UNIT 14
Information Gap

Student A
tiny = very small
boring = not interesting
noon = 12:00 P.M.
midnight = 12:00 A.M.
super = great
unhappy = sad
terrible = very bad
nice = good

Student B
large = big
relatives = your parents, brothers, sisters, grandparents, etc.
opposites = totally different
smart = intelligent
cousins = the children of your aunts and uncles
cute = good-looking
single = not married
second = between first and third

UNIT 15
With a Partner
Wolfgang Amadeus Mozart

UNIT 17
With a Partner
John F. Kennedy, Jr.
Maya Angelou

UNIT 23
5. Listen
Bonus question answer: Brad Pitt

7. What's True? What's False?

False statements	*Corrections*
left ~~France~~	England
trip across the ~~Pacific~~	Atlantic
during the ~~afternoon~~	night
~~Brad Pitt~~	Leonardo DiCaprio

UNIT 24
With a Partner
1. b   **2.** c   **3.** a   **4.** b   **5.** c

6. What's the Answer?
1. a   **2.** b   **3.** c   **4.** a   **5.** c   **6.** c   **7.** c   **8.** a   **9.** a

UNIT 31
7. Information Gap

Student A	*Student B*
1. November	**1.** a Sunday
2. December 21	**2.** December 21
3. 12:00 P.M.	**3.** 12:00 A.M.
4. February	**4.** July 6
5. March 21	**5.** September 21

REVIEW OR SELFTEST ANSWER KEY

PART 1 Review or SelfTest

I. 2. D   3. D   4. A   5. C   6. D

II. 2. These are   4. This is   6. This is
3. This is   5. These are

III. 2. They   4. He   6. We
3. It   5. She

IV. 1. Close your books.
2. Listen to the tape.
3. Write the homework in your notebook.
4. Practice with a partner.

V.
2. ~~Dont~~ **Don't** write your name.
3. Don't t~~o~~ open the window.
4. These **are** my new notebooks.
5. ~~This~~ **These** are my parents.
6. ~~No~~ **Don't** listen to the tape.

PART 2 Review or SelfTest

I. 2. D   4. D
3. A   5. B

II. 1. Is that   3. Are those
2. Is this   4. are these

III. 2. their   4. their   6. their
3. their   5. her

IV. 2. is on
3. is on . . . across from
4. is on . . . between
5. is next to
6. are across from
7. is on . . . across from
8. are on
9. is next to

PART 3 Review or SelfTest

I. 2. B   4. D   6. A
3. A   5. A   7. C

II. 2. it wasn't   5. he was
3. they weren't   6. she was
4. I was

III. 2. Where   5. How long
3. What   6. How
4. When

IV. 2. was   7. am
3. were   8. is
4. are   9. is
5. is   10. is
6. are   11. are

282

3. Do they have children?

Review or SelfTest

PART 4

I.
2. B	**4.** B
3. D	**5.** C

II.
2. is making	**6.** is reading
3. are singing	**7.** is watching
4. is playing	**8.** are sleeping
5. are sitting	

III.
1B. She's playing a game.
2A. Is Ben playing too?
2B. No, he's playing with the cat.
3A. Why are you laughing?
3B. The cat is wearing a hat.
4A. Where is Jessica going?
4B. She's going to the supermarket.

IV.
2. What are they playing?
3. Why is he making dinner?
4. What's he making?
5. Who's singing?

Review or SelfTest

PART 5

I.
2. D	**4.** C	**6.** D
3. A	**5.** B	

II.
2. He never comes at 9:00.
3. He usually arrives at 9:15. OR
Usually he arrives at 9:15.
4. Where do you usually eat?
5. Do you always have lunch at noon?

III.
2. is	**4.** have	**6.** have	**8.** is
3. is	**5.** has	**7.** is	

IV.
A. 2. Where does she work?
3. What time does she start?
4. How long does she stay?
B. 1. Who lives in that house?
2. What do they do?

3. Do they have children?
4. Is their son the boy on the bike?
OR
Is the boy on the bike their son?

Review or SelfTest

PART 6

I.
2. D	**4.** D
3. A	**5.** D

II.
2. How does it look?
3. Do you like the black shoes?
4. Yes, but I can't understand his message.
5. Can Jeremy play the guitar?

III.
2. They don't have any coffee.
3. They don't have any juice.
4. They don't have any fruit.
5. They have some bagels.
6. They have some milk.

IV.
2. a	**7.** one	**12.** one
3. ones	**8.** the	**13.** the
4. ones	**9.** an	**14.** one
5. an	**10.** a	
6. a	**11.** the	

V.
2. It's Annie's cat.
3. It's the men's department.
4. It's the women's department.
5. It's Jessica's parents' house.

PART 7 Review or SelfTest

I.
2. B   4. C
3. A   5. D

II.
2. liked   6. got
3. completed   7. directed
4. received   8. watch
5. studied

III.
2. is   6. worked
3. gave   7. Does . . . have
4. 's   8. is showing OR
5. like   's showing

IV.
2. are   4. Hurry
3. Try   5. save

V.
2. When did you leave? OR
   What time did you leave?
3. Why did it take five hours?
4. Who changed the tire?
5. When did you get home? OR
   What time did you get home?

PART 8 Review or SelfTest

I.
2. D   3. A   4. B

II.
2. How many miles did you drive?
3. How many people went on the trip?
4. How much did the trip cost?

III.
2. A few   4. many   6. a little
3. Some   5. much

IV.
2. They are   8. there are
3. There is   9. They are
4. There are   10. there was
5. there were   11. It was
6. They were   12. There were
7. There were

PART 9 Review or SelfTest

I.
2. A   3. A   4. C

II.
2. *The Thing* / scarier than
3. *Erin Brockovich* / more serious than
4. *Meet the Parents* / funnier than
5. *Erin Brockovich* / the longest
6. *Erin Brockovich* / the best

III.
2. on   4. On   6. at
3. at   5. on   7. at

IV.

JUDY: How was your party?

KEN: Cool. We had lots of ~~goods~~ *good*
CDs and ~~pizzas great~~ *great pizzas*. It
ended ~~on~~ *at* 3:00 ~~at~~ *in* the
morning. Did you have
a nice weekend?

JUDY: No. I just studied and
watched a ~~video bad~~ *bad video*.

KEN: What video?

JUDY: *The Thing*. It was the *most* boring
movie in the world.

KEN: You're kidding! My friends
and I saw it. We loved it.

PART 10 — Review or SelfTest

I.
2. D   4. C
3. B   5. A

II.
2. They're going to go to a rock concert.
3. She's going to cook dinner.
4. They're going to get married.

III.
2. Is it going to snow?
3. Where are Mark and Kathy going to go on their honeymoon?
4. Is Ken going to go to college?
5. Who's going to drive you to the airport?

IV.
Thanks for driving us to the airport. We arrived in Acapulco at 1:00 P.M. and went right to the hotel. The weather is beautiful so far, but it looks like ^*it* is going to rain. Tomorrow ^*are* we going to go swimming in the morning. In the afternoon ~~are we~~ *we are* going to go fishing out in the ocean. When ~~you and Bill are~~ *are you and Bill* going to come with us on a trip? We always have such a good time when we travel. The only thing I miss about Seattle is baseball. ~~Our team is~~ *Is our team* going to win?

PART 11 — Review or SelfTest

I.
2. D   4. B
3. A   5. A

II.
1. has to have
2. should remember
3. shouldn't drive
4. don't have to take

III.
1. OR Should we go ice skating?
2. Should I buy (OR get OR rent) a new car?
3. Do you like pizza?
4. Would you like some (OR a cup of) coffee?
5. Should Jeremy study more?

IV.
1. OR A traveler ~~must~~ *has* to have a passport to travel to most countries.
2. To visit many countries, a traveler has to ~~has~~ *have* a visa.
3. Travelers should ~~to~~ carry most of their money in traveler's checks.
4. A traveler shouldn't ~~carries~~ *carry* much cash.
5. Travelers ~~mustn't~~ *don't have to* take credit cards, but it's a good idea.

INDEX